CHRISTIAN
ROMAN EMPIRE
SERIES

Vol. 11

THE FRAGMENTARY HISTORY OF PRISCUS

Attila, the Huns and the Roman Empire
AD 430 – 476

translated with an introduction by
John Given

Evolution Publishing
Merchantville NJ
2014

©2014 Evolution Publishing
Merchantville, New Jersey.

Printed in the United States of America

ISBN 978-1-935228-14-1

Library of Congress Cataloging-in-Publication Data

Priscus, active 5th century.
 [Works. Selections. English. 2005]
 The fragmentary history of Priscus : Attila, the Huns and the Roman Empire, AD 430-476 / translated with an introduction by John Given.
    pages cm. -- (Christian Roman Empire series ; vol. 11)
   Includes bibliographical references.
  ISBN 978-1-935228-14-1
 1. Priscus, active 5th century--Criticism, Textual. 2. Attila, -453. 3. Huns--History--Early works to 1800. 4. Rome--History--Empire, 284-476--Early works to 1800. 5. Priscus, active 5th century. I. Given, John. II. Title.
 PA4399.P85A244 2014
 937'.09--dc23

                              2014027416

TABLE OF CONTENTS

Preface iii
Acknowledgements ix

Introduction
   I. Priscus, A Biographical Sketch xi
   II. Priscus's History Book xiv
   III. The Text xx
   IV. The Translation xxxvi
   V. Further Reading xxxviii

The Fragments: Their Sources and Numbering Systems xlv

Map of the Roman Empire, the Empire of Attila,
and neighboring kingdoms xlix

The Fragmentary History of Priscus 1
   Ancient Testimonia 3
   The Arrival of the Huns 5
   Two Young Emperors 19
   Negotiating with Attila 35
   Attila in the West 93
   The Death of Attila 111
   Diplomacy in the East 117
   Turmoil in the West 125
   Huns, Persians, Goths and Vandals 141
   The End of the West 169
   Miscellaneous Fragments 173

Bibliography 177

Index 187

PREFACE

Attila the Hun exists in modern imagination as the savage barbarian conqueror who brought about the fall of the Roman Empire. There is some truth there. Attila was an impressively successful conqueror whose Huns dominated Europe for a decade in the mid-fifth century AD. He harassed several emperors with his military ferocity and his tribute demands. He threatened both Rome and Constantinople, though he sacked neither. Yet his army was repulsed by a joint effort of Romans and Goths and, scarcely ten years after his rise to power, he died in his sleep, next to his newlywed bride, and his kingdom quickly disintegrated. He had made an impression on the Romans that led generations of historians and storytellers to amplify his name. As historians have increasingly recognized, however, Attila's own story is much more complex, as is the story of the entire fifth century. More complicated than Edward Gibbon's conception of a Roman "decline and fall," the fifth century was a period of political change and ethnic displacement, but also cultural continuity and (in the East and even in the West for the first half of the century) political stability.

A vital key to understanding Attila, the Huns and the fifth century is the historical writing of Priscus of Panion, an historian whose work is mostly lost but whose surviving words deserve to capture more popular imagination than they have. Priscus is the one ancient Roman who has left us a firsthand account of Attila's Hunnic culture and activities. He met Attila when he served on a diplomatic mission for the Eastern emperor Theodosius II, a mission whose secret purpose, Priscus himself only learned later, was to assassinate the Hunnic king. His account of the mission is written in clear, insightful prose that stands proudly alongside the best of ancient historical writing. Priscus's importance, though, does not lie solely in his descriptions of the Huns. He also writes about other significant fifth-century events, primarily from an Eastern perspective, including a revolt in Egypt and the failed attempt to retake North Africa from the Vandals. He tells of the miraculous omens that attended the rise of Eastern Emperor Marcian, but he also narrates Western Emperor Valentinian III's vicious murder of his general Aetius and, in turn, Valentinian's own murder at the hands of soldiers loyal to the aspiring usurper Petronius Maximus. Priscus covers events from the mid-430s until the mid-470s, just before the succession of Roman emperors in the West came to an end. Although his extant descriptions of these parts of Roman history are not as extensive as his Hunnic material, he nevertheless adds significant details to our understanding of these decades.

This small volume contains all that we have left of Priscus's history. It is the first translation based on the recently published new edition of Priscus's Greek fragments by Pia Carolla.[1] Two previous books have translated Priscus's fragments into English. In *The Age of Attila* (1960), C. D. Gordon produced a continuous history of the fifth century, organized geographically and chronologically, by interspersing his own historical narrative with the translated excerpts of Priscus and other fifth- and sixth-century historians. The result was an indispensible collection of knowledge and sources for fifth-century history, written for non-specialist readers. David S. Potter's revision (2013) has added extensive historiographical and textual notes that contain important material unknown to or omitted by Gordon and that compare Gordon's translation to Carolla's Greek edition of Priscus. Gordon/Potter is an excellent work for understanding Late Antiquity, but insofar as each ancient author gets subsumed into the all-encompassing narrative it lacks this book's focus on Priscus himself. The edition and translation by R. C. Blockley (1981/1983, reprinted 2007/2009) also encompasses other late antique Roman historians but separates the discussion of each one. It is a monument of erudition whose influence can be seen on every page of this book. With Blockley's edition and accompanying translations, scholars with or without Greek have gained access to the important historical texts of the fifth century. His detailed commentary contextualizes Priscus's text for scholars in a way not previously attempted.

In preparing this translation, I have strived to find a middle ground between Gordon and Blockley. I write for a more general audience than Blockley, whether students learning about Late Antiquity for the first time or the casual reader interested in the period of Attila and Rome's fall. I also, however, believe that it is worth focusing on the historian himself and so I keep Priscus at the forefront. I deliberately do not intersperse his fragments with other historians' excerpts, as Gordon did, lest we lose sight of Priscus's unique voice. I have kept footnotes to a minimum, primarily using them to indicate modern geographical names, alternative translations and places where I diverge from Carolla's text. Between fragments, I have supplied brief historical contextualization. These small paragraphs are in no way meant to represent the unrecoverable parts of Priscus's history or to provide a continuous narrative of the period. They are guides to the people and events described in the fragments, and no more.

As is explained in the Introduction, there are two basic groups of fragments: excerpts that we are certain derive from Priscus's original text, whether through verbatim quotation or paraphrase, and excerpts that in scholars' judgment seem to contain Priscan material but do not cite Priscus by name. The former group comprises fragments 1–49 (with the exception of fragment 11*). Most of them are verbatim quotations from Priscus; all of them are, with strong probability, numbered in the order they appeared in Priscus's complete work, although I have occasionally relocated a fragment to keep similar topics together or because the chronology does seem wrong. The latter group (fragments 50*–83* plus 11*), which I call conjectural, are marked with an asterisk, just as in Carolla's Greek edition. These I have interspersed with the certain fragments according to their probable location in Priscus's narrative. With each fragment, I list and occasionally comment on the later text that serves as its source. (All the source texts are described in detail in the Introduction.) I ask readers to remain alert to the different authorial voices through which we know Priscus. I expect that readers will be able to experience this book as a semi-coherent narrative of the middle decades of the fifth century, but I also expect that their reading experience will at times be disjointed. This is by design. The primary purpose of a translation is to enable the reader who does not have the original language to experience the text as the translator experiences it in the original. For me, at least, reading Priscus is a disjointed experience. Because of the fragmentary nature of his remains, recovered from eleven distinct sources, Priscus today has a multiplicity of voices that do not always harmonize with each other. I hope that readers will share in my disjointed reading experience and come to appreciate the challenges that face scholars as they work to understand the period of Attila.

—Prof. John P. Given
East Carolina University
December 2013

Notes

1. There have been five major modern editions of Priscus's Greek fragments: by Müller (1868 / 1870), Dindorf (1870), Bornmann

Preface

(1979), Blockley (1983) and Carolla (2008). All except Blockley use the same numbering system for the fragments; I follow Carolla's fragment numbers precisely. Each edition contains fragments not included in other editions, based on the editors' judgment about how extensively later authors used Priscus's text. For example, Bornmann's edition contains numerous quotations from the ancient encyclopedia called the *Suda*, but Blockley and Carolla reject most of them as non-Priscan. I have included all the fragments printed by Carolla, as it represents the most recent scholarship about Priscus's writing. For more information on the text's composition, see Introduction, Section III (p. xx).

ACKNOWLEDGEMENTS

Academic work can be a solitary experience; I have been fortunate not to work in a vacuum. I would like to extend sincere thanks to the many friends and colleagues with whom I discussed this project. Some are classicists who lent needed expertise and advice. Others are sharp-minded colleagues from other fields willing to help me think through problems. Deserving special mention are Juan Daneri, Peter Green, Brent Henze, Frank Romer, Wendy Sharer, John Stevens, Jennifer Valko, David Wilson-Okamura and Tricia Wilson-Okamura. I was fortunate to be able to give this translation a test run in my seminar "The Theory and Art of Translating Classical Literature." The discussions in that class not only helped me improve this book, but helped me understand more fully the act of translation itself. My hearty thanks to seminar students Charlotte Bruce, Cecelia Collins, Kirsis Concepción, Justin Goforth, Julio Maldonado and Thomas Mann. Thanks also to the staff at Evolution Publishing for their patience when I stretched deadlines and for their enthusiasm when they read my work. Priscus wasn't our first idea for this project, but he proved to be the right fit. I would like to give particular thanks to the anonymous peer reviewers whose diligent and careful reading greatly improved this book. It is a truism of translating that readers will attribute problems to the author, not the translator. My dear readers, I confess that any remaining errors and infelicities in this volume are my own.

Finally, I offer my thanks and love to my wife, Patricia Dragon, and our son, David. Their support made this work possible. Their love makes everything else possible.

INTRODUCTION

I. PRISCUS, A BIOGRAPHICAL SKETCH

Priscus hails from Panion, a small city on the northwestern shore of the Sea of Marmara, between the Black Sea and the Aegean Sea, an area known in the ancient world as the Thracian Chersonese (testimonium 1 [p. 3]; cf. fragment 64* [p. 101] and fragment 42 [p. 157]). We cannot be certain of his date of birth, but it was likely in the 410s. He would thus have been in his thirties when he visited Attila's camp and in his sixties at the time of the last historical events he records in his extant text. We have no knowledge of how long he survived after his history ends. Nor do we have any knowledge of his family or his social position, though his high level of literacy and knowledge of the historiographical tradition clearly indicate an excellent education. Finally, we are in the dark about his religious inclination. Unlike other fifth-century historians who boldly parade their religious zeal—Eunapius was a pagan who despised Constantine and Theodosius and praised Julian the so-called Apostate; the trio of Sozomen, Socrates and Theodoret were Christians who composed ecclesiastical histories and interpreted the world through a Christian lens—Priscus keeps his religious biases to himself. Nothing in his preserved text gives any clear evidence of his worship practices. He is sometimes hostile to the Christian Theodosius II but sympathetic toward the Christian Marcian. Perhaps, on the one hand, he was a pagan keeping silent about his religion in a Christian world. On the other hand, it is reasonable to believe that a well-connected man in the Eastern Roman Empire must have professed Christianity. All is speculation. Blockley summarizes perfectly when he says, "The tone of the History is determinedly secular, and religious considerations are effaced as much as is possible....Thus, the question of Priscus' religion is not answerable, nor does it seem especially important" (Blockley 1981, 60; cf. Rohrbacher 2002, 87).

We can make some solid guesses about Priscus's political connections. It is evident from his history that he was well-traveled, with journeys not only to Attila's camp somewhere in the Hungarian plain, but also to Rome (fragment 16 [p. 99]), Damascus (fragment 20 [p. 117]) and Alexandria (fragment 22 [p. 119]). In these travels he was a companion of the Eastern Roman ambassador Maximinos. It is not clear in what capacity he served under him. He tells us that Maximinos "with earnest entreaty persuaded me to accompany him" on his embassy to Attila (fragment 8 §5 [p. 48]). It is possible that Priscus held an official position on this and subsequent embassies, and that he was appointed to the missions because of some office he held in the Constantinopolitan bureaucracy. The language, though, suggests that Priscus did not receive an official appointment. It seems more likely that he followed Maximinos as an unofficial adviser and, given his training (see below), as an assistant in the skills of political and diplomatic rhetoric.[1] After Maximinos's death, he appears as an associate of the *magister officiorum* Euphemios (fragment 26 [p. 122]). The *magister officiorum*, or Master of the Offices, was one of the highest civil officials in the imperial court, responsible for overseeing numerous bureaucratic offices, including those dealing with legal affairs and imperial communications.[2] It is generally believed that Priscus did serve Euphemios in an official capacity, as his *assessor*, or legal and judicial adviser. Given that Euphemios may have been related to the reigning Eastern emperor Marcian,[3] Priscus seems to have been moving in the upper echelons of Roman society.

Introduction

Speculation about Priscus's role as an *assessor* derives from his apparent legal training. The Byzantine encyclopedia known as the *Suda* labels Priscus as a "sophist" (testimonium 1 [p. 3]), while the ecclesiastical historian Evagrius calls Priscus an "orator" (in Greek: *rhêtor*) (testimonium 2 [p. 3]; fragments 22 [p. 119], 44 [p. 161], 63* [p. 95]). The *Suda* testimonium adds that Priscus wrote, in addition to history, "rhetorical declamations and letters." The evidence is not conclusive, but it probably points to a career in the law. "Sophist" is not the derogatory term for a hair-splitting rogue, as the word is often used in English. That meaning derives from Plato's portraits of fifth-century BC itinerant teachers, such as Protagoras and Gorgias. By Late Antiquity, the term could be applied broadly to a skilled public speaker or writer. The *Suda* and the ninth-century bibliographer Photios also call the historian Malchus, a younger contemporary of Priscus, a "sophist" (Malchus testimonia 1, 2 in Blockley's edition). Combined with the notice that Priscus composed rhetorical declamations and letters—which may have been model speeches and letters for students to emulate—the appellation may indicate that Priscus was a teacher of rhetoric. Evagrius's term *rhêtor*, though, almost certainly identifies Priscus as a lawyer. It is the term consistently used to describe Evagrius himself and his contemporary Agathias, whom we know with certainty to have been lawyers. The possibility that Priscus was a lawyer also correlates well with his text's internal evidence, especially the long debate on political and legal institutions contained in fragment 8 §96–114 (pp. 62–65). His career as a lawyer would also place him in good company among Late Antique historians, including not just Evagrius and Agathias but also Sozomen, Socrates, Theophylact Simocatta and probably Procopius, John Malalas and Zosimus. While others' careers cannot serve as sure evidence for Priscus's course of life, it is suggestive that most Late Antique histories were written by lawyers late in their careers.[4]

Priscus, then, was an Eastern Roman man whose life spanned much of the fifth century AD. He clearly had an excellent education, including a classical education in literature and rhetoric. His post-graduate education, if you will, was probably in the law. He was well-connected in Constantinopolitan society and served as a subordinate, whether officially or not, to two highly ranked Roman officials. While we can only speculate about why he decided to write a history of his times, it is clear that he possessed the access and experience to have firsthand or easily attainable secondhand knowledge of the most significant events of his day. The remnants of his history demonstrate conclusively his wide-ranging access and his insightful intelligence.

II. PRISCUS'S HISTORY BOOK

The *Suda* (testimonium 1 [p. 3]) tells us that Priscus "wrote a *Byzantine History* and *On Attila*, in eight books." Printing a title in italics is a modern convention; my decisions about what to italicize are a result of what follows here, not evidence for it. While it seems likely that the *Suda* entry's author intended the words "Byzantine History" and "On Attila" to be seen as titles, we cannot be certain. Even if the author did intend that, they are unlikely to be Priscus's titles. Priscus nowhere uses the term "Byzantine" in his history. He would have called his work a "Roman" history. As for the title *On Attila*, it certainly suits the majority of pages found in this volume, but Priscus's history covers twenty years beyond the death of Attila and the disintegration of his Hunnic Empire. It is not an apt title for the whole work. One further problem arises with the conjunction "and," which in Greek can not only connect two equivalent entities, but can also assert that one entity is subordinate to or included in the other (e.g., "the gods and [i.e., including] Poseidon," Aeschylus, *Persians* line 750). Since all other ancient authors refer to Priscus's work as if it is a single corpus, this understanding of "and" seems best. The *Suda*'s titles, then, are probably descriptive titles appended to a single historical work by a later writer who sought to inform his contemporaries about Priscus's contents, including the most famous portion of his work, the description of the great conqueror Attila. In this book, I have therefore translated: Priscus "wrote a *Byzantine History*, including *On Attila*, in eight books." Whether Priscus himself conceived of his work in the same way, we cannot know.

The *Suda* reports, presumably accurately, that Priscus's history was written in eight books. The only clear evidence we have about the history's structure is that fragment 8.1 [p. 80] is labeled by its excerpter, again presumably accurately, as coming from Book 4. If, as seems likely, fragment 8.1 was the beginning of Book 4, it shows that Priscus's episode about the embassy to Attila and the assassination plot was so extensive that it broke across two books. It also shows that, by the end of Book 3, Priscus had reached the year 449. We should thus be able to calculate approximately how many years Priscus on average covered in each book.

This calculation depends on what years Priscus covered in his history. As with so much else, we must speculate. We face three particular barriers. First, the earliest dateable event in the certain fragments is the Hunnic king Roua's negotiations with the Eastern Romans in 434 (fragment 1 [p. 8]). Some scholars have surmised, though, that Priscus began with the rise of Attila in 439/440 (fragment 1.1 [p. 10]) and wrote about negotiations with Roua in flashback. It is likewise possible that Priscus began earlier than 434, if the several fragments (50*–57* [pp. 20–30]) that speak of a young Theodosius II and a clash among Valentinian III's generals are genuine and appeared in regular chronological order. In short, while Priscus's starting point is unknowable, the bulk of the narrative, as we have it, starts in 439/440. Second, Priscus's extant fragments do not contain any temporal markings. The excerpted fragments do proceed in a basic chronological order. However, while Late Antique chroniclers, both secular and Christian, used an annalistic (i.e., year-by-year) structure to order their histories and while other historians, like Zosimus, made correct chronology a central goal of their histories, we do not know whether Priscus structured his history according to a strict calendar or by other criteria such as geography or imperial reigns. Third, Priscus's end-date is especially obscure. Did he conclude with the death of Leo I in 474? Given that the historian Malchus begins his book with the year 473, was he continuing Priscus, and did Priscus thus end with the death of Anthemius in 472? Since he is able to criticize Basiliscus freely, was Priscus writing after Basiliscus's usurpation in 476, and did he continue his history past that date? Are later events flash-forwards, like the fragment about Roua may have been a flashback? The questions are unanswerable. And so we can at best say that Priscus probably narrated events beginning around 434 to 439 and ending around 472 to 476, though even these may be a few years off.[5]

If Priscus had a span of 33 to 42 years, he covered on average four to five years per book. As the end of Book 3 is set in 449, it seems that the earlier books, which told of events during the life of Attila, covered fewer years than the later books. This conclusion should not surprise us. The fragments concerning Attila and other Hunnic matters are far more detailed than the fragments concerning later events. Priscus could not have recounted the events of 33 to 42 years at that level of detail in only eight books. There are several possible reasons for this. To be sure, Priscus was closely involved in the Hunnic events and so as an eyewitness he was able to provide a level of detail that surpassed his knowledge of other events.[6] Still, even in the case of later events where Priscus was present, such as the revolt in Egypt or the negotiations with Gobazes, king of the Lazi, the details are fewer. We get the sense that Priscus was not as fascinated by these affairs as he had been with Attila. It may be that Priscus recognized which episodes would hold the greatest historical interest and so devoted his greatest energies and the most space to them. It may also be that, as the history progressed toward current events, Priscus felt unease writing about people still alive and even in power. It may have been safer to his own career and his own person to narrate the most recent events in the least detail.

While significant questions remain about the history's structure and coverage, the extant fragments enable us to draw good conclusions about Priscus's historiographical ideas and style. Priscus belongs to a group of Late Antique authors referred to as classicizing historians. Besides Priscus, this group includes the fragmentary fifth-century writers Eunapius, Olympiodorus and Malchus (all of whom are translated in the collections of Gordon and Blockley) as well as the sixth- and seventh-century writers Procopius, Agathias and Theophylact Simocatta. They all self-consciously stand in an historiographical tradition dating back to Herodotus and Thucydides in the fifth century BC. I will highlight three aspects of Priscus's classicizing: his secularism, his language usage and how he positions himself in the literary tradition.

First, secularism. With Herodotus and especially Thucydides, secularism meant rejection of theories of causation that could be traced back to the gods. For the fifth century AD revival of classical historiography, it meant not only a rejection of divine providence as an historical force but also an understanding of Christianity as one unprivileged influence among many on political and military affairs.[7] While some Christians, following the lead of Eusebius, were writing chronicles that re-interpreted world history in the light of Christian revelation and eschatology, Priscus and the other classicizers held to a more anthropocentric ideology. Priscus, to be sure, recognizes the importance of Christianity as a political force. For example, he notes that Emperor Marcian was careful to select an ambassador to the Vandal king Geiseric who belonged to Geiseric's particular Christian sect, i.e. Arianism (fragment 24 §3 [p. 131]). He does not, however, name the Christian God as motivating human action. Notably, even when the history covers portentous events, the historian is decidedly vague about the divine powers at work. In a story found in Procopius and possibly derived from Priscus (fragment 56* [p. 96]), an eagle shades a young Marcian from the blazing sun and thus marks him as a future emperor. Procopius (and Priscus?) merely says that the event is "godly."

Classicizing historiography is also noted for its peculiar language usage. Far from the *lingua franca* of the day and even far from the period's other prose writing, the classicizing historians wrote in an elevated style that their contemporaries would have identified as highly literary. Priscus mostly uses vocabulary and grammatical conventions that could have been found a millennium earlier. Because of this practice, he avoids most Late Antique technical terms and titles for the military, the imperial bureaucracy, ecclesiastical matters, and so forth, although a few Latinisms do find their way into his text. As a result, the reader can get frustrated when Priscus refers to an official with a generic term such as "leader" when a more precise, technical term is available. Priscus also tends to prefer classical to contemporary names in his geographical and especially his ethnic designations. His term "Scythian" dates back to Herodotus's descriptions of the peoples who lived north of the Black Sea. Priscus uses it to describe the Huns who entered Roman consciousness via that geographical area, but he also occasionally uses "Scythian" in reference to other northerners, such as Goths. To add to the confusion, he sometimes calls Attila's people simply "the Huns." Likewise, the "Parthians" are the Persians, i.e. the Sassanid Persians who had ruled Persia since the end of the Parthian Empire in AD 224. The Parthians were a minor tribe in the old (Achaemenid) Persian Empire. They were known to Herodotus (3.93) and so had a classical heritage; their 400-year hegemony between the Achaemenids and Sassanids earned them synonymy with Persia in Priscus's history.

Classicizing historians needed to demonstrate their knowledge of the historiographical tradition itself. Priscus frequently alludes to earlier Greek historians, particularly Herodotus and Thucydides. His allusions are sometimes so extensive as to have led some scholars to doubt Priscus's truthfulness about the events he describes. He preferred, they argue, to quote his ancient predecessors rather than accurately describe his events. A fine example of Priscus's allusiveness occurs in fragment 1b [p. 14], his account of the siege of Naissos, where within 35 lines of printed text Priscus's language is reminiscent of at least 28 passages in Herodotus, Thucydides, Xenophon and Dexippus (a third-century AD historian), with particularly frequent parallels to Thucydides's description of the Spartan siege of Plataea and Dexippus's account of the siege of Philippoupolis, which was itself modeled on Thucydides's Plataea narrative. One scholar, who believed the fragment is "a mere cento of Thucydidean phrases," argued that Dexippus and

Priscus "are purely literary compositions of less value to the historian than is commonly thought" (Thompson 1945b, 92–93). He concluded that Priscus's description of the Hunnic siege must be falsified, since the Huns did not possess siege technology. Such thinking is generally rejected today, as scholars have come to understand the classicizing historians' practice better. Priscus is not merely substituting "Naissos" for "Plataea." He is using Thucydides's language to validate his own judgment of the significance of the Hunnic siege of Naissos. Even if Priscus uses ancient terminology for siege warfare and even if it is fair for the scientific historian to dispute Priscus's details, the reader nevertheless learns more about the place of the Naissos siege in the course of Roman history than a mere list of accurate facts could provide. As for Hunnic technologies, it is generally recognized that Thompson's preconceptions of the Huns' abilities led him to misjudge their expertise. They certainly did take Naissos, as well as several other cities south of the Danube; it is hard to believe that they conquered these well-fortified places in any way other than a siege.[8]

III. THE TEXT

Priscus's history is a "lost" work. There exists no manuscript containing all or any of its eight books. Although such manuscripts survived until at least the tenth century, they are now gone. What we have instead—and what appears in this volume—are excerpts and allusions preserved in other Greek and Latin authors. For some of the fragments translated here, we can be fairly certain that we possess something close to Priscus's original words. The fragments preserved by Constantine VII Porphyrogennetos, in particular, are from collections of excerpts copied nearly word for word from Priscus's history. Other fragments are here because their authors say they used Priscus as a source for their own prose. In these, we are less likely to possess Priscus's original words, although it is not unusual for ancient authors to quote their sources verbatim. Still other passages are included here because scholars have made educated guesses that authors used Priscus as a source. This last group of fragments (nos. 50*–83*, along with 11*) are, according to scholarly convention, marked with an asterisk (*) and called "conjectural" because of their uncertain relationship to Priscus's original work.

In this section, I briefly review the eleven authors who have preserved Priscan material. None of the authors who quote or cite Priscus was his contemporary. We are relying on a centuries-long literary tradition for our scant knowledge of this important fifth-century historian.

1. Constantine VII Porphyrogennetos

The majority of this book exists because of an enterprise commissioned by a tenth-century Byzantine emperor named Constantine VII Porphyrogennetos. He initiated a work now called the *Constantinian Excerpts*. In this monumental undertaking, Constantinopolitan scholars read dozens of Greek historians, divided the texts into short passages and cataloged each excerpt under one of 53 pre-defined categories. We know the names of about half of the categories. They cover politics (e.g., "On the inauguration of emperors"), military events (e.g., "On victory"), religion (e.g., "On ecclesiastical affairs"), ethnography (e.g., "On customs") and literature (e.g., "On letters," i.e. epistles).[9] Under each category the excerptors produced a compilation of passages from Greek historians from the fifth century BC to the ninth century AD. Only a few of these compilations have survived; even the survivors are not complete. We have "On aphorisms" (*De sententiis*), "On plots" (*De insidiis*),

"On virtues and vices" (*De virtutibus et vitiis*) and most importantly for our purposes "On embassies of Romans to barbarians" (*De legationibus Romanorum ad gentes*) and "On embassies of barbarians to Romans" (*De legationibus gentium ad Romanos*).[10] These last two compilations are our main sources for Priscus's excerpts.

Constantine and his compilers, as far as we can tell, intended to include every word of each historical work somewhere in the 53 categories. Each excerpt was to be copied verbatim from the exemplar into the compilation. Several of the authors contained in the extant compilations have come down to us in separate manuscript traditions, and so we are able to judge how faithfully the excerptors copied their exemplars. They were extraordinarily faithful. There are often minor adjustments at the beginnings and ends of excerpts—e.g., the addition of a proper name or a time indicator like "when X was emperor"—so that the decontextualized passage is comprehensible. At times, a passage was removed from the middle of an excerpt, presumably because it had been designated for a different category. The excerptor did not mark the gap and sometimes rephrased the remaining text for the sake of comprehension. Overall, though, the transcriptions are faithful. In the case of a lost author like Priscus, it is impossible to know which words were added for contextualization and where excluded intermediary passages once existed. Besides this flaw, though, we can be reasonably certain that we are reading Priscus's words—or at least the words that existed in a tenth-century manuscript.[11]

The reason for the *Excerpts*' existence is hotly debated, but it is worth discussing because Constantine's motivation and ideology are important for our understanding of Priscus. Constantine's mere rearrangement of others' writings has frequently drawn scholars' scorn. It is an exercise in intellectual vacuity, they charge, an example of unoriginal, antiquarian encyclopedism. Even Edward Gibbon acknowledged that "we open with curiosity and respect the royal volumes" produced by Constantine, but "a closer survey will indeed reduce the value of the gift, and the gratitude of posterity."[12] More recently, scholars have been willing to study Constantine on his own terms and in his own historical context. They have recognized the intellectual, political, ideological and moral purposes that underlie his work.[13] Constantine's reign as emperor was never simple.[14] His surname, Porphyrogennetos, means "purple-born," indicating that he was born in the imperial household. And so he was, in AD 905, to Emperor Leo VI and his controversial, not-yet fourth wife Zoe. "Porphyrogennetos" was less an innocent description than a plea for legitimacy for the illegitimate son. Named co-emperor by his father before Leo died in 912, he was overshadowed by regents and co-emperors for over 30 years. He did not become sole emperor until 945, a position he would hold until his death in 959. Constantine exerted much effort in ideologically legitimizing his rule through the written word. Several of his works—*On Ruling the Empire*, *On Ceremonies*, *On the Provinces*, *The Life of Basil*—have survived. Although Priscus does not appear in the treatises, it is clear that the historical indexing performed for the *Excerpts* enabled Constantine to place himself, in writing, in a long tradition of Roman emperors. Although it is unlikely that the *Excerpts* were commissioned simply for Constantine's research purposes, the list of excerpted historians suggests that the compilers had a particular view of history in mind.

Anthony Kaldellis has shown that the Greek historians whose work survived the Byzantine period did so because of "identifiable Byzantine interests" that ensured their preservation.[15] As heirs of the Roman Empire, the Byzantines held the study of Roman history as a higher priority than study of the Greek city-states or the Hellenistic monarchies. Preserving the direct line of Roman emperors, they valued imperial history over Roman republican history. They also had a strong interest in the history of their neighbors, especially Persia, and the history of their Church, including its Jewish predecessor. As a result, the historians that were preserved—and chosen for inclusion in the *Constantinian Excerpts*—are focused on Judeo-Christian history, Near Eastern history, and Roman imperial history, especially in the post-Constantine the Great era. Thus, the *Excerpts* contain passages from Josephus and Socrates (the ecclesiastical historian) and from Herodotus (because of his Persian history) and Iamblichus (his quasi-historical *Babylonian History*). There are Roman and world histories by Nicolas of Damascus (his biography of Augustus), Cassius Dio, Dexippus, Eunapius, Zosimus, Procopius, Peter the Patrician, John Malalas, Malchus, Agathias, Menander the Guardsman, Theophylact Simocatta, John of Antioch, George the Monk—and our man Priscus. There are also a few representatives of earlier Roman history, including Polybius, Diodorus of Sicily, Dionysius of Halicarnassus and Appian. Three outliers appear, but their presence is easily explained. Arrian's histories of Alexander the Great are present not as representatives of Hellenistic history, but to educate readers about history's first great imperialist. And Thucydides and Xenophon are present not as representatives of Greek city-states' history (though Xenophon's *Cyropaideia* is notable for the light it sheds on Persia), but as canonical authors who displayed exemplary prose style and who were central to Byzantine education.[16]

Priscus, then, made it into the *Excerpts* and therefore into this book because he narrated a period of history that was important in the Byzantine view of world history. Like Eunapius before him and Procopius after him, Priscus is one of a string of historians covering nearly without break what we now call the period of Late Antiquity but which the Byzantines saw as an integral period in their own state's history. We can read Priscus because the Roman imperial succession continued into the tenth century and beyond.

2. John of Antioch

John is a (probably) seventh-century writer who compiled a universal history beginning with Adam and stretching to his own day. It focused on Roman history, including substantial work on the Republican period. His work survives only in fragments, preserved in the *Constantinian Excerpts*,[17] another excerpt collection called the *Excerpta Salmasiana*, the *Suda* and several other sources. Scholars have noted that the fragments in the two excerpt collections differ substantially in content and style, and so they have questioned whether the fragment sets even come from the same author. The questions when John ended his history (in the sixth or the seventh century) and even when he lived depend on how one resolves the controversy.[18] Fortunately, only one fragment (fr. 55* [p. 29]) identified as Priscan comes from the disputed, Salmasian parts of John's remnants and so the controversy does not greatly concern us.[19]

Fifteen of our Priscus fragments are preserved in John's corpus, all but two of them from the *Constantinian Excerpts*. (Fr. 55* [p. 29] comes from the *Excerpta Salmasiana* and fr. 52* [p. 22] from the *Suda*.) Comparison of John's fragments with his independently surviving sources (e.g., Plutarch, Cassius Dio) shows that John closely paraphrased his sources and sometimes synthesized them into a single narrative rather than, like Constantine's excerptors, copying them verbatim one author at a time. John's text, as it is excerpted, never names Priscus as a source. All of our fragments are therefore marked conjectural. Nevertheless, verbal and topical parallels make most of the identifications likely.[20]

3. Jordanes

Seven Priscus fragments—five certain (9, 10, 17, 23 and 45 [pp. 60, 70, 107, 112 and 9, respectively]) and two conjectural (66a* and 68* [pp. 104 and 114])—come from a history of the Goths by sixth-century author Jordanes. The work, written in Latin, is known as the *Getica* (full title: *De origine actibusque getarum*, "On the Origin and Deeds of the Goths"). We have scant knowledge of Jordanes himself. He tells us that he was secretary (*notarius*) to the Ostrogothic officer Gunthigis, also known as Baza, and that his grandfather had been secretary to the Alan king Candac, probably in the 450s.[21] He was probably of Gothic ethnicity, though there is some doubt. He probably wrote the *Getica* in Constantinople in 551 or a little later.[22] In its preface, he tells us that his book is an abridgement of Cassiodorus's twelve-volume *History of the Goths*,[23] a work written in Latin in the 520s or 530s and now lost. Jordanes claims to have supplemented Cassiodorus's accounts with information from Gothic oral tradition and from other Greek and Latin authors. Scholars have shown that most if not all of Jordanes's pre-fifth-century history is unhistorical, whatever sources may be claimed for it.[24] We reach more secure, though hardly consistently accurate, historical grounds when Jordanes narrates the fifth and sixth centuries, which is where we find his Priscan citations. All of Jordanes's Priscan passages, including the conjectural fragments, concern the Huns. The nineteenth century classicist Theodor Mommsen went so far as to suggest that in Jordanes there is nothing about Attila that is not from Priscus and there is nothing from Priscus that is not linked to Attila.[25] More recent editors have been more selective,[26] but it is clear that Priscus was one of Jordanes's main sources for fifth-century Hunnic material. Conversely, Jordanes is an essential witness for Priscus's Hunnic material.

There is some small overlap between Jordanes's citations of Priscus and the fragments preserved in Constantine's *Excerpts*, just enough to judge how reliable a witness Jordanes is for Priscus, even keeping in mind the fact that Jordanes is translating from Greek into Latin. *Getica* XXXIV.178–79 (= Priscus fr. 9 [p. 60]) is reminiscent of some scattered sentences in the long fragment 8, namely §64 and 83 (pp. 56 and 59). The passage is Jordanes's first mention of Attila. To describe his grandeur, he cites Priscus's journey to Attila's camp. He presents the citation as a continuous quotation from Priscus, when in fact he has selected only a few small details from Priscus's long account. Yet Jordanes's "quotation" also contains many details not found in Constantine's *Excerpts*. Though we cannot discount the possibility that Constantine's excerptors failed to report the entire Priscus text, it seems most likely that Jordanes has severely abridged Priscus's long account and then augmented it with invented details to support his own purposes. It is by no means a straightforward translation of the Greek historian.[27] The Jordanes fragments, then, even those which cite Priscus by name, should be used with caution by those who seek Priscus's original text. They are valuable and worth including here because they most likely do contain significant content from Priscus's history. But that content has been revised, supplemented and repurposed.

4. Procopius

Procopius is the giant among Late Antique / Early Byzantine classicizing historians. He was born around the turn of the sixth century in Caesarea in Palestine and was trained in rhetoric and law. He served on the staff of Justinian's general Belisarius during his campaigns in Persia, Africa and Italy, and so was an eyewitness to many of the events he describes. His three major works survive intact. The *Wars* was written in eight books. Books 1–2 cover the Persian campaign; as a unit, the books are sometimes called the *Persian Wars*. Books 3–4 narrate the *Vandalic Wars*. Books 5–7 are the *Gothic Wars*. The eighth book is a conclusion to the entire work, and updates each of the three main narratives. Besides the *Wars*, Procopius wrote *On Buildings*, a treatise in praise of Justinian and his art and architecture, and the *Anecdota* or the *Secret History*, a venomous attack on Justinian, Belisarius and their wives.[28]

Scholars have identified seven passages in Procopius's *Wars* as containing Priscan material (fragments 56*, 57*, 58*, 59*, 66b*, 76* and 83* [pp. 96, 30, 32, 25, 105, 158 and 174, respectively]). Procopius does not name Priscus in any of them. Five of the seven come from the *Vandalic Wars* and one each from the *Persian Wars* and *Gothic Wars*. We cannot compare Procopius's words with his sources', as was possible for John of Antioch and Jordanes. Even if we could, the result seems certain. Procopius, like Jordanes, wrote a coherent, literary narrative with a consistent narrative voice. Sources were adapted to his own purposes. For example, one recent scholar has demonstrated that, when using fifth-century sources, Procopius tended to eschew care about chronological precision in favor of his interest in explaining historical causation.[29] Insofar as he wrote in a classicizing style similar to Priscus, it remains

INTRODUCTION

possible that some phrases may have come over verbatim, but the much more likely scenario is that Procopius used Priscus as a source of facts, which he incorporated into his own unique narrative.

5. The Suda

The *Suda* is a late-tenth-century Byzantine encyclopedia-*cum*-dictionary. With 31,342 articles, arranged (mostly) alphabetically from alpha (*a a*, "ah! ah!") to omega (*ôpsônêkotes*, "having bought food"),[30] it collects words and phrases found throughout Greek literature, defines them and often includes quotations from authors who used the word(s). It also lists the names of historical people and gives mini-biographies of them. Although some authors, such as Homer, Aristophanes and the Bible, were consulted directly, most entries derive from other Byzantine compilations of texts. The historians in the *Suda* are quoted from the excerpts of Constantine VII Porphyrogennetos.[31]

For Priscus, the *Suda* preserves one testimonium (test. 1 [p. 3], on Priscus himself), four fragments that cite Priscus by name and four conjectural fragments. Unfortunately, the four fragments (fr. 47, 48a, 48b and 49 [pp. 173–174]) that cite Priscus by name are the least interesting. They preserve out-of-context sentences in which Priscus used an unusual word or phrase. None of them can be placed with any certainty within Priscus's narrative, but they do give us a handful of Priscus's words otherwise unattested.

The four conjectural fragments (fr. 11*, 52*, 70* and 79*) are more interesting, or at least more colorful. Fragment 52* (p. 22), which is a fragment of John of Antioch for which he may have used Priscus, tells of Theodosius II's relationships with his chamberlains in his youth.

Fragment 11* (p. 75) is the story of Zerkon, the Hunnic king Bleda's court jester. Fragment 70* (p. 127) glosses the rare word *thladias* ("eunuch") and preserves the story of how Valentinian was persuaded to kill Aetius by his eunuch courtiers. Fragment 79* (p. 165) preserves an anecdote about the long-distance runner—and Isaurian rebel—Indachos. Priscus certainly mentions all these characters. Whether he is the source for the specific information preserved in the *Suda* cannot be proved. Even if he is, their style indicates that the passages have been heavily abridged or rewritten. They may preserve Priscan material but it is highly unlikely that they present Priscus's verbatim words.

6. Evagrius

Five Priscus fragments (fr. 22, 43, 44, 63* and 75* [pp. 119, 151, 161, 95 and 146, respectively]) plus a testimonium (test. 2 [p. 3]) are preserved in the *Ecclesiastical History* of Evagrius. Evagrius was born *circa* 535 in Epiphaneia, in Syria. Trained in the law, he spent most of his life working for the Patriarch Gregory in Antioch.[32] His only work to survive is the *Ecclesiastical History* in six books, written around 593 and covering church but also secular events from around 430 down to his own day. Most of his fifth-century coverage deals with the Christological debates about the nature of Christ as human and divine. When he does include fifth-century secular material, Priscus and Zosimus are his main sources.[33] Evagrius keeps the ecclesiastical and secular sections distinct, an arrangement necessitated by his using only one source at a time and not, as John of Antioch sometimes did, synthesizing different accounts into a single narrative.[34]

It is not wholly clear how Evagrius used Priscus, since he adapted his sources in several ways. Only one of Evagrius's secular sources survives intact, namely Procopius. Comparison of Evagrius's text with Procopius's shows that Evagrius frequently quoted verbatim, but sometimes paraphrased. In some instances, Evagrius has drastically condensed large portions of Procopius's text. Moreover, Evagrius is not always free from factual error.[35] As for Priscus, Evagrius appears not to have quoted him verbatim. A couple of the fragments, particularly fr. 43 and fr. 44, seem to this translator at least to be bare-bones summaries. None of Evagrius's citations reports the same information as fragments preserved in other authors, and so it is impossible to verify whether Evagrius's are truncated or accurate. That lack of overlap, though, offers an important benefit. Evagrius does not cite Priscus for his Hunnic material. He knew that Priscus wrote about Attila, as testimonium 2 shows. Evagrius, however, has little interest in Roman–barbarian relations. Priscus's visit to Attila does not suit his purposes. Instead, Evagrius cites Priscus for religious riots in Alexandria (fr. 22), natural disasters (fr. 43) and the legendary early life of Emperor Marcian (fr. 63*). Because Evagrius is more concerned with urban events and imperial court dramas, we know that Priscus's history encompassed more than international relations.

7. Theophanes

The *Chronicle* of Theophanes the Confessor was written in the early ninth century and is the source for four Priscus fragments. Theophanes lived *circa* 759 or 760 to 818. Though married at a very young age, he entered a monastery, and his wife entered a convent. He probably wrote his *Chronicle* while in sickbed in the waning years of his life. The *Chronicle* is a compendium of earlier chronicles, histories, biographies and archival materials. It continues the chronicle of George Synkellos, which covered history down to Diocletian. At the request of Constantine VII Porphyrogennetos, Theophanes's *Chronicle* was itself continued into the tenth century by several anonymous writers.

Theophanes generally adheres closely to his source, being careful in the selection of his material and often directly quoting it with little alteration.[36] Yet, although Theophanes preserves a wealth of information, largely ecclesiastical but some secular, his ability to synthesize his sources into a correct chronology was weak. For example, in Priscus fragment 61* (p. 41), he confounds three Hunnic invasions of Thrace, in 441, 442 and 447, into a single year. Fragment 42 (p. 157), on the Eastern Empire's 468 expedition against Vandal North Africa, is the only passage for which Theophanes names Priscus as a source. Even here, he may have been reading Priscus through an intermediary. Still, there is a strong possibility that Priscus is the ultimate source for stories of Basiliscus's treachery during this mission. The other fragments believed to contain Priscan material are 54* (p. 25), on a conflict between Theodosius II and the Persians, and 65* (p. 102), a brief and confused account of Attila's campaigns against the Western Empire.

8. John Malalas

In his *Chronicle*, John Malalas names Priscus as an historian who wrote about the war between the Romans and the Huns (Book 14 §10 (ed. Thurn)), but it is not clear how Malalas used Priscus as a source. Malalas was a sixth-century writer who composed a history from creation to the death of Justinian in 565. "Malalas" seems to derive from a Syriac root associated with high learning. Evagrius refers to him as John the *rhêtor*; as with Priscus, the title probably indicates that Malalas was trained in the law. That his name contains Syriac elements is no surprise. To judge from the strong Antiochene perspective in his *Chronicle*, Malalas was a native of Antioch and probably worked there in the civil service. He seems to have been born in the 480s or 490s. His motivation for writing the *Chronicle* is unknown, although he demonstrates a strong interest in correcting others' chronological calculations.[37] Several ancient versions of the *Chronicle* have come down to us: in the original Greek but also in Latin, Syriac and Slavonic. The Slavonic translation is particularly useful in reconstructing parts of the *Chronicle* that do not survive intact in the Greek manuscripts.

Through Book 14, which concludes with the death of Leo II (in 474), Malalas frequently cites written sources for his knowledge. (Thereafter, he relies on his own memory, oral reports and documentary evidence.) Although he cites dozens of sources, both historians and poets, he did not have access to all of them firsthand. For example, he cites several Latin authorities, including Vergil, Ovid and Livy, but it is unlikely that Malalas could read Latin. Many of his "sources," then, are secondhand citations from books he did read. It is not clear into which category Priscus falls. Although Malalas writes about the Hunnic Wars and this is the context in which he actually names Priscus, Priscus does not seem to have been his source. Instead, Priscus seems to supply him, either directly or indirectly, with information about Constantinopolitan politicking. The two fragments identified as Priscan (53* and 60* [pp. 23 and 27]) concern Theodosius II's punishment of imperial magistrates in the 440s. The accounts are confused and (if we assume that Priscus's accounts adhered to the author's usual clarity) do not justify a belief that Malalas was using Priscus directly. Malalas's possible main source for the fifth century was the now lost *Chronicle* of Eustathius of Epiphaneia, an author known to have consulted Priscus's work.[37]

9. The Paschal Chronicle

The *Chronicon Paschale*, translated as the *Paschal Chronicle* or *Easter Chronicle* is an anonymous seventh-century chronicle that covered events from creation to AD

630, although the extant text breaks off in 628. It has its title because, in the preface and occasionally throughout the chronicle, the author pays particular attention to the dating of Christian feasts, especially the complex dating system of Easter Sunday. Accurate chronology was a major concern of the chronicle's author. He coordinated multiple dating systems and labeled each year's entry in multiple ways. Thus, during the Late Antique period, each year is catalogued by its Olympiad number, indiction number (an indiction is a 15-year taxation cycle), years of the current imperial reign and the eponymous consuls. Even for years when there are no events listed, the author gives the chronographic information.

The *Chronicle*'s author adapted a variety of sources, both Greek and Latin, for its own chronology. John Malalas is a major source, as are several other anonymous chronicles. The author, however, did not merely transcribe his source into his own work. He adapted, arranged, combined, reordered and rewrote his source material to suit his own purposes.[39] The *Chronicle* has two fragments attributed to Priscus: fragment 3a (p. 26) and fragment 64* (p. 101). In the *Chronicle*'s text, 64* is followed immediately by 3a, which cites Priscus by name and says "he says that," as if Priscus's own words follow.[40] It is one of the few times the *Chronicle* names a source, and yet it is highly unlikely that the anonymous author read Priscus. Both fragments are taken from John Malalas, where they are a few pages apart. Malalas mentions Priscus in connection with our 64*, but not in connection with our 3a. While there may be a genuine Priscan passage underlying either or both fragments, readers should not have much confidence in either.[41]

10. Nikephoros Kallistos Xanthopoulos

Nikephoros Kallistos was a priest and teacher of rhetoric who lived in the late thirteenth and early fourteenth centuries. He wrote an ecclesiastical history in eighteen books, completing it probably in the 1320s. For the Late Antique period, Nikephoros was almost wholly dependent upon Evagrius.[42] The few times when he cites Priscus by name, the text comes directly from Evagrius, and so the passages are not translated here. Our collection contains one other Nikephoros passage (fragment 67*, about the Egyptian god Serapis [p. 120]) that may come from Priscus. It is not derived from Evagrius but immediately follows Evagrius's account of the Alexandrian riots in Nikephoros (= Priscus fragment 22 [p. 119]). Nikephoros would not have read Priscus directly. Instead, like John Malalas, Nikephoros may have used Eustathius of Epiphaneia as an intermediary.

11. Stephanos of Byzantium

A single fragment (fr. 46 [p. 173])—actually, a single word—comes down to us in the *Ethnika* of Stephanos of Byzantium. Stephanos was a sixth-century grammarian and teacher, working in Constantinople, who compiled a massive work listing geographical names.[43] Only an epitome, an abridgment, of the work has come down to us, apparently depriving us of many of Stephanos's literary citations.[44] One of Stephanos's aims was to use published literature along with morphological rules to identify each location's proper demonym, i.e. the term for someone who hails from a certain place, as if we were to record that someone from New York is a New Yorker, from Paris a Parisian and from Moscow a Muscovite. He tells us that Priscus called a person from Salonae a *Saloneus*.

IV. THE TRANSLATION

It has been my practice to attempt to express in fluent English the meaning of each Greek sentence in its context. I have not tried to render Greek words consistently with the same English words, except in cases of the rare technical terms. So *presbeus* and its cognates are always "ambassador" or "embassy," particularly important terms given the nature of Constantine's excerpts. In contrast, Priscus uses the term *basileus* to refer to monarchs. When he refers to Attila or other barbarian monarchs, I have used "king." When the reference is to the Roman monarch, I have used "emperor." Like most classicizing Greek writers, Priscus prefers to translate Latin technical terms into non-technical Greek terms rather than transliterate them, but some Latin words do appear in his text transliterated. For example, at fr. 8 §75 (p. 58), Priscus calls the Western ambassador Romulus a *komês*, a transliteration of the Latin title *comes*. Yet in the same sentence, he refers to his fellow ambassadors Promoutos and Romanos as *tês Nôrikôn archôn chôras* and *stratiôtikou tagmatos hêgemôn*, which are commonplace Greek words. My practice has been to translate the commonplace Greek words into commonplace English words—here, "the governor of Noricum" and "leader of a military division"—even when there is a detectable Latin title behind Priscus's Greek. The Latin terms Priscus transliterated into Greek I have put back into the Latin alphabet, but left them untranslated. Thus, *"comes"* in my translation. The foreign word in the Greek remains a foreign word in the English.

Translating proper nouns always requires some compromise. The principles of translation ask me to give readers of my English the same qualitative experience that I have in reading Priscus's Greek. For proper nouns, it means that I ought to leave them as close as possible to their Greek spelling. Yet I also recognize that most classical names are used in English—including in standard reference works—with Latinate spellings. For names of people and places,

Introduction

therefore, I have used Latinate spelling when readers are likely to encounter the names in other works, but I have used Greek spelling for all other names so that readers will keep a sense that they are reading a Hellenic text. (The only exceptions are the fragments from Jordanes's Latin-language *Getica*, which keep Jordanes's Latin spellings.) When there might be some confusion about a person's identity, I provide a cross-reference to *The Prosopography of the Late Roman Empire* (*PLRE*).

One more note about geographical locations: For most place-names, I have included in the notes descriptions of where to find the places on a modern map. (The most frequent equivalency is worth mentioning here: the Istros or Ister River is the Danube.) I have also included references to the Pleiades Project, an invaluable online compendium of ancient geographical information maintained by the Institute for the Study of the Ancient World at New York University (http://pleiades.stoa.org), based on Richard Talbert's research for his *Barrington Atlas of the Greek and Roman World*. The references are numbers that can be integrated into a URL (http://pleiades.stoa.org/places/*ref#*) to bring up maps and other information on thousands of ancient locations. I also highly recommend the excellent online maps in the Digital Atlas of the Roman Empire (http://imperium.ahlfeldt.se/), which has been my primary source for matching ancient and modern place names. Where useful, I have also included distances between points that Priscus mentions. These have been calculated using Google Earth's measuring tools, using the longitudinal and latitudinal coordinates from Pleiades; the calculations are not meant to reflect distances on ancient roads, only straight-line distances on a map.

V. FURTHER READING

Those wishing to pursue further research in English about Priscus, Attila and the fifth century will find a good starting point here. There is an enormous amount of material, both academic and popular, about Late Antiquity, and I can only scratch the surface of even the best books and articles. The ones listed below are those I have found most useful.

In the historical notes that appear among the translated fragments, I have tried to print what has emerged as scholarly consensus about fifth-century events. The nature of this publication has precluded me from incorporating detailed footnotes. Let the list below, then, also serve as my acknowledgement and my expression of gratitude to those scholars whose works I have consulted to judge current consensus. A complete bibliography appears at the end of the volume.

ON PRISCUS AND FIFTH-CENTURY HISTORIOGRAPHY

Baldwin, Barry. 1980. "Priscus of Panium." *Byzantium* 50: 18–61.

Blockley, R. C. 1981 and 1983. *The Fragmentary Classicising Historians of the Later Roman Empire: Eunapius, Olympiodorus, Priscus and Malchus*. 2 vols. Reprint edition, 2007 and 2009. Liverpool: Francis Cairns.

Gordon, C. D. 2013. *The Age of Attila: Fifth-Century Byzantium and the Barbarians*. Revised edition, with introduction and notes by David S. Potter. Ann Arbor: University of Michigan Press.

Rohrbacher, David. 2002. *The Historians of Late Antiquity*. London and New York: Routledge.

Treadgold, Warren. 2007. *The Early Byzantine Historians*. Basingstoke and New York: Palgrave Macmillan.

ON FIFTH-CENTURY HISTORY

Blockley, R. C. 1992. *East Roman Foreign Policy: Formation and Conduct from Diocletian to Anastasius*. Leeds: Francis Cairns.

Introduction

Cameron, Averil and Peter Garnsey, eds. 1998. *The Late Empire, AD 337–425*. Vol. 13 of *The Cambridge Ancient History*. Cambridge: Cambridge University Press.

Cameron, Averil, Bryan Ward-Perkins and Michael Whitby, eds. 2001. *Late Antiquity: Empire and Successors, AD 425–600*. Vol. 14 of *The Cambridge Ancient History*. Cambridge: Cambridge University Press.

Cameron, Averil. 2012. *The Mediterranean World in Late Antiquity, AD 395–700*. 2nd ed. London and New York: Routledge.

Christie, Neil. 2011. *The Fall of the Western Roman Empire: An Archaeological and Historical Perspective*. London and New York: Bloomsbury Academic.

Goldsworthy, Adrian. 2009. *How Rome Fell: Death of a Superpower*. New Haven and London: Yale University Press.

Halsall, Guy. 2007. *Barbarian Migrations and the Roman West, 376–568*. Cambridge: Cambridge University Press.

Heather, Peter. 1996. *The Goths*. Cambridge, Mass.: Blackwell Publishers.

Heather, Peter. 2006. *The Fall of the Roman Empire: A New History of Rome and the Barbarians*. Oxford and New York: Oxford University Press.

Hughes, Ian. 2012. *Aetius: Attila's Nemesis*. Barnsley, UK: Pen and Sword.

Jones, A. H. M. 1964. *The Later Roman Empire, 284–602: A Social, Economic and Administrative Survey*. 2 vols. Norman: University of Oklahoma Press.

Kelly, Christopher. 2009. *The End of Empire: Attila the Hun and the Fall of Rome*. New York and London: Norton.

Kim, Hyun Jin. 2013. *The Huns, Rome and The Birth of Europe*. Cambridge and New York: Cambridge University Press, 2013.[45]

Lee, A. D. 2013. *From Rome to Byzantium AD 363 to 565: The Transformation of Ancient Rome*. Edinburgh: Edinburgh University Press.

Maenchen-Helfen, J. Otto. 1973. *The World of the Huns*. Edited by Max Knight. Berkeley, Los Angeles and London: University of California Press.

Martindale, J. R. 1980. *The Prosopography of the Later Roman Empire (PLRE)*. Volume 2: *AD 395–527*. Cambridge: Cambridge University Press.

Thompson, E. A. 1996. *The Huns*. Revised edition, with an afterword by Peter Heather. Originally published as *A History of Attila and the Huns*, 1948. Oxford: Blackwell Publishers.

Ward-Perkins, Bryan. 2005. *The Fall of Rome and the End of Civilization*. Oxford: Oxford University Press.

OTHER LATE ANTIQUE HISTORIANS AND THEIR TRANSLATIONS

Allen, Pauline. 1981. *Evagrius Scholasticus: The Church Historian*. Leuven: Spicilegium Sacrum Lovaniense.

Stephanos of Byzantium. 2006. *Stephani Byzantii Ethnica*. Volume 1, A–Γ. Edited by Margarethe Billerbeck. Berlin and New York: Walter de Gruyter.

Cameron, Averil. 1985. *Procopius and the Sixth Century*. Berkeley and Los Angeles: University of California Press.

Christensen, Arne Søby. 2002. *Cassiodorus, Jordanes and the History of the Goths: Studies in a Migration Myth*. Copenhagen: Museum Tusculanum Press.

Evagrius. *The Ecclesiastical History of Evagrius Scholasticus*. 2000. Translated by Michael Whitby. Liverpool: Liverpool University Press.

Goffart, Walter. 1988. *The Narrators of Barbarian History (AD 550–800): Jordanes, Gregory of Tours, Bede, and Paul the Deacon*. Princeton: Princeton University Press.

John of Antioch. 2005. *Ioannnis Antiocheni Fragmenta ex Historia Chronica*. Edited and translated (into Italian) by Umberto Roberto. Berlin and New York: Walter de Gruyter.

Jordanes. 1915. *The Gothic History of Jordanes*. Translated by Charles Christopher Mierow. Reprint edition, 2006. Merchantville, NJ: Evolution Publishing.

Kaldellis, Anthony. 2004. *Procopius of Caesarea: Tyranny, History, and Philosophy at the End of Antiquity*. Philadelphia: University of Pennsylvania Press.

Kaldellis, Anthony. 2012. "The Byzantine Role in the Making of the Corpus of Classical Greek Historiography: A Preliminary Investigation." *Journal of Hellenic Studies* 132: 71–85.

Malalas, John. 1986. *The Chronicle of John Malalas: A Translation*. Translated by Elizabeth Jeffreys, Michael Jeffreys and Roger Scott. Melbourne: Australian Association for Byzantine Studies.

Theophanes. 1997. *The Chronicle of Theophanes Confessor: Byzantine and Near Eastern History, AD 284–813*. Translated by Cyril Mango and Roger Scott, with Geoffrey Greatrex. Oxford: Clarendon Press.

Whitby, Michael and Mary Whitby (Trans.). 1989. *Chronicon Paschale, 284–628 AD*. Liverpool: Liverpool University Press.

INTRODUCTION

NOTES

1. Baldwin 1980, 21–22; Blockley 1981, 48; Rohrbacher 2002, 82. It used to be scholarly opinion that Priscus worked as a *scriniarius*, a minor bureaucrat in a financial or legal office. This belief turned on the identification of the ambassador Maximinos with a man of the same name who worked on the Theodosian Code as a *magister scrinii*. As this identification has been called into question, so too has Priscus lost his official employment. See, though, Treadgold 2007a, 97, who revives the possibility.
2. For an overview of the *magister's* duties, see *CAH* XIV, 172.
3. Speculation at *PLRE* II 424 (Euphemius 1), based on the fact that Marcian's daughter was named Euphemia.
4. On the rise of professional "lawyer-historians" in Late Antiquity, see Greatrex 2001. He mentions Priscus in passing (p. 50).
5. This discussion is informed by: Baldwin 1980, 27–28; Blockley 1981, 49–51; Blockley 2003, 293; Rohrbacher 2002, 88; Treadgold 2007a, 99–100.
6. On the importance of first-person narration for the Late Antique historian's claim to authority, see Austin 1983.
7. Blockley 1981, 87–88, partially following Momigliano, argues that the revival of classical historiography, especially in the case of Eunapius, the earliest revivalist, came about through a hostility toward Christianity.
8. On the weakness of Thompson's argument, see Baldwin 1980, 53–54; Blockley 1972; Blockley 1981, 54–55. On the Huns' military capabilities, see Maenchen-Helfen 1973, 201–58 (highly speculative but worthwhile); Heather 2006, 302–4. Adshead 1983 provides another good example of how to understand a Late Antique historian (in this case, Agathias) and his imitation of Thucydides. Thompson's understanding of the historiographical tradition is not unique nor is it wholly dead today; see, e.g., Cataudella 2003, on Procopius's imitation of Thucydides and Herodotus.
9. For lists of known and hypothesized categories, see Flusin 2002, 553–55; Németh 2010, 73; Schreiner 1987, 21–23.
10. The so-called Mynas codex (Par. suppl. gr. 607) preserves a collection of historical excerpts on sieges, including Priscus fr. 1a (p. 12) and 1b (p. 14). Although we do not know whether Constantine's project had an "On sieges" category, it is plausible that the compilation derives from his work. See Wescher 1868; Németh 2010, 147–72. There are also a few fragments preserved in a Milan codex that could belong to "On public speeches" (a known category), but the connection is tenuous. See Németh 2010, 175–76.

11. So too Flusin 2004, 122, though one should note his cautionary tone on 129. On the excerptor's methods of adaptation, see also Németh 2010, 228–35; Pittia 2006.
12. Ševčenko 1992 is a highly amusing but insightful "letter" from Constantine himself reappraising the worth of Constantine's intellectual contributions. Gibbon quote from p. 173 n. 11. See also Lemerle 1986, 331–32, for an appreciation of Byzantine humanism that still fails to treat Constantine on his own terms.
13. See, e.g., Holmes 2010; Németh 2010; Ševčenko 1992. Toynbee 1973, 581 is an early proponent of looking deeper into Constantine's antiquarianism.
14. For an overview of Constantine's life, see Toynbee 1973, 2–14.
15. Kaldellis 2012, 71.
16. On Byzantine prioritization of Roman imperial history over Greek city-state history, see also Jeffreys 1979; Ševčenko 1992, 180.
17. The Johannine fragments come from the collections "On virtues and vices" and "On plots," collections that do not contain (in their surviving parts) any direct quotations from Priscus.
18. John's two recent editions, Roberto 2005 and Mariev 2008, discuss the issue thoroughly; a more accessible introduction to the issues can be found at Whittow 2009 (a review of Mariev's edition).
19. On the unlikelihood that our fr. 55* (= John of Antioch fr. 290 in Roberto's edition) derives from Priscus, see Bleckmann 2010, 60. Bleckmann notes that the only other fifth-century fragment from the Salmasian John (fr. 293.2 [ed. Roberto]) tells the same story as a fragment from the Constantinian John (fr. 293.1 [ed. Roberto]), the latter of which has greater claim to be Priscan in origin and is printed here as fr. 69* (p. 125) and fr. 71* (p. 128).
20. See Blockley 1981, 114; Roberto 2005, CLV–LVII.
21. Jordanes, *Getica* L.265. (Jordanes is quoted from the edition of Giunta and Grillone.) Christensen 2002, 84–102 carefully reviews all the evidence for Jordanes's life, ancestry and career. See also Goffart 1988, 42–47.
22. On Jordanes's date of composition, see most recently Croke 2005.
23. *Getica* Pref.1–2.
24. Oral tradition: *Getica* IV.28, XI.72. Other authors: *Getica* Pref.3. Croke 1987, 122–24 catalogs the contributions of other classical authors, including Priscus. Non-historical narrative: Christensen 2002, *passim*; Goffart 1988, 88–96; Heather 1989; Heather 1991, 52–61. For a defense of Gothic oral tradition as a genuine and valid source for Jordanes, see Heather 1991, 61–67; Croke 2003, 374–75.
25. Mommsen 1882, 35.

INTRODUCTION

26. Blockley 1981, 113–14 gives reasons for excluding much of Jordanes's Hunnic material from the Priscan corpus.
27. Cf. Heather 1991, 35–38. Goffart 1988, 40–41 reaches a similar, if tentative, conclusion regarding Jordanes's abridgement of Cassiodorus.
28. Biographical and literary sketch: Cataudella 2003, 392–404.
29. Brodka 2007.
30. The number is the total number of articles on Suda Online (http://www.stoa.org/sol/), a crowdsourced project to translate the entire encyclopedia. The entries are "almost" alphabetical because diphthongs are treated as a single letter. For example, words beginning with alpha-iota are grouped together after the other alpha-initial words.
31. de Boor 1912 and de Boor 1914–1919.
32. Biographical overviews: Allen 1981, 1–4; Whitby 2000, xiii–xv.
33. Whitby 2000, xxvi–xxvii.
34. Allen 1981, 7–11 criticizes Evagrius's inability to synthesize his historical sources.
35. Allen 1981, 15–16; Whitby 2000, xxviii–xxxi.
36. On Theophanes's biography and historiography, see Mango, Scott and Greatrex 1997, xliii–xciv.
37. For biographical information and speculation, see Croke in Jeffreys, Croke and Scott 1990, 1–11; Jeffreys 2003; Thurn 2000, 2*–4*.
38. Blockley 1981, 116–17; Jeffreys in Jeffreys, Croke and Scott 1990, 168–72 and 191.
39. For discussion, see Whitby and Whitby 1989, xv–xxii.
40. Because I disagree with how editors have divided the *Chronicle's* text between fr. 64* and fr. 3a, I have moved what editors print as the first paragraph of 3a to the end of fr. 64*, where its context is more meaningful. In the *Chronicle* it is a single continuous passage, albeit one that describes events several years apart.
41. See also Blockley 1981, 116–17.
42. On Nikephoros, see Panteghini 2009.
43. Billerbeck 2006, 2–4 reviews our scant knowledge of Stephanos's life and work.
44. Billerbeck 2008 compares the epitome of Stephanos to a few pages from the full work that happen to survive.
45. Of all the works listed here, Kim's new book goes the furthest in challenging scholarly consensus, in seeking to revise radically our understanding of the Huns by placing them in their historical central Asian context. While its views are not generally represented in this book, I include it in the Further Reading list for its inherent interest, even when I cannot support its conclusions.

THE FRAGMENTS

THEIR SOURCES AND NUMBERING SYSTEMS

The table below lists all the testimonia and fragments contained in this volume in numerical order, as in Carolla's Greek edition. With each testimonium and fragment appears the corresponding fragment number in Blockley's edition. Blockley uses brackets rather than asterisks to mark uncertain fragments. "N/A" indicates that Blockley does not include the fragment in his collection. Each line also cites the source of the fragment and, since they are not translated here in numerical order, it gives the page number in this volume.

Abbreviations
Evagr. = Evagrius, *Ecclesiastical History*.
Chron. Pasch. = *Chronicon Paschale* (*Easter Chronicle*).
　　　The *Easter Chronicle* is cited by the page numbers from Dindorf's edition (1832).
EI = Constantine VII Porphyrogennetos, "Excerpts on plots" (*Excerpta de inidiis*)
ELR = Constantine VII Porphyrogennetos, "Excerpts on embassies of Romans to foreigners" (*Excerpta de legationibus Romanorum ad gentes*)
ELG = Constantine VII Porphyrogennetos, "Excerpts on embassies of foreigners to Romans" (*Excerpta de legationibus gentium ad Romanos*)
EV = Constantine VII Porphyrogennetos, "Excerpts on virtues and vices" (*Excerpta de virtutibus et vitiis*)
John Ant. = John of Antioch. Fragment numbers are cited from the edition of Roberto.
John Mal. = John Malalas, *Chronicle*

Jord. = Jordanes, *Getica*
Nik. Kall. = Nikephoros Kallistos, *Ecclesiastical History*
Par. suppl. gr. 607 = "Excerpts on sieges"
Procop. = Procopius, *Wars*
Theoph. = Theophanes, *Chronicle*. (a.m. = *anno mundi*, "year of the world," Theophanes' chronological system.)

Carolla	Blockley	Source	Page #
test. 1	test. 1	Suda Π 2301	3
test. 2	test. 2	Evagr. I.17	3
fr. 1	fr. 2	ELR 1	8
fr. 1.1	fr. 2	ELR 1	10–11
fr. 1a	fr. 5	Par. suppl. gr. 607	12
fr. 1b	fr. 6.2	Par. suppl. gr. 607	14–15
fr. 2	fr. 6.1	ELG 1	13–14
fr. 3	fr. 9.1	ELG 2	35–36
fr. 3a	n/a	Chron. Pasch. p. 588	26–27
fr. 4	fr. 9.2	ELR 2	36
fr. 5	fr. 9.3	ELG 3	37–40
fr. 6	fr. 10	ELG 4	42
fr. 7	fr. 11.1	ELG 5	44–46
fr. 8	fr. 11.2 + fr. 12.1 + fr. 13.1 + fr. 13.3 + fr. 14	ELR 3	47–59, 60–70, 71–74, 76–79
fr. 8.1	fr. 15.1	ELR 3	80–81
fr. 9	fr. 11.3	Jord. XXXIV.178–179	60
fr. 10	fr. 12.2	Jord. XXXV.183	70–71
fr. 11*	fr. 13.2	Suda Z 29	75
fr. 12	fr. 15.2	ELG 6	81–82
fr. 12.1	fr. 15.2	ELG 6	82
fr. 13	fr. 15.3	ELR 4	83–84
fr. 14	fr. 15.4	ELR 5	84–85
fr. 15	fr. 20.1	ELG 7	98–99
fr. 16	fr. 20.3	ELG 8	99–100
fr. 17	fr. 22.1	Jord. XLII.222–223	107
fr. 18	fr. 23.3	ELR 6	103–104
fr. 19	fr. 23.1	ELG 9	108
fr. 20	fr. 26	ELG 10	117
fr. 21	fr. 27.1	ELG 11	118–119

The Fragments

Carolla	Blockley	Source	Page #
fr. 22	fr. 28.1	Evagr. II.5	119–120
fr. 23	fr. 24.1	Jord. XLIX.254–258	112–113
fr. 24	fr. 31.1	ELR 7	131–132
fr. 25	fr. 33.1	ELR 8	121–122
fr. 26	fr. 33.2	ELG 12	122–123
fr. 27	fr. 36.1	ELG 13	134
fr. 28	fr. 37	ELR 9	136
fr. 29	fr. 38.1	ELR 10	136–137
fr. 30	fr. 39.1 + fr. 40.1	ELG 14	138–139
fr. 31	fr. 41.1	ELG 15	142–143
fr. 32	fr. 41.2	ELR 11	143–144
fr. 33	fr. 41.3	ELR 12	144–146
fr. 34	fr. 44	ELG 16	147
fr. 35	fr. 45	ELG 17	148
fr. 36	fr. 46	ELG 18	149
fr. 37	fr. 47	ELG 19	150
fr. 38	fr. 48.1	ELG 20	151–152
fr. 39	fr. 49	ELG 21	152–154
fr. 40	fr. 52	ELR 13	157
fr. 41	fr. 51.1	ELG 22	155
fr. 42	fr. 53.1	Theoph. a.m. 5961	157–158
fr. 43	fr. 48.2	Evagr. II.14	151
fr. 44	fr. [50] + fr. 53.2 + fr. 61	Evagr. II.16	161
fr. 45	fr. 1	Jord. XXIV.122–126	9–10
fr. 46	fr. 39.2	Steph. Byz. s.v. Σάλωνα	173
fr. 47	fr. 67	Suda A 1660	173
fr. 48a	fr. 31.2	Suda X 144	173
fr. 48b	n/a	Suda Δ 1594	174
fr. 49	fr. 68	Suda Π 687	174
fr. 50*	n/a	John Ant. fr. 285 = EV 69	20
fr. 51*	n/a	John Ant. fr. 286 = EV 70	21
fr. 52*	[fr. 3.2] + [fr. 4] + [fr. 3.1]	John Ant. fr. 288 = EV 72 = Suda Θ 145	22–23
fr. 53*	[fr. 7]	John Mal. XIV.16	23–24
fr. 54*	n/a	Theoph. a.m. 5921	25
fr. 55*	n/a	John Ant. fr. 290	29
fr. 56*	n/a	Procop. III.4.1–11	96–98
fr. 57*	n/a	Procop. III.4.12–14	30–31
fr. 58*	n/a	Procop. III.5.8–17	32–33
fr. 59*	n/a	Procop. I.2.11–15	25–26
fr. 60*	[fr. 8]	John Mal. XIV.16	27

THE FRAGMENTARY HISTORY OF PRISCUS

Carolla	Blockley	Source	Page #
fr. 61*	[fr. 9.4]	Theoph. a.m. 5942	41
fr. 62*	fr. 16 + fr. 17	John Ant. fr. 292 = EI 84	93–94
fr. 63*	fr. 18	Evagr. II.1	95–96
fr. 64*	fr. 21.1	Chron. Pasch. p. 587	101
fr. 65*	[fr. 21.2]	Theoph. a.m. 5943	102
fr. 66a*	fr. 22.1	Jord. XLII.219–222	104–105
fr. 66b*	fr. 22.2	Procop. III.4.29-35	105–106
fr. 67*	[fr. 28.2]	Nik. Kall. XV.8	120–121
fr. 68*	[fr. 25]	Jord. L.259–263	114–116
fr. 69*	[fr. 30.1]	John Ant. fr. 293.1 = EI 85	125–127
fr. 70*	n/a	Suda Θ 389	127
fr. 71*	[fr. 30.1]	John Ant. fr. 291.1 = EI 85	128–130
fr. 72*	[fr. 32]	John Ant. fr. 294 = EI 86	132–133
fr. 73*	fr. 36.2	John Ant. fr. 295 = EI 87	134–135
fr. 74*	fr. 38.2	John Ant. fr. 296 = EI 88	137
fr. 75*	[fr. 42]	Evagr. II.13	146–147
fr. 76*	fr. 53.3	Procop. III.6.1–2, 5–25	158–161
fr. 77*	[fr. 54.1]	John Ant. fr. 297 = EI 89	162
fr. 78*	[fr. 55] + [fr. 56] [fr. 57] + [fr. 51.2] + + [fr. 59]	John Ant. fr. 298 = EI 90	163–164
fr. 79*	n/a	Suda I 368	165
fr. 80*	[fr. 62]	John Ant. fr. 299 = EI 91	169
fr. 81*	[fr. 63]	John Ant. fr. 300 = EI 92	166
fr. 82*	[fr. 64.1] + [fr. 65]	John Ant. fr. 301 = EI 93	170–171
fr. 83*	[fr. 66]	Procop. VI.15–23	174–175

THE ROMAN EMPIRE,
the Empire of Attila and neighboring states
AD 450
miles
kilometers
500
800
FRANKS
VISIGOTHS
Aurelia
Mediolanum
Aquileia
Ravenna
Rome
Western Roman Empire
Vandalic Kingdom
Carthage
Empire of Attila
Sirmium
Singidunum
Margos
Danube (Ister) River
Novidounon
Ratiaria
Asemos
Novae
Naissos
Serdica
Odessos
Philippoupolis
Arkadioupolis
Hadrianopole
Athyras
Constantinople
Panion
Eastern Roman Empire
Smyrna
Isauropolis
Damascus

THE FRAGMENTARY HISTORY OF PRISCUS

ANCIENT TESTIMONIA

We begin with two brief notices, or testimonia, that mention Priscus but do not preserve any of his history. They were written at least a century after Priscus's life by people who never knew him. Most likely, their only knowledge of him came from his writings. We know of no independent biographical tradition. They had the entirety of his writings and so were in a better position than modern readers to ascertain facts about Priscus, but it is striking how few details they extracted from the writings of a man who figured prominently in his own historical work.

TESTIMONIUM 1
From the *Suda*

Priscus, of Panion,[1] a sophist, lived in the time of Theodosius II. He wrote a *Byzantine History*, including *On Attila*, in eight books,[2] and also rhetorical declamations and letters.

TESTIMONIUM 2
From the *Ecclesiastical History* of Evagrius

At this time, the well-documented war with Attila, king of the Scythians, was stirred up. Priscus the orator wrote about it eloquently and especially eruditely. With great refinement he told how Attila marched against the Eastern and Western Empires, how many and what sort of cities he captured and subdued, and how many things he accomplished before he died.[3]

NOTES

1. A town in the Thracian Chersonese, on the north shore of the Sea of Marmara, modern Barbaros, Turkey, located 128 km west of Constantinople. Pleiades ID: 511351. It was briefly called Theodosiopolis in honor of Theodosius II (Jones 1971, 25). The *Chronicon Paschale* (s.a. 450 = Priscus fr. 64* [p. 101]) and Theophanes (a.m. 5961 = Priscus fr. 42 [p. 157]) also attest Priscus's Thracian heritage.
2. On these titles, see Introduction, Section II (pp. xiv–xv).
3. Or "before he left there."

THE ARRIVAL OF THE HUNS

Priscus probably began his history with the greatest foreign threat of his lifetime: the Huns. The Huns had thunderously entered onto the Roman stage in AD 376 when their westward migrations from the central Asian steppe caused thousands of Goths to seek refuge on the Roman side of the Danube River. The Romans knew next to nothing about the new arrivals. The fourth-century Roman historian Ammianus Marcellinus, in a tour de force *of ethnographic chauvinism, imagination and inherited stereotypes of distant foreigners, begins his description of the Huns by calling them "abnormally savage. From the moment of birth they make deep gashes in their children's cheeks, so that when in due course hair appears its growth is checked by the wrinkled scars; as they grow older this gives them the unlovely appearance of beardless eunuchs. They have squat bodies, strong limbs, and thick necks, and are so prodigiously ugly and bent that they might be two-legged animals, or the figures crudely carved from stumps which are seen on the parapets of bridges" (Ammianus Marcellinus 31.1, trans. Hamilton).*

Our own information on the Huns' origins, appearance, culture and migration is only slightly better than the tales of Ammianus. There are no written accounts by the Huns or the non-Romans they overran. It is reasonably clear that the Huns were a nomadic people from central Asia who began moving westward by the 350s. We do not know what caused their movements, but it is unlikely to have been a political decision. They seem to have been only very loosely organized or even wholly unorganized bands. Ammianus reports that the Huns overcame the Alans, another nomadic group who dwelled somewhere north or northeast of the Black Sea. But he also says that "other Huns," hired by the Gothic king Vithimir, fought against the approaching Huns. This is the dominant pattern in our sources about the fourth century: the Huns fight both alongside and against various groups. In 378, they joined the Goths after (but not at) the Battle of Hadrianople to ravage the Balkan countryside. Around 381–382, the Huns were among Skiri and Carpodacian raiders who were driven back from the Danube. Ambrose, the Bishop of Milan, records a Hunnic band threatening Gaul, possibly in 384. Huns were even hired as mercenaries by the Romans. They formed part of Theodosius I's army when he marched against the usurper Maximus in 388 and against the usurper Eugenius in 394; yet they also are said to have raided the Balkan provinces in 392 and, in 395, they crossed the Caucasus Mountains and harassed both the Persian Empire and the easternmost Roman provinces.[1] *Throughout these events, the Huns worked without discernible strategy for conquering territory or establishing power. They did not set out to construct a European empire. They moved and fought where there was opportunity for wealth.*

That pattern holds true when Hunnic kings appear in historical records. The ascendance of a king suggests a more highly organized political structure, with the king probably ruling over numerous previously disorganized groups. Even with a king, though, the Huns' tactics remained the same. The first king we know was Uldin, who apparently allied himself with the Roman general Stilicho and helped defend Italy from the Goths in 406. But he is also said to have raided Roman lands

THE ARRIVAL OF THE HUNS

in Thrace in the winter of 404/405 and again in the summer of 408. His demands—demands we will see oft repeated by later kings in the fragments below—were for tribute payments, not territory. The next king we hear of is Charaton, who ruled sometime in the 410s or 420s; he may have succeeded Uldin or been king of a different group of Huns. Like Priscus later, the Roman historian Olympiodorus took part in an embassy to Charaton's Huns, but his account of the visit is wholly lost. Around this same time, the future Western Roman general Aetius spent time among the Huns as a hostage. We will see below how Aetius's Hunnic connections benefitted his military and political career.

Sometime in the early 420s, the brothers Roua and Octar became kings of the Huns. Octar would die by the end of the decade, leaving Roua as sole ruler. We hear of a Hunnic incursion across the Danube in 422, possibly even approaching the walls of Constantinople itself, while Emperor Theodosius II was dealing with Persian persecutions of Christians (see fragment 54* [p. 25, below]). Retreat was only brought about by an agreement to pay the Huns 350 pounds of gold annually. The annual payments continued for the next decade, which brings us to the point where Priscus's narrative begins. The year is 434. The Romans' attention was again focused elsewhere, this time on the Vandals in North Africa (see fragments 55* and 57* [pp. 29–31], below). Roua was pursuing what was clearly a longstanding strategy: to keep his inferiors in line. Any subordinate tribes who sought help from the Romans were to be subdued. Any Huns who tried to flee to the Romans and establish connections outside the king's own network of connections were to be recovered and punished. The strategy has an effect even on the

7

Romans, who compete for the opportunity to negotiate with the Hun.

FRAGMENT 1

From the *Excerpts on Romans' Embassies to Foreigners* of Constantine VII Porphyrogennetos

(1) While Roua was king of the Huns, he chose to campaign against the Amilzouri, Itimari, Tounsoures, Boïski and other peoples who dwelled along the Istros River[2] and who were seeking refuge in alliances with the Romans. He sent Eslas, his usual minister in disputes between himself and the Romans, to threaten to dissolve the existing peace unless the Romans handed over everyone who had fled to them. (2) While the Romans were considering sending an embassy to the Huns, Plinthas and Dionysios volunteered to serve as ambassador. Plinthas was a man of Scythian[3] origin, Dionysios a Thracian. Both had held the Roman consulship and were currently serving as generals.[4] (3) When it became apparent that Eslas was returning to Roua before the embassy would be sent out, Plinthas sent with him Sengilachos, one of his confidants, to persuade Roua to negotiate only with him, not with any other Roman.

About five years elapse before the fragments' story resumes. Perhaps it was during this interval that Priscus told a story of the Huns' origins. Like Ammianus, quoted above, Priscus clearly had no good information about the Huns' identity. The account, transmitted by the Gothic historian Jordanes, is a fanciful folktale.

FRAGMENT 45

From the *Getica* of Jordanes

And so the Huns, sprung from that stock, came to the Goths' borders. The ferocious nation, as Priscus the historian reports, was situated on the far bank of Lake Maeotis.[5] They were skilled in hunting only, no other labor, but after their population had grown, they became good at disturbing their neighbors' peace with crimes and pillaging. Now, some hunters of this race, as was their wont, were seeking game on the far bank of Maeotis, when they noticed how a deer was suddenly offering itself to them. It went into the lake, now moving forward, now standing still, offering itself as a guide on the road.

Following it, the hunters crossed Lake Maeotis on foot, although they had thought it impassable like the sea. As soon as the Scythian land appeared to them—they had been unacquainted with it—the deer disappeared. I [Jordanes] believe that those spirits from whom the Huns draw their lineage brought about this event to make the Huns envious of the Scythians.

The hunters, who had been completely unaware that the world extended beyond Maeotis, were in awe at the Scythian land. As they were intelligent, they realized that their journey, known to no one before their own day, had been revealed by divine providence. They returned home, explaining what had taken place and praising Scythia. After they won over their people, they hastened to Scythia by the road they had found under the deer's guidance. Early during their incursion, however many Scythians they encountered, they sacrificed to victory; the rest they conquered and enslaved. Soon after they crossed the enormous lake, in that territory they conquered the Alcildzuri, Itimari, Tuncarsi and Boisci, who all dwelled on that Scythian bank like a whirlwind of nations. And by harassing them with frequent battle, they also subdued the Alans, who were equal to them in fighting but unlike them in humaneness, mores and appearance.

The main narrative resumes in the winter of 439/440. Roua died sometime between 434 and 439, supposedly killed by a lightning strike. His nephews Bleda and Attila took up the kingship. The Romans' continuing military entanglements against the Vandals in North Africa gave Bleda and Attila an opportunity to make new tribute demands on Theodosius's court and to begin campaigns against Roman cities south of the Danube.

FRAGMENT 1.1

From the *Excerpts on Romans' Embassies to Foreigners* of Constantine VII Porphyrogennetos[6]

(1) After Roua died and the kingship of the Huns devolved upon Attila and Bleda, the Roman Senate[7] decided to send Plinthas as an ambassador to them. After their vote on his appointment was ratified by the emperor, Plinthas said he wanted Epigenes to join him on the embassy since he brought with him a superlative reputation for wisdom and held the office of *quaestor*. Once his appointment was completed, both men set out on the embassy and came to Margos.[8] (2) This city of Mysia in Illyria[9] lies on the Istros River, with the fortress Constantia on the opposite bank. The royal Scythians[10] also arrived, and they held their summit outside the city on horseback. The barbarians think it best not to have talks while dismounted; therefore the Roman ambassadors too, taking into consideration their

The Arrival of the Huns

own dignity, reached the same decision as the Scythians, based on the same principle, lest one party negotiate from horseback and the other on foot. (3) <They reached an agreement that in the future the Romans not only not admit>[11] Scythian fugitives but also give back past fugitives together with Roman prisoners of war who had returned home without paying ransom, unless for each escapee eight gold coins[12] were paid to his captors; that the Romans not form alliances with any barbarian nation if that nation was stirring up war against the Huns; that the marketplaces be havens with equal rights, safe for both Romans and Huns; that the treaty be kept and remain in effect so long as seven hundred pounds of gold be paid each year by the Romans to the royal Scythians. (Previously the payment had been three hundred fifty pounds.) (4) Both the Romans and the Huns agreed to these provisions and after swearing an ancestral oath they returned to their own territories.

(5) Those who had sought refuge with the Romans were given back to the barbarians. Among them were Mama and Atakam, children of royal lineage. The men who received them crucified them in the Thracian fortress Karso as punishment for their flight. (6) After they concluded the peace treaty with the Romans, Attila's and Bleda's forces passed through the nations in Scythia, subduing them, and contrived a war against the Sorosgi.

Priscus records another foreign threat along the Danube frontier, an attack by the Roubi far downstream against the city of Novidounon, led by a barbarian named Valips. The action cannot be dated with precision. It is possible that Priscus connected this attack to Hunnic affairs. Jordanes (see fragment 68* [p. 114, below]) records that a people called the Rugi were one of the groups to emerge from Hunnic domination after the *death of Attila. If Valips's Roubi, who are otherwise unattested, are identical to these Rugi, it may be that Valips was deliberately revolting against the Romans in preference for the Huns' leadership or attacking the Roman city on the Huns' behalf.*

FRAGMENT 1A

Perhaps from the *Excerpts* of Constantine VII Porphyrogennetos[13]

(1) From the writings of Priscus: the siege of the city of Novidounon.[14] Valips, who long ago caused the Roubi to revolt against the eastern Romans, seized Novidounon, a city situated on the river bank, and slew some of the citizens. He gathered all the money in the town and was preparing to overrun Thrace and Illyria with his fellow revolters. (2) The emperor dispatched a force to bring Valips to terms. Besieged, he kept the besiegers away from the city walls as long as he and his men were able to endure. (3) When they were exhausted by the toil of fighting the Roman army's repeated attacks, they stopped the rush of enemy spears by positioning their captives' children on the parapets. Because of their kinship with the children, the soldiers neither launched missiles nor cast spears against them. (4) Valips thus gained some time and the siege was lifted with the arrangement of a treaty.

Meanwhile, back at Margos, the newly concluded treaty was not in force for long. Hunnic fugitives continued to live among the Romans, and so the Huns found a pretext for taking the city. These events probably took place in 441.

FRAGMENT 2

From the *Excerpts on Foreigners' Embassies to the Romans* of Constantine VII Porphyrogennetos

(1) After the Scythians outwitted the Romans at the time of the marketplace and killed many men, the Romans sent messages to them, accusing them of seizing the fortress and neglecting the treaty. (2) The Scythians replied that they had not acted preemptively but in self-defense. For, they said, the bishop of Margos had crossed into their land, tracked down their royal tombs and looted the buried treasures. (3) And, they said, unless the Romans surrendered him and, according to their agreements, also surrendered the fugitives (for there were numerous fugitives in Roman territory), they would launch a war. (4) When the Romans denied the truth of the accusation, the barbarians, trusting in their own claims, scorned arbitration and turned to war. They crossed the Istros and ravaged the numerous fortresses and cities along the river. They even took Viminakion,[15] a city of Mysia in Illyria.

(5) While these things were taking place, some were proposing that the bishop of Margos should be surrendered so that the danger of war would not fall upon the entire Roman state for the sake of one man. But that man, suspecting he would be surrendered, unbeknownst to the townspeople went to the enemy and promised to betray the city to them if the Scythian kings should devise an equitable reward. (6) They said they would treat him well in every way if he made good on his promise. Handshakes and oaths confirming the agreement were exchanged with the barbarian throng, and the bishop returned to Roman territory. When night fell, having positioned an ambush right opposite the river bank, he rose up at the agreed signal

and caused the city to fall to its enemies. (7) Thus Margos was sacked, and the barbarians' accomplishments rose to a still greater level.

After taking Margos and Viminakion, the Huns moved south. In 442, they attacked and sacked the city of Naissos. Naissos was a major strategic point, located at a crossroads from which one could travel north to the Danube, south to Thessalonike (modern Thessaloniki, Greece) and its Aegean port, and east to Serdica (modern Sofia, Bulgaria) and eventually to Constantinople itself. To control Naissos was to control access to the Balkans, Greece and Thrace.

FRAGMENT 1B

Perhaps from the *Excerpts* of Constantine VII Porphyrogennetos

(1) From the writings of Priscus: the siege of Naissos.[16] The Scythians were besieging Naissos, an Illyrian city on the †Danouba† River.[17] They say that the city was founded by Constantine,[18] who also built the city named for himself at Byzantium. (2) Now, seeing how they intended to take this well-populated and, more to the point, well-fortified city, the barbarians advanced with every attempt. (3) As the town's inhabitants lacked the courage for going out to battle, the barbarians bridged the river to the southern side, just where it flows past the city, so that a large number could easily cross. At this spot, they brought machines up to the city wall. First, since the approach was easy, they brought up beams laid on wheels. Men standing on the beams shot arrows at the defenders on the ramparts. Other men stationed at each of the two ends pushed the wheels with their feet and brought

the machines up to wherever they were needed, to make it possible to shoot with good aim through the embrasures in the coverings. For the machines were covered with braided chaste-tree withes, which held hides and leather as a protection against whatever fire-bearing missiles or other projectiles were launched against them. The battle was thus without danger for the men on the beam.

(4) After many similar engines had been constructed for use against the city, scores of their projectiles caused the rampart defenders to give up and retreat. Now the machines called rams were also brought up. This machine, also very large, consisted of a beam hanging down by slack chains from wooden posts inclining toward each other. It had spearheads and protective coverings, in the way already described, to ensure the operators' safety. (5) From the rear, men vigorously drew back the beam with small cords at a spot opposite their target and then let it go so that, by its force, the whole part of the wall would collapse and disappear.

(6) The defenders on the walls were throwing stones large as wagons, which had already been prepared for this purpose, whenever the engines were brought up to the city wall. They crushed one machine together with its men, but they were no match for the whole number of them. (7) In fact, the attackers also brought up ladders. Here the wall lay destroyed by the rams, there the defenders on the ramparts were overwhelmed by the number of machines. And so the city was taken, with the barbarians gaining access through the part of the wall shattered by the ram's blow, (8) and also via the ladders that were brought up to the parts of the wall not yet falling.[19]

After the siege of Naissos in 442, we lose Priscus's narrative for five more years. We know from brief mentions in other, later sources that the Huns took the major cities of Sirmium (modern Sremska Mitrovica, Serbia) and Singidunum (modern Belgrade), either immediately before or immediately after the sack of Naissos. These were cities along the Danube, upstream from Margos and Viminakion. The Huns thus effectively sealed off the major road to the West. They also renegotiated the terms of the Treaty of Margos. The new provisions called for a greatly increased tribute payment, perhaps as much as 1400 pounds of gold annually. They then, for reasons unknowable, withdrew from Roman territory. But they had grabbed the Eastern Romans' attention.

NOTES

1. Otto Maenchen-Helfen 1973, 18–81 carefully traces all evidence about the Huns movements in the late fourth and early fifth century, much more than I can include here. He uses histories, letters, poems, speeches and any other textual source that mentions the Huns. His conclusions are sometimes over-confident, but his thoroughness is unmatched.
2. The Istros is the Danube River. Notice the clear similarity between these tribal names and the tribes Jordanes puts beside the Sea of Azov (fragment 45 [p. 9], below).
3. i.e., Gothic.
4. Priscus translates the Latin term *magister militum* into Greek. Plinthas (*PLRE* II 892–93 [Fl. Plinta]) held the consulship in 419. He was also appointed *magister militum praesentalis* in 419, an office that he held at least until 438. Dionysios (*PLRE* II 365 66 [Fl. Dionysius 13]) had been consul in 429. He had served as *magister militum per Orientem* from 428 to 431 and held another, uncertain *magister militum* post at the time of this embassy.
5. Today, the Sea of Azov, the northern arm of the Black Sea. A story of Huns crossing the Sea of Azov is also mentioned briefly at fragment 8 §140 (p. 68).
6. Fragment 1.1 is quoted in Constantine's collection as if it immediately follows our fragment 1, but it is likely that the compilers have omitted substantial sections of Priscus's text. Indeed, the opening clause of fr. 1.1 sounds like a compiler's

7. That is, the Senate in Constantinople.
8. Situated in modern-day Serbia near the mouth of the Great Morava River (called the Margos River in the ancient world), where it empties into the Danube. Pleiades ID: 207267.
9. "Mysia in Illyria" is Priscus's classicizing name for the province of Moesia Superior.
10. That is, the Hunnic royalty. The phrase "royal Scythians" is straight from Herodotus.
11. Several words have fallen out of the text. I translate the conjecture of Niebuhr.
12. The Greek *chruseos* ("gold coin") is a translation of the Latin *solidus* (or *aureus*), the standard gold coin of Late Antiquity. On currency and their purchasing power, see Jones 1964, 1: 438–48. Jones reports that a soldier's annual rations in mid-fifth-century Africa cost 4 *solidi*, although a poor rural person might subsist on one and a third *solidi* for a year. Attila's demand for eight *solidi* per fugitive is a very steep price. His demand will increase by 50% in fr. 5 §3 (p. 37).
13. On the source for this fragment and fragment 1b, see Introduction p. xli, n. 10.
14. Probably Noviodunum ad Istrum, on the lower Danube, now the small town of Isaccea, Romania. Pleiades ID: 216900.
15. A city and military base, just downriver from Margos, near modern Kostolac, Serbia. Pleiades ID: 207549.
16. Modern Niš, Serbia on the Nišva River, about 190 km south of ancient Margos. Pleiades ID: 207303.
17. The manuscript preserves the word "Danouba" (i.e., Danube), a name not used by Priscus. Regardless, Naisssos was not on the Danube. The ancient name of the Nišva River is not known. See Thompson 1947, 61.
18. This is incorrect. Naissos was Constantine the Great's birthplace.
19. On this passage's echoes of Thucydides and Dexippus and their implications for Priscus's classicizing historiography, see Introduction pp. xix–xx.

TWO YOUNG EMPERORS

At some point in the early part of his history—perhaps here—Priscus seems to have given background information on the Eastern and Western Empires. The pretense may have been to demonstrate the weakness of the emperors, Valentinian III in the West (419–455, reigned 425–455) and Theodosius II in the East (401–450, reigned 402–450), as they faced the Huns' threat. These men were cousins, grandsons of Theodosius I (346–395, reigned 379–395). During his life, Theodosius I had raised his young sons Arcadius and Honorius to the rank of Augustus (i.e., emperor): Arcadius in 383 at age five and Honorius in 393 at age eight. When Theodosius died in 395, the Empire was divided between Arcadius in the East and Honorius in the West. The Theodosian Dynasty would rule the empires for more than half a century, but there would never again be a single Roman Empire spanning Europe, North Africa and the Middle East. The East and West were permanently divided administratively and, more and more, culturally.

Theodosius I did not live to see either of his grandsons born. His namesake, Theodosius II, was born to Arcadius in April 401 and proclaimed Augustus the following January, before his first birthday. When Arcadius died in 408, Theodosius II acceded to the throne in Constantinople at age seven. Valentinian was born in 419, not to Honorius but to his half-sister Galla Placidia (daughter of Theodosius I) and her husband Flavius Constantius. Honorius himself was childless. While Honorius was still alive, Galla Placidia took her young son from Ravenna, by then the Western capital, and fled to Constantinople. When Honorius died in 423, a power struggle began in the West. A usurper named John was proclaimed Augustus. He was overthrown in 425 when an army supplied by Theodosius II and led by the general Aspar brought Valentinian back to Italy and installed him as Honorius's rightful heir. The six-year-old Valentinian was also betrothed to Theodosius's three-year-old daughter Licinia Eudoxia, thus cementing the partnership between the cousins.

The passages comprising the digression about Theodosius and Valentinian, sometimes containing more gossip than history, come mostly from the conjectural fragments, i.e. passages from other authors that seem to contain Priscus-derived information but do not name him as their source. They begin with two comments on Theodosius's time as a boy emperor.

FRAGMENT 50*

A fragment of John of Antioch, preserved in the *Excerpts on Virtues and Vices* of Constantine VII Porphyrogennetos

Because of his very young age Theodosius the Younger was competent neither in reasoning nor in waging war. He provided indictments to those who wanted them, mostly to the eunuchs around the palace. Due to these indictments everyone, so to speak, saw their property being seized. Some had their property bequeathed while they were still alive, others were forcibly made to hand their wives over to other men and were forcibly deprived of their children since they were unable to speak against the emperor's injunctions. The affairs of the Romans were in this condition.

The eunuchs castigated in this fragment were foreign slaves who were employed as the emperor's chamberlains. They were frequently abused because of their appearance and because they held positions of great privilege in the imperial court. When an emperor was deemed weak, it was easy to blame his chamberlains as having undue influence over him. Constantius II (son of Constantine the Great, ruled 337–361) was similarly said to be controlled by his chamberlain Eusebius.

Other members of the court were seen as positive influences on the young ruler.

FRAGMENT 51*

A fragment of John of Antioch, preserved in the *Excerpts on Virtues and Vices* of Constantine VII Porphyrogennetos

Emperor Theodosius bid farewell to playthings and directed his mind toward words fit for a free man. Paulinos and Plakitos read with him, and to them he graciously gave magistracies and wealth.

Paulinos and Plakitos each held the post of magister officiorum, *Master of Offices (though Plakitos may not have held it until the reign of Marcian). This important position placed its holder at the head of the imperial bureaucracy. As we shall read at fragment 7 §13 (p. 46, below), when Theodosius and his courtier Chrysaphius are plotting Attila's assassination, they summon the Master of Offices into their conspiracy since he "has knowledge of all the emperor's plans insofar as emissaries, translators and soldiers in the emperor's garrison are under his authority." It comes as no surprise that Theodosius would tap old childhood friends for this post, as he needed men whom he could trust completely. Paulinos, rumor had it, would fail Theodosius in his trust. He was said to have had an affair with Eudocia, Theodosius's wife, and was exiled and executed.*

Still, the eunuchs were seen as a corrupting influence even into Theodosius's adulthood. Chief among these retainers was the aforementioned Chrysaphius. He was Theodosius's spatharius, *the captain of the imperial bodyguard, and will play an important role in the events to come. This next fragment is from the Byzantine encyclopedia* Suda's *entry on Theodosius II.*

FRAGMENT 52*

A fragment of John of Antioch, preserved in the *Suda*

Theodosius the Younger, Roman emperor. He succeeded his father in office although he was unwarlike and spent his life in cowardice. He won peace with money, not with arms, and as patron for the Roman state he introduced many evils. Raised under the guidance of eunuchs, he was readily obedient to their every command. As a result, the elite required the eunuchs' aid and the eunuchs introduced many innovations in the political and military commands. Men capable of governing did not progress into magistracies; rather, those who gave gold took office. Because of the eunuchs' greed and the piracy of Sebastian's bodyguards, the Hellespont and the Propontis[1] were thrown into confusion. The eunuchs arranged affairs to this level of absurdity: by bewildering Theodosius in the way children are bewildered with toys, they planned to accomplish nothing worthy of memory. Even when Theodosius reached age fifty, he continued engaging in some vulgar handicrafts and devoting himself to hunting, so that Chrysaphius and the eunuchs held the emperor's power. Chrysaphius was the man Pulcheria went after, once her brother was dead.

This is the only glimpse Priscus gives us of Pulcheria, the older sister of Theodosius II and one of the most powerful women of the fifth century. Though just two years older than her brother, she is said to have guided his education and possessed influence to rival a series of male courtiers throughout Theodosius's reign. Known for her charitable work and doctrinal orthodoxy, she eschewed marriage and, with her sisters, lived a religious life of virginity. She had herself proclaimed Augusta, or empress, in 414, a title she would retain after Theodosius's death when she married his successor Marcian, after having Chrysaphius murdered. Some ancient sources say the marriage with Marcian was never consummated. She died in 453 and was later canonized a saint.

Another powerful eunuch who (other sources tell us) ran up against Pulcheria was Antiochos. He is called a praepositus *and a* cubicularius, *titles that can be combined as* praepositus sacri cubiculi, *"overseer of the sacred bedchamber" or "grand chamberlain." This important post held great power, including oversight of some financial and judicial functions within the palace and control of the emperor's audiences.*

FRAGMENT 53*

From the *Chronicle* of John Malalas

This same emperor Theodosius badly treated Antiochos, the *praepositus* and patrician who held power in the palace and ruled over state affairs. He was the man who, as *cubicularius*, educated Theodosius while his father was still alive and who administered the Roman state after his father Arcadius's death. He remained in place as a patrician after Theodosius had matured, with full power over Theodosius. But growing irritated by him, Theodosius confiscated his property and, imposing tonsure on him, made him priest of the Great Church of Constantinople, ordering that no eunuch *cubicularii*, i.e., the palace's *praepositi*, were to advance into the ranks of senators or patricians after completing their service. This same Antiochos died as a presbyter.

Antiochos, who was a Persian, had influence over Constantinopolitan relations with the great empire to the east. From other sources, we hear of his work in successfully negotiating with the Persian king Yazdgard I (ruled 399–421, called Isdigerdes in Greek) so that the latter would not persecute Christians within his borders. Some sources even report that Antiochos had been sent by Yazdgard to be Theodosius's tutor.

The lone fragments regarding Eastern foreign relations in this period tell about a brief conflict in 421–422 with Persia. After nearly constant warfare in the fourth century, the early fifth century had seen a cooling of tensions between the two empires. As both faced other external threats, they relied on the stability of their ancient neighbor to have at least one peaceful border. Yazdgard died in 421 and was succeeded by his son Bahram V (ruled 421–438, called Vararanes in Greek). In this brief flare-up, the issue again was the persecution of Persian Christians, which probably restarted during the last years of Yazdgard's reign and was simultaneous with Roman religious persecution against Persians in Roman territory. When the Romans accepted refugees from the persecutions, the Persians attacked.

FRAGMENT 54*

From the *Chronicle* of Theophanes

In this year, Emperor Theodosius, motivated by much goodness, although he vigorously conquered the Persians, signaled his embrace of peace by sparing the Christians living in Persia. He sent Helion the patrician, whom he held in great esteem, and Anatolios, the general of the East, as ambassadors to make a peace treaty. Vararanes recognized that he had been defeated and so he received the embassy. Thus the persecution of the Christians ceased.

Theophanes's version gives too much credit to the Romans. In reality, the Hunnic invasion across the Danube in 422 caused Theodosius to come to terms in a war that had not yet been decided militarily.

Procopius preserves a more detailed account of Anatolios's mission. (Some believe that fragment 59* is more properly placed in 441, a brief hostility between Theodosius and Yazdgard II, who succeeded Bahram V in 438.)

FRAGMENT 59*

From the *Persian War* of Procopius

When Theodosius had become a man and reached his prime of life, and Isdigerdes became ill and passed away, the Persian king Vararanes invaded Roman land with a great army. He did nothing disagreeable, but returned to his own land without accomplishment in the following way.

Emperor Theodosius sent Anatolios, the general of the East, as an ambassador to the Persians, and him alone. When Anatolios came very near the Medes' army, by himself, he leapt from his horse and went to Vararanes on foot. Vararanes saw him and asked those nearby who in the world was approaching. They said that he was a Roman general. Astounded by the excess of honor, the king himself turned his horse around and rode back, and the entire Persian army followed. When he reached his own land, he welcomed the ambassador with great cordiality and conceded peace in just the way Anatolios requested, stipulating, however, that neither nation should construct any new fortification on their own land in the neighborhood of the border. Once this condition was worked out, each nation went about its business wherever it wanted.

Two other fragments that may come from Priscus's pre-Attila flashback concern internal political affairs in Constantinople in the early 440s. The Paschal Chronicle, *in a confused passage, preserves Priscus's story about Kyros (or Cyrus),[2] a poet who served as the prefect of the city of Constantinople as well as praetorian prefect from 439–441.*

FRAGMENT 3A

From the *Paschal Chronicle*[3]

He[4] says that in Constantinople Kyros was appointed both praetorian prefect and prefect of the city. He used to go forth as praetorian prefect in the prefects' carriage, but he would return sitting in the carriage of the prefect of the city. He held power in the two offices for four terms because he was very pure. He directed that evening lights be kindled in the workshops, just as nighttime lights were.[5] And the factions in the Hippodrome shouted for him the whole day, "Constantine founded the city, Kyros revived it." Because of their cries the emperor grew angry at him. He ousted him by confiscating his property and he made him a priest. He sent him as bishop to Asian Smyrna,[6] a place where four bishops had already been murdered, in the hope that Kyros too would be killed.

John Malalas preserves a variant account of the same events.

FRAGMENT 60*
From the *Chronicle* of John Malalas

This same emperor appointed as praetorian prefect and prefect of the city the patrician Kyros, the philosopher, a man wisest among all. He held the two offices for four years. He used to go forth in the carriage of the prefect of the city, caring for the buildings and reviving all Constantinople; for he was a very respectable man. For a whole day, the Byzantines cried out for him in the hippodrome while Theodosius was watching: "Constantine founded it, Kyros revived it. Put him in that place, Augustus."[7] Kyros shouted back in astonishment, "Fortune, though it smiles much, does not suit me." The emperor grew angry because they shouted for Kyros and named him with Constantine as the reviver of the city. Then this same Kyros was framed and entwined in an accusation that he was a Greek.[8] Stripped of his office, his property was confiscated. He fled and became a priest. He was sent to Phrygia, where he became a bishop in the town called Kotyaeion.[9]

Such was the situation in the East in the years leading up to Attila's rise. In the West, when Valentinian III had been installed on the throne in 425, the government had only a tenuous hold on large swaths of its former territory. Britain was already lost. Goths who had entered the Eastern Empire in 376 and killed the emperor Valens at the Battle of Hadrianople in 378 were now settled, in relative peace, in Gaul. More threateningly, groups of Vandals, Alans and Sueves had crossed the Rhine on December 31, 406 and crossed the Pyrenees into Spain in 409. Though a joint Roman and Gothic army recovered part of Spain in 416, the coalition continued to challenge Roman rule. At the time of Valentinian's accession, they firmly controlled southern Spain and were making moves toward crossing the Strait of Gibraltar into northern Africa, home to the richest of the Roman provinces. The general Boniface had been active in North Africa since at least 417; by 423 or 424, he was commanding the field army there, with the title comes Africae. *His loyalty to Valentinian's mother Galla Placidia when she fled to Constantinople in 423 earned him a promotion to* comes domesticorum *when her son came to power. He remained in Africa, protecting its vital resources.*

Two other generals vied for power in the late 420s: Felix and Aetius. Felix commanded in Italy, and Aetius in Gaul. Aetius will prove to be the most interesting figure in the story. In his youth, he had established important relationships with barbarian leaders. He was given as a hostage to the Goths in 405 and later to the Huns. In 425, after Honorius's death, the usurper John sent Aetius to the Huns to obtain an alliance. When Aetius returned with a Hunnic army, he found that John had already been overthrown and

Valentinian III installed on the throne. Aetius, however, used the presence of the Huns to secure his generalship in Gaul before he dismissed the Huns. As Aetius, Boniface and Felix strove for power, Galla Placidia, who ran the empire in her son's name, played them off against one another. At times, though, it seemed the men were using her. This passage is dateable to 427.

FRAGMENT 55*

A fragment of John of Antioch, preserved in the *Excerpta Salmasiana*

Placidia had two generals. To one of them, Boniface, she entrusted Libya; the other, Aetius, she held back. Aetius was jealous and wrote to Boniface, "The empress is against you. Here is proof: she will summon you for no reason. If she writes to you to come, don't obey. She will kill you." He then sought out the empress and said that Boniface was planning a revolt. "And you will know this clearly: if you summon him," he said, "he will not come." When the empress wrote to him to come, Boniface handed over Libya to the Goths[10] and disobeyed the order to go, since he believed Aetius's revelations to be true. Later when some men were dispatched to him and they reached an understanding, the lie was discovered. And so the empress cherished him more, but loathed Aetius because he had acted so fraudulently, even though she was unable to do anything harmful to him. He never had the strength to recover Libya from that man.

The passage lacks some important details. When Boniface refused to return to Italy, Placidia sent Felix against him. (Some scholars have argued that Felix *initiated the deception, not Aetius, who seems to have been in Gaul at the time.) Aetius took advantage of the power vacuum in Italy. In 429, he came to Italy, took control of the armies and, arresting the defeated Felix, had him executed in 430. Boniface, meanwhile, almost certainly did not betray the province to the barbarians, as fragment 55* states. Instead, Placidia reconciled with him and restored his command to face the Vandals, who moved into Africa en masse in 429.*

The fragment's final sentence lacks a typical grammatical connection to the previous sentence and indeed seems badly out of context. Its subject and the "man" of the final phrase are ambiguous. Most likely, it refers to the fact that Boniface was unable to recover the African provinces after his reconciliation with Rome. The final "man," then, is probably the Vandal king Geiseric. For, once Boniface was restored to his command, he took up arms against the Vandals in 430. He was defeated and besieged in Hippo Regius, the episcopal see of the recently deceased Augustine. In 431, he received reinforcements from the East, under the command of Aspar. The joint Roman force, though, was defeated by the Vandals in 432.

FRAGMENT 57*

From the *Vandalic War* of Procopius

After Geiseric conquered Aspar and Boniface with noteworthy forethought, he bolstered his good fortune as much as possible. He feared that if an army from Rome and Byzantium came against him again, the Vandals would not be able to rely on similar strength and luck, since human affairs are wont to be tripped up by divine plans and human bodies are wont to grow weaker. Therefore, not emboldened by his successes but humbled by his fears, he concluded a treaty with Emperor Valentinian which stipulated that each year he was to bear tribute from Libya to the emperor. He also handed over one of his sons, Huneric, as a hostage according to the terms of this agreement. Geiseric thereby was proved a brave man in the battle and guarded his victory as securely as possible, and he received back his son Huneric when the friendship between the nations grew into something great.

After Boniface's unsuccessful campaign against the Vandals, he was recalled to Italy. Aetius marched against him in open civil war. Boniface was victorious, but was mortally wounded. After his death, his son-in-law Sebastian (see fragment 52* [p. 22, above]) took over his command. Aetius, as he had in 425, summoned aid from the Huns. With them, in 433, he defeated Sebastian, who fled east. Aetius emerged as the unchallenged general under the young Valentinian's nominal command.

Even after Boniface's recall, the Eastern general Aspar stayed on in Africa, a decision which would haunt the Eastern Empire when the Huns renewed their attacks on the Danube frontier. Aspar finally came to terms with Geiseric in early 435, temporarily keeping him out of Africa's richest provinces. In autumn 439, however, the Vandals marched on Carthage and took the city; by the following spring, they were launching raids against Sicily. In response, Aetius (in the name of Valentinian) and Theodosius (through Aspar) began assembling an enormous force in Sicily to recover Carthage. But the army never set out against the Vandals. In 442, the same year as the Huns' siege of

Naissos, the Romans quickly negotiated a new treaty with the Vandals, an agreement that left Geiseric in control of Carthage and its surrounding provinces as a client king of the Roman Empire. His son Huneric was betrothed to Valentinian's daughter Eudocia. Aspar and the Eastern troops were recalled to protect the Danube frontier against the Huns.

In a passage derived from Priscus, Procopius describes the Vandals' actions against the North African Roman population.

FRAGMENT 58*

From the *Vandalic War* of Procopius

Later Geiseric devised the following idea. He pulled down the walls of all the Libyan cities except Carthage,[11] so that the Libyans themselves, if they should choose Roman governance, would not be able to set out from a safe location and revolt, and also so that men sent by the emperor would have no hope of seizing the city and harassing the Vandals from a garrison installed in it. So he seemed to have planned well and maintained the Vandals' prosperity as securely as possible, but later when Belisarius captured the unwalled cities easily and with little toil, Geiseric brought considerable laughter upon himself. What had seemed like good planning he now pronounced folly. For when fortunes change, people are always wont to change their opinions of their earlier decisions too.

If any Libyan had anything notable and opulent, he handed them over to his children Huneric and Genzon, along with their fields and all their money, as if they were prisoners of war. (Theodoros, his youngest son, was now dying, without any children at all, either male or female.) He took away from other Libyans their largest and best fields, and he apportioned them to the Vandals. Those fields are still today called the "Vandals' allotments." It came to pass that those who had possessed these lands for a long time became as poor as could be even though they were freemen and it was in their power to depart and go wherever they wished. Geiseric ordered that all the lands he had handed over to his children and other Vandals should be subject to no payment of tribute. Any land he deemed not good he returned to its earlier owners, but he arranged that they would pay so much tax to the state that nothing at all would remain for the original landowners. Many fled and were killed because many onerous charges were brought against them. The single greatest charge of all seemed to be that someone had private money hidden away. Thus a whole class of misfortune closed in on the Libyans.

NOTES

1. The Propontis is today called the Sea of Marmara, the inland sea between the Black Sea and the Aegean Sea on which Constantinople (Istanbul) sits. The Hellespont is the strait connecting the Propontis to the Aegean Sea, today called the Dardanelles.
2. On the career of this important Egyptian poet and politician, see *PLRE* II 336–39 (Fl. Taurus Seleucus Cyrus 7). Despite Theodosius's attempt to have him killed, he outlived the emperor and survived into the reign of Leo.
3. As noted in the Introduction (p. xliii, note 40), a continuous passage of the *Paschal Chronicle* gives us fr. 64* and fr. 3a. I have divided the fragments at a different place than Carolla and earlier editors by printing the first paragraph of their fr. 3a as the final paragraph of my fr. 64* (p. 101, below), where the context is better.
4. In the *Paschal Chronicle*, "he" refers to Priscus. It is, however, possible that the *Chronicle* has juxtaposed two sources without clearly noting the difference. It is possible that Priscus is not the source for this story.
5. Obscure. Blockley 1983, 381 n. 18 suggests that this was a measure to improve workers' safety. Martindale (*PLRE* II 338) suggests it is a system of street lights. Baldwin 1980, 45 also nominates street

lights, adding that Kyros made it a public expenditure and thereby relieved the merchants of the cost.

6. Smyrna was a major city on the west coast of Asia Minor, modern-day İzmir, Turkey. Pleiades ID: 550893.
7. i.e., put him in the emperor's place; give him the throne.
8. i.e., one devoted to Greek, pagan religion, a non-Christian.
9. Modern-day Kütahya, in central Turkey, approximately 200 km southeast of Constantinople. Pleiades ID: 609444.
10. i.e., the Vandals.
11. The major city of North Africa throughout antiquity, near modern-day Tunis, Tunisia. Pleiades ID: 314921.

NEGOTIATING WITH ATTILA

Once the Eastern Roman troops returned home, Theodosius deployed them along the Danube frontier. With his position fortified, Theodosius broke the treaty with the Huns. He stopped paying tribute to Attila and Bleda. The Huns developed problems of their own. Bleda was murdered by Attila in 444 or 445. The Huns' silence toward the Romans for the next few years may indicate that Attila needed time to consolidate his power over the Huns and their subject peoples. By 447, when Priscus's main narrative resumes, Attila had emerged as the most powerful of the Huns. He now turned his attention to enforcing the lapsed treaties with the Romans and to threatening the eastern Balkans and Thrace, with an eye on Constantinople itself.[1]

FRAGMENT 3

From the *Excerpts on Foreigners' Embassies to the Romans* of Constantine VII Porphyrogennetos

(1) During the reign of Emperor Theodosius II, Attila, King of the Huns, mustered his army and sent a letter to the emperor about the fugitives and the tribute. He commanded that all the fugitives and tribute that had not been sent—the Romans were alleging the present war as an excuse—should be sent to him immediately; furthermore, regarding the arrangement of future tribute, ambassadors with the power to negotiate should come to him, since, if they delayed or if they moved toward war, not even he, though still willing, would keep the Scythian multitude in check.

(2) When the emperor's courtiers read the letter, they replied that they would not surrender the fugitives, but would consent to war alongside them; yet, they said, they would send ambassadors to resolve the disputes. (3) When the Romans' decisions were reported to Attila, he became angry and ravaged Roman territory. He destroyed some fortresses and attacked Ratiaria, a very large and populous city.[2]

The scholar J. Otto Maenchen-Helfen, a specialist in the Huns, sees in Attila's threat several groups of Huns, not all fully under Attila's control.[3] It may be that Attila was so insistent about the tribute because he needed the wealth to solidify his control over rival groups. In the next fragment, we find a Roman ambassador, a former consul, unwilling to travel overland to negotiate with Attila, perhaps because Attila's Huns or other groups of Huns had made travel across Thrace impossible.

FRAGMENT 4

From the *Excerpts on Romans' Embassies to Foreigners* of Constantine VII Porphyrogennetos

Theodosius sent Senator, a man of consular rank, to Attila as an ambassador. Although he had the name of ambassador, he was fearful of traveling overland to the Huns. Instead, he sailed to the Sea and the city of the Odyssenians, where Theodoulos who had been sent out as a general was spending time.[4]

We do not have any information about Senator's negotiations with Attila, whether he even made it to the Huns' camp. Whatever the course of the talks, they

evidently failed. Multiple sources describe widespread destruction in Thrace. The armies Theodosius had stationed against the Huns were ineffective. But the Huns were not the Romans' only problem. In January 447, before the invasion began, an earthquake struck Constantinople and destroyed its city walls. The Romans rebuilt the walls with remarkable speed; the job was done by March. As a result, when Attila marched east toward Constantinople he found fully functioning defenses. He did not attempt to take the capital itself. Instead he contented himself with the devastation of the Chersonese region on the north shore of the Dardanelles. The Eastern Romans had no choice but to agree to all of Attila's demands. Attila extracted fugitives and cash from the Romans, and dispatched his lieutenant Skottas to collect.

FRAGMENT 5

From the *Excerpts on Foreigners' Embassies to the Romans* of Constantine VII Porphyrogennetos

(1) After the Romans' battle in the Chersonese against the Huns, a treaty was reached, for which Anatolios served as ambassador. They agreed to the following: that the fugitives be returned to the Huns and six thousand pounds of gold be paid to them to satisfy the old agreements; (2) that tribute be assessed each year in the amount of two thousand one hundred pounds of gold; (3) that, for each Roman prisoner of war who escaped and returned to his own land without ransom, there be a fee of twelve gold coins, and that those who took in fugitives surrender them if they do not pay the fee; and that the Romans accept no barbarian seeking refuge with them.

(4) The Romans professed to make this treaty voluntarily. (5) Really it was by necessity that they gladly accepted every injunction, difficult as each one was, because of the inordinate fear constraining their commanders. They were eager to obtain peace and so assented to the tribute arrangement, however burdensome it was, even though both their private assets and the imperial treasury had been exhausted, not paid out for needful purposes but on strange spectacles, unworthy public exhibitions, and unconstrained pleasures and expenditures that no right-thinking person would ever consent to, not even in good times, let alone those who think little of arms. As a result, with regard to the payment of tribute, they submitted not only to the Scythians but in fact to the rest of the barbarians dwelling alongside Roman territory.

(6) As for the agreements and the money owed to the Huns, the Romans compelled everyone to contribute who paid taxes towards tribute payments as well as those who at any time had been relieved of the burdensome property taxes, whether through judges' decision or emperors' generosity. (7) Men registered in the Senate on account of their net worth also contributed promised gold. For many of them, the illustrious circumstances of their lives changed. They suffered humiliation in having to pay what the emperor's appointed assessors held them liable for. Once prosperous men were setting out their wives' jewelry and their furniture in the marketplace. (8) So much adversity awaited the Romans after the war that many men gave up their lives, either by starving or by hanging. But as soon as the treasury had been emptied and Skottas arrived, the gold and the fugitives were sent. When many of the fugitives refused to comply with the surrender, the Romans killed them. Among them were some royal Scythians who had come to the Romans after they refused to be marshaled under Attila.

(9) Adding to his injunctions, Attila ordered the people of Asemos to surrender however many prisoners of war they were holding, whether Roman or barbarian. (10) Asemos is a strong fortress, not very distant from Illyricum, in the Thracian region.[5] The men stationed there had accomplished many formidable deeds against the enemy, not defending themselves from the walls, but undertaking battle outside the trench against an innumerable multitude and generals with the greatest fame among the Scythians, and causing the Huns to stream away from the fortress in retreat. The Asemountians sallied out after them and found themselves far from the fortress, when their scouts reported that the enemy was escaping with Roman plunder. They fell on them unsuspecting and made their spoils their own, since though inferior to their opponents in number they excelled them in courage and strength. (11) The Asemountians thus killed countless Scythians in this war and freed countless Romans, and also received countless enemy deserters. (12) Now, Attila said that he would not lead his army away, nor would he ratify the peace treaty, unless either the Romans who had escaped to the Asemountians were surrendered or fees were paid in exchange for them and the barbarian prisoners of war captured by the Asemountians were sent back. (13) Neither Anatolios, the ambassador, nor Theodoulos, the commander of the armies stationed in Thrace,[6] was able to speak against him. They could not persuade him, not even by making sensible arguments, since the barbarian was acting brazenly, ready to start another war, and since they themselves were cowering in fear because of what had already happened. So they sent letters to the Asemountians, advising them either to surrender the Roman prisoners of war who had escaped to them or to pay twelve gold coins for each one and, in addition, to release the Hunnic prisoners of war.

(14) The Asemountians read the letters. They replied

that they had freed the Roman escapees and had killed the Scythian prisoners of war they had taken. Two of the men they had seized, however, were still being held. After the siege had been going on for some time, the enemy had set up an ambush and snatched some children who were pasturing flocks in front of the fortress. Unless, they said, they received the children back, they would not return the two men captured in compliance with the laws of war.

(15) When the envoys to the Asemountians made their report, the Scythian king and Roman leaders decided to search for the children who the Asemountians claimed had been captured. When none was found, the Scythians pledged oaths that the children were not among them and so the barbarians held by the Asemountians were given back. (16) The Asemountians also swore that the Roman escapees had been freed. They made this oath even though the Romans were in fact with them. They did not think that they were swearing a false oath since they were protecting men of their own race.

The success of Asemos aside, the Huns' destruction of the Balkan region was complete. Priscus gives hints that the Romans tried to put a veneer of victory on the events, but the historian sees through the propaganda. This was a total defeat. The Roman military, the Roman economy, even the Roman sense of security was left in ruins. The Huns were left free to roam throughout the Balkans and southward into Greece, as far as Thermopylae.

The Huns' devastation of Thrace is emphasized by Theophanes in his Chronicle. *Theophanes is almost certainly using Priscus's history to compile the events in the next fragment, but unfortunately he conflates events beginning in 441 or 442 through the devastation of 447. The text gives us more information about how badly Theophanes put together his facts than about the events themselves.*

FRAGMENT 61*

From the *Chronicle* of Theophanes

While the army, as we said before, was in Sicily awaiting the arrival of Geiseric's ambassadors and the emperor's commands, Attila, the son of Moundios, a Scythian, manly and proud, having thrown off his older brother Bdellas and alone ruling the kingdom of the Scythians, whom they also call Huns, overran Thrace. Primarily because of him Theodosius concluded a treaty <with> Geiseric and brought the army back from Sicily. He sent Aspar and his force, together with Areobindos and Argagisklos,[7] against Attila, who had now overturned Ratiaria, Naisos, Philippoupolis, Arkadioupolis, Constantia[8] and numerous other towns and had taken an exorbitant amount of plunder along with many prisoners of war. After the generals were badly defeated in battles, Attila advanced to both seas, the Pontos and the one near Kallipolis and Sestos.[9] He enslaved every city and fortress except Hadrianople and Herakleia (formerly Peirinthos), so that he even reached the fortress Athyras.[10] Theodosius was therefore forced to send an embassy to Attila and to promise to pay six thousand pounds of gold as an annual tribute to pacify him.

In the next fragment, Priscus gives us the sense that Attila was enjoying the games he could play with the recoiling imperial court. This seems to have gone on for a long time, even after Attila returned to his home base in the Hungarian Plain, and we should think of fragment 6 as dating to 448. Priscus, while he tells of Attila's fun, also notes that the Romans had other problems on their hands.

FRAGMENT 6

From the *Excerpts on Foreigners' Embassies to the Romans* of Constantine VII Porphyrogennetos

(1) After the treaty was completed, Attila again sent ambassadors to the Eastern Romans to demand the return of fugitives. The Romans received the ambassadors and blandished them with numerous gifts, but sent them away saying they did not have any fugitives. (2) Attila again sent others; after they too transacted their business, a third embassy went and a fourth after that. (3) The barbarian, seeing the Romans' generosity as they avoided transgressing the treaty, kept sending whichever of his retainers he wanted to treat well, inventing reasons and finding empty pretenses. (4) The Romans heeded every injunction and considered the despot's every command, whatever it was. Not only were they avoiding starting a war against him, but they also feared the Parthians who were in a state of preparation, the Vandals who were drawing up in formation by the sea, the Isaurians who were again practicing banditry, the Saracens who were overrunning the eastern end of their dominion, and the Ethiopian races who were unifying. (5) Humbled, therefore, the Romans were blandishing Attila while gathering their forces and appointing generals to try to marshal their troops against the rest of the nations.

In the next fragment, dateable to 449, we read about the last in the series of embassies Attila sent to Constantinople. Our interest, though, is not caught by Attila's demands, but by the Romans' new strategy. With the emperor's knowledge, they hatch a plot to assassinate Attila. The fragment also introduces a number of characters who will play major roles in the coming narrative. We have already met Aetius, the Western Roman general who, in his youth, lived among the Huns as a hostage and who relied on Hunnic armies as mercenaries during the Western civil conflicts. Apparently in payment for their support, Aetius arranged for the Huns to receive portions of the Roman province Pannonia (northwestern Serbia and eastern Croatia). Among those living in the newly Hunnic Pannonia, along the Saos River (modern: Sava River, which empties into the Danube at Belgrade), was Orestes, son of Tatoulos; the father will enter the story at fragment 8 §76 (p. 58, below). Orestes, fluent in the Hunnic language and working as a secretary to Attila, appears here as part of Attila's embassy to the Romans. Alongside him is the Hun Edekon, an accomplished soldier, member of Attila's personal bodyguard and here his lead ambassador to the Romans.

We cannot pass over a curious historical coincidence here. Orestes and Edekon arrive in Constantinople in 449 as comrades serving Attila. Their sons, 27 years later, would figure very prominently in the final moments of the Western Roman Empire. Orestes went on to become magister militum *in the Western Empire in 475. In this command, he marched against Emperor Julius Nepos, deposed him and installed his young son Romulus Augustulus as emperor. The following year, Edekon's son Odovacer, commanding a barbarian army, captured and killed Orestes, and deposed Romulus Augustulus.*[11] *In the absence of a Roman emperor, Odovacer proclaimed himself king (*rex*), thus bringing* *an end to the 500-year succession of emperors in Italy.*

In 449, Orestes and Edekon arrived in Constantinople with a letter from Attila. While Orestes was taken aside, Edekon presented the letter to Theodosius II, with assistance from the Constantinopolitan translator Bigilas. Bigilas had been working as Theodosius's Hunnic translator at least for a few years. He had accompanied the ambassador Anatolios to Attila's camp, presumably to negotiate the treaty whose terms were laid out in fragment 5 (p. 37, above). He was, he thought, well-respected by both Romans and Huns. Among the Romans who trusted him was Chrysaphius, the eunuch who was among the most highly influential counselors in Theodosius's court (see fragment 52* [p. 22, above].) He is the mastermind of the assassination plot.

FRAGMENT 7

From the *Excerpts on Foreigners' Embassies to the Romans* of Constantine VII Porphyrogennetos

(1) There came next the ambassador Edekon, a Scythian man who had accomplished splendid deeds in war. With him was Orestes, a man of Roman heritage who dwelled along the Saos River in Paionia,[12] which had come under the sway of the barbarian in the negotiations with Aetius, the Western Roman general. (2) This Edekon entered the palace and delivered a letter from Attila in which he accused the Romans of harboring fugitives. He threatened to take up arms if the fugitives were not surrendered to him and if the Romans would not stop cultivating conquered land, namely, the territory along the Istros, five days' journey wide, from Paionia down to Novae in Thrace.[13] (3) Furthermore, the

marketplace in Illyria was not to be on the bank of the Istros River, as it had been previously, but at Naissos, which after Attila's devastation of it formed a boundary between Scythian and Roman territories. Naissos was a five days' journey from the Istros for a light-armed man. (4) Attila ordered ambassadors to come to him to discuss their differences. The ambassadors were to be the greatest, not of some random men, but of men with consular rank. If the Romans were hesitant to dispatch such men, he would cross to Serdica to receive them.[14]

(5) After the letter was read to the emperor, Edekon withdrew with Bigilas, who had been translating whichever of Attila's commands the barbarian reported verbally. Edekon came to another house, where he was met by Chrysaphius, the emperor's chamberlain, the most powerful man in the palace. Edekon expressed astonishment at the lavishness of the imperial buildings. (6) As the barbarian conversed with Chrysaphius, Bigilas said in translation that Edekon commended the palace and congratulated Chrysaphius on its wealth. Chrysaphius said that he too would possess wealth, including gold-roofed houses, if he were to put aside Scythian interests and prefer Roman. (7) When he answered that it was not right that the subject of another master act without his lord's permission, the eunuch asked whether his access to Attila was unhindered and whether he had any power among the Scythians. (8) He answered that he was in fact one of Attila's retainers and had been entrusted with his garrison and the men assigned to it. (For, he said, each of the guards attended Attila in rotation on specified days.) The eunuch said that, if he gave him pledges, he would tell him of splendid blessings. They needed leisure, and they would find some if he would come for dinner without Orestes and his fellow ambassadors.

(9) Edekon, promising to do it and later coming to the

eunuch's house for a banquet, they shook hands and, with Bigilas translating, exchanged oaths:[15] the eunuch pledged that his words would cause Edekon no harm but would substantially benefit him, and the other that he would not reveal what was said to him, even if he did not achieve its completion. (10) The eunuch said to Edekon that if he should cross into Scythia, kill Attila and return to the Romans, he would live a prosperous life and would gain considerable wealth. Edekon promised to do it. He said that he needed money for the deed, not much, merely fifty pounds of gold to pay the men serving under him so that they would assist him in the attack with complete loyalty. The eunuch promised to deliver the gold immediately, but the barbarian suggested that he be sent back to Attila to report on the embassy and that Bigilas be sent with him to receive Attila's answer on the question of the fugitives. (11) Through him Edekon would also reveal how the gold should be conveyed. Attila, he said, interrogated him—or anyone else—whenever he traveled abroad, inquiring into what gifts had been bestowed on him and how much money the Romans had given. It would not be possible, he said, because of his traveling companions, to conceal it.

(12) The eunuch thought he spoke well and so, accepting the barbarian's advice, he sent him away after dinner and brought the plan to the emperor, who in turn sent for Martialios, who held the office of *magister*,[16] and explained the agreement with the barbarian. (13) By necessity he placed confidence in this official, because the *magister* has knowledge of all the emperor's plans insofar as emissaries, translators and soldiers in the emperor's garrison are under his authority. (14) They decided, as they discussed the events, to dispatch as ambassadors to Attila not only Bigilas but also Maximinos.

The next fragment continues immediately from the previous one. It is a separate fragment because it is preserved in a different collection of Constantine VII Porphyrogennetos. (Note how the excerptor provides a few words of context that are not present at the end of the previous fragment.) It is by far the longest and most substantial of Priscus's fragments, the story for which he is most famous. Here, we meet Priscus himself as a character in his own history and learn about his travels with Maximinos and Bigilas to meet Attila. Priscus's skill as a vivid narrator is on full display.

FRAGMENT 8

From the Excerpts on *Romans' Embassies to Foreigners* of Constantine VII Porphyrogennetos

(1) After the eunuch Chrysaphius urged Edekon to kill Attila, Emperor Theodosius and the *magister* Martialios decided, as they discussed the events, to dispatch as ambassadors to Attila not only Bigilas but also Maximinos. They also decided that Bigilas, as a pretense, should keep occupying the translator's post and should do whatever Edekon thought best, and Maximinos, since he knew nothing of their plans, should deliver the emperor's letter.

(2) In the letter, they wrote, concerning the ambassadors, that Bigilas was a translator and Maximinos was of greater rank than Bigilas, being from a notable family and serving as the emperor's adviser in the most important affairs; secondly, it was not right to undermine the treaty and set foot upon Roman land; finally, concerning the fugitives, they were sending back[17] seventeen in addition to those already surrendered, and no more remained. (3) That was the content of the letter. They also instructed Maximinos

to tell Attila verbally that he ought not to demand that the highest ranking ambassadors travel to him. This right did not belong to his ancestors nor to any other Scythian rulers; both random soldiers and message-bearers served as ambassadors. (4) In order to mediate the disputes carefully, they urged that he should send Onegesios to the Romans. Since Serdica had been laid waste, he was not able to meet there with a man of consular rank.

(5) With earnest entreaty, Maximinos persuaded me to accompany him on this embassy. And so, closely following the road alongside the barbarians, we reached Serdica, a thirteen days' journey from Constantinople for a lightly armed man. There, as we settled into our quarters, we thought it would be a good idea to invite Edekon and his barbarian companions to a feast. (6) We bought sheep and cows from the locals, slaughtered them and made our meal. At the height of the banquet, when the barbarians were extolling Attila and we the emperor, Bigilas said it was not right to juxtapose a god and a man—meaning by "man" Attila and by "god" Theodosius. (7) The Huns were agitated and, their temperatures rising little by little, grew angry. (8) We turned the conversation to other topics and appeased their anger with friendliness. As we arose after the meal, Maximinos blandished Edekon and Orestes with gifts of silken clothing and Indian pearls.[18] (9) Orestes, while waiting for Edekon to take his leave, said to Maximinos that he was wise and excellent for not causing offense like the emperor's courtiers. They had invited Edekon to dinner without him and had honored him with gifts. (10) His words were incomprehensible to us since we knew nothing of those events. We asked how and when he had been overlooked while Edekon had been honored. He made no reply and went away.

(11) On the next day, as we were walking, we told

Bigilas what Orestes said to us. He said that Orestes should not get angry just because he does not get the same things as Edekon. Orestes, he said, is Attila's servant and secretary, but Edekon is their best warrior and, as a member of the Hunnic race, far surpasses Orestes. (12) So he spoke. Later, after speaking privately with Edekon, he said to us, whether speaking the truth or playing his part, that he told him what was said. He said Edekon grew angry at his words and he could scarcely calm him down.

(13) Arriving at Naissos, we found the city bereft of people because it had been overturned by the enemy, though there were some people in the sacred lodgings who were suffering from diseases. (14) We camped a little bit upriver in a clearing, since the bank was everywhere covered with the bones of war casualties. In the morning not far from Naissos we met with Agintheos, the commander of the armies in Illyria,[19] in order to report the emperor's instructions and to receive fugitives. He was obligated to hand over five of the seventeen men referenced in the letter to Attila. (15) We talked with him and made him hand over the five fugitives to the Huns. Although he had been showing them favor, he sent them away with us.

(16) After passing the night, we traveled from the region of Naissos to the Istros River. We came into a thickly shaded area with many bends, twists and turnabouts. When day appeared, we believed we were journeying toward the west, but the rising sun appeared before us. Those inexperienced with the lay of the land cried out, believing that the sun was traveling backward and signifying more unexpected events. But thanks to the topographical irregularity that part of the road was looking east.

(17) After this difficult ground, we came to a flat wooded area, where barbarian boatmen received us and ferried us across the river in canoes that they constructed by cutting

down trees and hollowing them out. They had not prepared the transportation for our sake, but had been ferrying across a group of barbarians, whom we had encountered along the road, because Attila wanted to cross into Roman land as if to hunt. (18) This was the royal Scythian's tactic to prepare for war under the pretense that all the fugitives had not been given to him.

(19) After we crossed the Istros and traveled about seventy stades with the barbarians, we were forced to wait on a plain so that Edekon's men could inform Attila of our arrival. (20) The barbarians stayed with us and acted as our guides. As we were taking our dinner in the late afternoon we heard the rumble of horses coming toward us. Two Scythian men arrived and ordered us to go to Attila. (21) First, though, we asked them to join us for dinner. They dismounted and we sumptuously entertained them. On the next day they led us along the road. (22) Around the ninth hour of the day we reached Attila's tents (and there were many tents there). We wanted to pitch ours on the crest of a hill, but the barbarians who met us prevented it, since Attila's tent was on lower ground.

(23) Once we settled down where the Scythians wanted, Edekon, Orestes, Skottas and some other select men came and asked what our embassy was eager to procure. (24) We expressed our confusion at the senseless question and kept looking at one another, but they continued to trouble us for an answer. (25) When we said that the emperor bade us to speak to Attila and to no one else, Skottas replied angrily that their order was from their leader; they would not have come to us out of their own desire to meddle. (26) We said that it was not customary for ambassadors to be questioned by intermediaries about why they had come without their meeting nor even seeing the parties to whom they had been sent. This, we said, was not unknown even to the Scythians,

who often sent ambassadors to the emperor. It was necessary that we receive identical treatment; otherwise we would not disclose the embassy's purpose. So we spoke, and they withdrew to Attila.

(27) Again they returned, though without Edekon, repeated to us all the reasons for which we had come on the embassy, and ordered us to go away by the quickest route possible unless we could name anything else. We were still more mystified by these words since it was not easy to see how decisions made by the emperor in secret had become clearly known. We believed that it was to our benefit to answer nothing further about the embassy unless we gained access to Attila. (28) So we said it was their leader who asked whether we came to negotiate the things listed by the Scythians or other matters too; we would not discuss it with anyone other than him. (29) They immediately ordered us to leave.

(30) As we prepared for our journey, Bigilas reproached us for our response. "I say it is better to be caught in a lie than to leave with nothing accomplished. If I had by chance exchanged words with Attila," he said, "I would have easily persuaded him to put aside his differences with the Romans, since I was his confidant on Anatolios's embassy." (31) He said this, <believing> Edekon remained friendly toward him,[20] so that, under the pretext of the embassy and of saying anything, true or false, he might find an excuse to discuss their intentions against Attila and how to convey the gold Edekon said he needed to pay the men appointed to perform the task. (32) But Edekon had secretly betrayed him. Either he had made his promise deceitfully or he feared Orestes would tell Attila what he said to us in Serdica after the feast and accuse him of conferring with the emperor and the eunuch without him. And so he revealed the plot he had pursued and the amount of gold to be sent, and he also

explained why we were making our embassy.

(33) We had already loaded our baggage onto the pack animals and were attempting—out of necessity, at nighttime—to begin our journey, when some of the barbarians came and said Attila told us to remain because of the late hour. To the place from which we were getting ready to set out, some men brought us a cow and some river-caught fish sent by Attila. (34) Then, after dining, we turned to sleep. When day came, we thought that the barbarian would reveal some kind, pleasant news. (35) Once again, however, he sent the same men, advising us to go away unless we had something to say beyond what they already knew. We said no and began preparing for the journey, although Bigilas vehemently argued we should say that we had more to say.

(36) Seeing Maximinos very dejected, I went out with Roustikios since he knew the barbarians' language fluently. (He had come with us to Scythia not on the embassy, but for some business with Constantius, Attila's Italian secretary, whom Aetius, the Western Roman general, had sent.) I came to Skottas—Onegesios was not present at the time—and, addressing him through the translator Roustikios, I said that he would receive numerous gifts from Maximinos if he helped him get access to Attila. The embassy, I said, would benefit not only the Romans and the Huns but also Onegesios, since the emperor wanted him to come and mediate the nations' differences,[21] and he would receive magnificent gifts when he went. (37) Since Onegesios was away, I said, he needed to support us, and more his brother, in pursuit of this good business. I said we knew Attila followed his guidance too, but we would not firmly believe the reports about him unless we[22] came to know his power through experience. (38) He replied that no one any longer doubted Attila deemed his words and deeds equal to

Negotiating with Attila

his brother's. And he immediately mounted his horse and rode to Attila's tent.

(39) I returned to Maximinos, who with Bigilas was perplexed and at a loss regarding the recent events. I repeated what I said to Skottas and what I heard from him, and said that we needed to prepare the gifts for the barbarian and to calculate what we would say to him. (40) Both of them leapt up (they happened to be lying in the grass), praised my actions and called back those who had already departed with the pack animals. They considered how to address Attila and how to give him the emperor's gifts as well as what Maximinos had brought for him. (41) As we were worrying about these things, Attila summoned us through Skottas. And so at last we came to Attila's tent, which was guarded by a barbarian multitude arrayed in a circle.

(42) When we reached the entrance, we found Attila seated on a wooden chair. Maximinos approached, as the rest of us stood a short distance from the seat, and he greeted the barbarian. Giving him the emperor's letter, he said that the emperor prayed that he and those around him were safe. (43) Attila replied that the Romans would have what they desired for him. He turned his attention straight to Bigilas, called him a shameless beast and asked why he wanted to come to him, considering that he knew his and Anatolios's peacetime agreement that no ambassadors should come to him until all fugitives had been surrendered to the barbarians. (44) Bigilas said that there was not a single Scythian fugitive among the Romans; those who had been there had been surrendered. Growing angrier and reviling him all the more, Attila shouted that he would have crucified him and given him as food to the birds, if he did not think inflicting this penalty on his shamelessness and on the effrontery of his words would violate sacred diplomatic

law. There were, he said, fugitives of their race among the Romans—many of them—whose names, which had been recorded on papyrus, he ordered the secretaries to read out. (45) When they had gone through <all the> absent men,[23] he ordered Bigilas to depart without a moment's delay. He would send Eslas with him too, he said, to tell the Romans they should send him all the barbarian fugitives, from the time of Karpileon (the son of Aetius, the Western Roman general), who had lived as a hostage at his court. He would not allow his own subjects to fight against him, although they were incapable of helping anyone who trusted them to protect his land. (46) What city, he asked, or what fortress had they saved, once he himself had begun a siege? (47) He told us to return again after we had repeated his demands about the fugitives and to say whether the Romans wanted to surrender them or undertake war on their behalf. (48) He had earlier told Maximinos to stay, so that he might reply to the emperor's letter through him, and so he permitted us to present the gifts Maximinos was carrying and to withdraw.

(49) We presented the gifts and retired into our tent, where we reviewed what had been said. Bigilas was amazed how Attila angrily reviled him, even though he seemed gentle and kind to him on his previous embassy. I expressed the fear that some of the barbarians who had feasted with us in Serdica had made Attila hostile to him by reporting that he called the Roman emperor a god but Attila a man. (50) Maximinos thought that was right, since he was <not>[24] a partner in the eunuch's conspiracy against the barbarian. (51) Bigilas was doubtful and seemed to me at a loss to explain why Attila had reviled him. He thought, as he later told us, that neither the events in Serdica nor the details of the plot had been reported to Attila, because, on the one hand, no one else from the group, he thought, was bold enough to speak with Attila due to the fear that

54

governed them all; on the other hand Edekon, he thought, would keep his silence completely because of his oaths and the uncertainty of the deed, in fear that he himself too, since he was a participant in such plans, would lose his favored status and suffer death as punishment.

(52) Edekon came to us while we were in that state of uncertainty. He led Bigilas outside and, pretending to be speaking truthfully about their plans, commanded that the gold be brought to pay the men who would act with him. He then withdrew. (53) Bigilas, himself deceived, was eager to deceive us when we earnestly asked what Edekon said to him. Concealing the true reason, he claimed that he said Attila was angry with Edekon too about the fugitives and that Attila either had to get them all back or ambassadors of the highest rank had to come to him.

(54) During our discussion, some of Attila's men came and ordered Bigilas and the rest of us not to purchase a Roman prisoner of war, a barbarian slave, horses or anything except provisions until the disputes between the Romans and Huns had been resolved. (55) The barbarian acted cleverly and skillfully, so that Bigilas was easily caught acting against him, unable to explain why he was carrying gold, while the rest of us, thinking there would be a reply to our embassy, awaited Onegesios's return in order to deliver the gifts we ourselves wanted to give and those the emperor had sent. (56) Onegesios, along with the eldest of Attila's children,[25] had been sent to the Akateri, a Scythian people, whom he was bringing into an alliance with Attila for the following reason.

(57) Seeing that the Akateri had many different leaders over their tribes and clans, Emperor Theodosius sent gifts hoping that they would all put aside their alliance with Attila and welcome peace with the Romans. (58) The man who delivered the gifts, though, did not distribute them according

to the each king's rank, and Kouridachos, who was more senior in his rule, received his gifts second. Overlooked and deprived of his honors, he called in Attila against his fellow kings. (59) Without delay, Attila dispatched a great force. Some he killed, others he brought to terms. He then called Kouridachos to share in the spoils of victory. (60) But he, suspecting a plot, said it was difficult for a man to look upon a god: if it is not even possible to look directly at the sun's disk, how could anyone see the greatest of the gods without suffering? (61) So Kouridachos stayed in his own territory and protected his rule while the entire rest of the Akateri nation was coming to terms with Attila. (62) Attila desired to make his eldest son their king, and so sent Onegesios to do it. It was for this reason that he told us to stay on, as mentioned above, while he sent Bigilas and Eslas back to Roman territory, allegedly to demand the fugitives' return but actually to fetch the gold for Edekon.

(63) Once Bigilas had gone, we remained there for one day after his departure. On the next day, we traveled with Attila to more northerly parts of the region. We journeyed with the barbarian up to a certain point but then we took a different road. The Scythians who were guiding us told us to do this because Attila was going to a village where he wanted to marry the daughter of Eskam. Attila already had very many wives, but he was marrying her too in accordance with Scythian custom.

(64) From there we traveled on a level road lying in a plain and reached navigable rivers, the biggest of which (after the Istros) were called the Drekon, the Tigas and the Tiphesas.[26] We crossed them in the canoes the local inhabitants used, but the region's other rivers we navigated on rafts that the barbarians carry on their wagons for use in the stagnant marshlands. (65) Nourishment was abundantly supplied to us in the villages: instead of grain we were given

millet; instead of wine, a drink locally called *medos*. The servants following us also brought millet and supplied a drink made from barley, which the barbarians call *kamon*.

(66) Making our way along the long road, we encamped around late afternoon beside a pond with potable water, which the people of the nearby village drew. (67) Suddenly wind and a storm arose, with thunder, frequent lightning and heavy rain. It not only overturned our tent but even cascaded all our belongings into the pond. (68) Frightened by the tumult dominating the sky and by what had happened, we started fleeing but became separated from one another. Because we were in darkness and a downpour, each man turned down the road he thought would be easy for himself. (69) When we arrived at the village's cabins (we all reached the same village in different ways), we assembled at the same spot and we started calling out to those unaccounted for. (70) The Scythians leapt out of bed because of the noise. They made some light by kindling the reeds they use for fire, and asked why we were shouting. (71) The barbarians with us replied that we had been scattered by the storm, and so the Scythians, calling out to each other, welcomed us and provided warmth by lighting more reeds.

(72) The woman who ruled the village (she had been one of Bleda's wives) sent us refreshments and beautiful women for sex. This is a Scythian honor. We treated the women kindly and shared the provisions that had been set out, but we declined intercourse with them. We remained in the cabins, and at daybreak we searched for our belongings. We found them all, some where we had camped the day before, more on the bank of the pond, and still more in the water. We gathered everything and spent that day in the village drying it all out. The storm had ended and the sun was shining bright. (73) After we tended to the horses and the other pack animals, we visited the queen. We greeted her

and exchanged as gifts three silver bowls, some red hides, pepper from India, the fruit of date-palm trees and other fruits that were valuable to the barbarians because they did not grow locally. We then thanked her for her hospitality and slowly withdrew.

(74) After seven days of travel, we tarried at a village, as our Scythian guides commanded, because Attila was on his way there and we were obliged to travel behind him. (75) While there, we met some Western Romans who were themselves serving on an embassy to Attila. Among them were Romulus, a man honored with the office of *comes*;[27] Promoutos, the governor of Noricum; and Romanos, leader of a military division. (76) With them were Constantius, whom Aetius sent to Attila as a secretary, and Tatoulos, the father of the Orestes who was with Edekon. These two were traveling with the others not as part of the embassy but due to personal connections: Constantius because he had previously come to know the men in Italy, Tatoulos because of the kinship ties formed when his son Orestes married Romulus's daughter, [. . .] from Patavion, the city in Noricum.[28] (77) They were on their embassy to appease Attila because he wanted the Romans to surrender Silvanos, a bank director in Rome. Silvanos had received some golden bowls from one Constantius, who came from the western Galatians[29] and who himself had been sent to Attila and Bleda as a secretary, just like the second Constantius. During the Scythians' siege of Sirmium in Paionia,[30] Constantius received the bowls from the city's bishop, on the condition that he would pay the bishop's ransom if the city was captured and he survived, or that, if he was killed, he would ransom any townspeople who were led away as prisoners of war. (78) After the city was enslaved, Constantius, thinking little of the agreement,[31] went to Rome on some business and borrowed gold from Silvanos in exchange for the bowls,

on the terms that within a specified time he could return the gold that was lent at interest and recover the collateral, or Silvanos could use them for whatever he wanted. (79) Now, this Constantius—because Attila and Bleda suspected he would betray them, they crucified him. After a time, when someone told Attila about the bowls, he wanted Silvanos to be surrendered to him on the grounds that he stole his property. (80) Ambassadors were sent from Aetius and the Western Roman emperor to say that Silvanos, as Constantius's creditor, took and kept the bowls as collateral, not as stolen goods, and that he had sold them for silver to priests and <not>[32] other random people, since it was not religiously permissible for people to use cups dedicated to God for their own service. (81) So if he would not stop demanding the bowls despite a reasonable explanation and out of respect for the divine, they were sending gold in place of the bowls and interceding for Silvanos; they would not, they said, surrender a man who had done nothing wrong.[33] (82) This was the reason for the men's embassy. They were following the barbarian to hear his response before they were dismissed.

(83) Since we were on the same road, we waited for Attila to pass by us and then followed closely with the entire crowd. We crossed some rivers and arrived in a very large village, in which it was said Attila's compound was more conspicuous than everyone else's, fitted together with logs and well-polished boards and encircled with a wooden wall that contributed not to safety but to majesty.

We briefly interrupt fragment 8 to insert a passage from the Gothic historian Jordanes, who adds details to the information found in § 64 and §83. See the discussion of this fragment in the Introduction (p. xxvii).

FRAGMENT 9
From the *Getica* of Jordanes

Priscus the historian was sent on an embassy to him [Attila] by Theodosius the Younger and, among other things, reported the following: After crossing large rivers (that is, the Tisia, Tibisia and Dricca), we came to the place where once Vidigoia, the most powerful of the Goths, died because of the guile of the Sarmati. A little ways on, we approached the village in which King Attila was tarrying, a village, I say, resembling a very populous city. We found there wooden walls made of shining planks, the interconnection of which mimicked something so solid that the planks' seam could hardly be seen even by someone looking for it. You could see dining rooms of great circumference and porticoes adorned with every beautification. The court's open space was embraced by so large a circuit that its very size displayed royal dignity. This was the dwelling of King Attila, who held the entire barbarian world. He preferred this abode to the cities he had captured.

FRAGMENT 8 (CONTINUED)
From the *Excerpts on Romans' Embassies to Foreigners* of Constantine VII Porphyrogennetos

(84) After the king's compound, Onegesios's was magnificent and also itself had an enclosing log wall. His was not equipped with towers like Attila's; rather there was a bath, not far from the enclosing wall, which Onegesios, as the preeminent man among the Scythians after Attila, built large by conveying stones from Paionia. (85) The barbarians of that region do not have a stone nor even a tree, but they use imported wood in this way. (86) The bath's architect,

brought in from Sirmium as a prisoner of war, was expecting to receive his freedom as a wage for his contrivance, but he unexpectedly fell into worse hardship than slavery among the Scythians. Onegesios made him the bath attendant to serve him and his comrades while they were bathing.

(87) As he entered this village, Attila was welcomed by girls who moved in lines under fine white linen sheets stretched over a great distance so that under each individual linen sheet, held up by the hands of the women on either side, seven or more girls were walking (there were many such rows of the women under the linen sheets) and singing Scythian songs. (88) As Attila approached Onegesios's compound (for the road to the palace ran through it), Onegesios's wife came out with a multitude of servants, some of whom were carrying food and others wine. This is a very great honor among Scythian women. She greeted him and begged him to partake of what she was kind-heartedly offering him. Showing favor to the wife of his adviser, he ate sitting on his horse as the barbarians accompanying him raised the platter up to him. It was made of silver. (89) After he sipped from the cup that had been given to him, he entered the palace, which was higher than the other buildings, situated upon an elevated site.

(90) We remained at Onegesios's compound, as he ordered us. (He had returned with Attila's son.) After his wife and his relatives greeted us, we took our meal. He himself did not have the leisure to dine with us. He was at that moment going to see Attila for the first time since his return to report on the results of his mission and on Attila's son's injury: he had taken a spill and broken his right hand.

(91) After dinner, we left Onegesios's compound and pitched our camp near Attila's so that there would be little delay if opportunity called and Maximinos had to meet Attila or to speak with his other comrades. (92) We spent

that night where we had pitched camp. When day broke, Maximinos sent me to Onegesios to give the gifts, both what he himself was giving and what the emperor had sent, and to learn where and when he wanted to speak with him. (93) I went with some servants who were carrying the gifts and, since the doors were still closed, I waited patiently until someone came out and reported our arrival.

(94) I was passing the time walking around outside the compound's wall when someone who I thought was a barbarian from his Scythian clothing approached and greeted me in Greek. "Hello," he said. I was amazed because a Scythian man was speaking Greek. Since they are a hodgepodge of peoples, they try to learn, besides their own barbarian language, Hunnic or Gothic or even—whoever has business with the Romans—Ausonian,[34] but none of them readily speaks Greek except their prisoners of war from the parts of Thrace and Illyria near the sea. (95) Such people were recognizable to anyone who met them due to their torn garments and their personal squalor, since they had fallen into misfortune. This man, though, looked like a prosperous Scythian, well-dressed, with a circular hairstyle.

(96) I returned his greeting and asked who he was and from where he had come to the barbarian land and taken up the Scythian life. He answered that I seemed eager in my curiosity. (97) I said his speaking Greek was the cause of my inquisitiveness. Then he laughed and said that he was Greek by birth. He had come as a trader to Viminakion, the Mysian city on the Istros River, had spent a long time there and married a very wealthy woman. (98) When the city came under the barbarians, he said, he stripped off his future success[35] and because of his accrued wealth he was selected for Onegesios himself in the distribution of war spoils;[36] "after Attila the high-ranking Scythians choose from among

the wealthy captives because they are in command of very many men."[37] (99) He added that, after he had distinguished himself in later battles against the Romans and Akateri, he gave the barbarian ruler, according to Scythian custom, the spoils he took and so obtained his freedom. He married a barbarian woman, and now had children.

As one who shared Onegesios's table, he said, he believed his present life to be better than his previous life. (100) After war Scythians spend their time at ease, with each man enjoying what is at hand and causing trouble or being troubled either not at all or only a little. (101) In contrast, Romans are easily killed in war because they rely on others for safety. Because of their tyrants, not everyone carries arms, and those who do bear arms are in still more peril due to the cowardice of generals who undermine war efforts. (102) What happens in peace is even more painful than wartime troubles because of the burdensome tribute collection and unprincipled men's abuses, since laws are not established equally. If a criminal belongs to the upper class, he does not pay the penalty for his injustice; but if he is poor, with no experience in legal affairs, he awaits his penalty under law—unless he loses his life prior to the decision, as time stretches interminably along during the trial and piles of money are spent. This may be the most grievous fact of all, that one obtains legal decisions for a price. (103) "For," he said, "no one will open a court to someone who has been wronged, unless he puts down some money for the judge and the judge's assistants."[38]

(104) After he laid out these thoughts and many others, I delicately replied that he would hear my thoughts too. (105) And so I said that the devisers of the Roman constitution, being wise and good men, prevented the state from faltering by arranging that some men be guardians of the laws, that others oversee arms and military exercises—

aiming at nothing other than battle preparedness and going to war emboldened by their habitual practice so that their fear is consumed by their exercise—and that still others devote themselves to agriculture and care of the land and nourish themselves and those who fight on their behalf.

(106) "They also appointed," I said, "some men to levy the military provision-tax[39] and others to see to those treated unjustly: some to direct the judicial process on behalf of those who are unable to bring their own cases due to infirmity, and others to act as judges to protect what the law desires: that they not be deprived of attention or advocates, but that they too have counselors who will ensure that anyone who wins the judges' decision will win justice and anyone who is found guilty is not fined more than the judicial decree desires. (107) If there were no one who provided such attention, there would exist a pretext for another case on the same charge, either because the victorious party pursued too harshly or because the loser endured an unjust decision." (108) I added that a fee was paid to these men by the litigants, just as soldiers are supported by farmers (or is it not right to maintain someone who helps you and to repay his good will, just as the care of a horse is good for a cavalryman, the tendance of cows is good for a cowherd, the tendance of dogs for a hunter and so forth for other animals people keep for their own protection and advantage?). If they are convicted, they pay the court costs, attributing the loss to their own wrongdoing and no one else's.

(109) As for the protracted length of trials, I said, if they happen to be long, it is due to our thoughtfulness about justice so that judges do not act carelessly and neglect precision. They reckon it is better to conclude a trial only after a long time than to act in haste and not only treat a man unjustly but offend God, the inventor of justice. (110) The

laws are established for everyone. Even the emperor obeys them and it is certainly not the case, as he had said in his accusation, that the rich overpower the poor without risk, except if someone escapes justice by avoiding detection. But those exceptions can be found not just among the wealthy but even among the poor. In the absence of cross-examination not even the poor suffer punishment when they have done wrong (and this happens among all peoples, not just the Romans). (111) He should thank luck for his freedom, not a master who led him out to war so that his inexperience would either get him killed by the enemy or, if he escaped, punished by the man who owned him. (112) "The Romans," I said, "have always treated even their household slaves better, just as they do for their own children, when they hold up before them their fathers' or their teachers' accomplishments, in the hope that they might abstain from base actions and pursue what has been deemed noble by recalling themselves to their senses when they err.[40] It is not sanctioned for the Romans, as it is for Scythians, to use capital punishment. (113) Among them, there are very many ways of granting freedom. They grant it freely, not only when they are living but also when they are dying, by making arrangements about their property, however they want. What each man, when he is dying, decides to do with his possessions, that amounts to law."

(114) In tears he said that the laws were noble and the Roman constitution good, but the rulers, since they do not think like rulers of old, had corrupted it.

(115) During our discussion, someone from inside came out and opened the gate. I ran up and asked what Onegesios was doing. I wanted to deliver a message, I said, from the Roman ambassador. (116) The attendant replied that I would meet him if I waited a little longer, since he was about to come out.

(117) In fact, I soon saw him coming out. I went to him and said that the Roman ambassador sent his greetings and that I had come bearing gifts from him along with the gold sent by the emperor. He was eager, I said, to speak with him, wherever and whenever he wished. (118) He told his attendants to take the gold and gifts, and told me to tell Maximinos that he would come to him immediately. (119) And so I returned and reported that Onegesios was coming. Just then he came into the tent. (120) Addressing Maximinos, he said that he owed the emperor and him thanks for the gifts and he asked why he summoned him, what he wished to say. (121) Maximinos said that the time had come for Onegesios to have greater fame among men, if he would go to the emperor, use his intelligence to understand their disputes and establish harmony between the Romans and Huns. (122) It would, he said, not only be thenceforward advantageous to both nations but it would also provide many benefits for his own house: he himself and his children would forever be friends of the emperor and his descendants.

(123) Onegesios asked what must be done to gain the emperor's favor, and how he was to resolve the disputes. (124) Maximinos replied that he would cross into Roman territory, establish favor with the emperor, and study the disputes by discovering their causes and resolving them according to the law of peace. Onegesios said that he would say to the emperor and his courtiers what Attila wanted. (125) Or, he said, did the Romans think that they would cajole him so much that he would altogether betray his master and scorn his rearing among the Scythians and his wives and children? Did they think he would not consider slavery with Attila greater than wealth among the Romans? (126) He would be more useful, he said, staying home (since he soothed his master's heart whenever he grew

angry at the Romans) than traveling to Roman territory and being suspected of acting contrary to Attila's principles. (127) Once he had spoken, he proposed that I meet with him to discuss what we wanted to learn from him. (Continuous access was not appropriate for Maximinos since he was serving in an official capacity.) He then departed.

(128) The next day I arrived at the wall of Attila's compound, carrying gifts for his wife. Her name was Kreka. She had borne three children to him, of whom the eldest was ruling the Akateri and the other nations in the parts of Scythia near the Sea.[41] (129) Inside the wall there were very many buildings, some built of wooden timbers carved and fitted together with an eye for style, others made of beams[42] cleaned, scraped to straightness and placed onto logs that formed <circles>. The circles, starting from the ground, rose up to a height of good proportion. (130) This is where Attila's wife dwelled. I passed the barbarians at the door and found her lying on a soft mattress. The ground was covered with woolen felt pieces for walking on. (131) A number of male servants were gathered round her while female servants sat on the ground opposite her, dyeing some fine linens that were to be placed over the barbarians' clothing as adornment. (132) I approached her and, after a greeting, presented her with the gifts. I then withdrew and walked to the other buildings where Attila was spending his time. I waited for Onegesios to come out since he had already set out from his compound and was inside.

(133) Standing in the middle of the whole crowd (since I was known to Attila's guards and his barbarian followers, no one stopped me), I noticed a crowd coming and a murmur and clamor all around. Attila was coming out. He came forth from the house, walking haughtily, looking around here and there. (134) As he stood with Onegesios before the house, many men feuding with each other approached and received

his judgment. Then he went up to the house and received barbarian ambassadors who had come to him.

(135) While I was waiting for Onegesios, Romulus, Promoutos and Romanos, the ambassadors who had come from Italy to Attila about the golden bowls controversy, began speaking with me. With them were Roustikios, who was there to see Constantius, and Constantiolus, a man from the part of Paionia controlled by Attila. They asked whether we had been dismissed or were being forced to wait. (136) I said that I was waiting patiently at the walls to learn just this from Onegesios. I asked them in turn <whether> Attila had given a humane, mild answer to their embassy. They said that he had not changed his mind at all, but was threatening war unless Silvanos or the cups were sent to him. (137) As we marveled at the barbarian's senselessness, Romulus, a very experienced ambassador, said that Attila's brilliant good fortune and the power derived from it had raised him so high that he would not endure righteous words unless he believed they benefitted him. (138) "No ruler of Scythia," he said, "or any other land ever accomplished so many things in such a short time: ruling the islands in the Ocean and requiring even Romans, let alone all Scythia, to pay tribute." He added that Attila longed to add still more to his present possessions, to increase his empire, and so wanted to attack the Persians too.

(139) One of us asked what route he would be able to take to Persia. Romulus said that the Medes' country[43] was not very far from Scythia. The Huns were not unfamiliar with this road, because they had once traveled it when famine was striking their country and the Romans were not engaging them due to the war taking place at that time. (140) He said Basich and Kursich, royal Scythians, rulers of many people, who later went to Rome to negotiate an alliance, had visited the Medes' country. Upon their return, they said they had

come to a desolate land and crossed a lake, which Romulus thought was Maiotis.[44] Fifteen days later, they scaled some mountains and came to Media. (141) A Persian force attacked them as they were plundering and overrunning the land. They filled the air above them with missiles. In fear of the immediate danger they retreated to the mountains with only a little plunder since the Medes had reclaimed most of it. (142) Because they were apprehensive about the enemy's pursuit, they turned up another road. They made a few days' journey beyond the flame that arises from the underwater rock[45] and arrived home. And so they knew Scythia was not very far from Media. (143) Therefore, Romulus said, if Attila wished to invade Media, he would not toil hard nor travel far to bring Medes, Parthians and Persians under his sway and compel them to pay tribute, for he has a fighting force that no nation will halt.

(144) We prayed he would go against the Persians and turn his warmongering against them, but Constantiolus said he feared that, even if Attila easily brought the Persians under his sway, he would return as a master, not a friend. Even now, he said, they were paying him gold because of his rank, but if he should bring the Parthians, Medes and Persians under his sway, he would no longer tolerate the Romans' depriving him of power. Rather, he would openly consider them his servants and would issue harsher and unbearable commands to them. (145) The rank Constantiolus mentioned was a Roman generalship, the favor of which Attila had received from the emperor. It was a disguise for the word "tribute," so that levies were being sent to him under the pretense of tax proceeds distributed to generals.

(146) Constantiolus said that after the Medes, Parthians and Persians, Attila would shake off this name which the Romans wanted to call him and the rank with which they

thought they had honored him and he would force[46] them to address him as king instead of general (for when he was angry, he already said that that man's generals[47] were his servants, and his generals were equal in honor to Roman emperors). And soon there would be a great increase in his present power. God made it plain, he said, by revealing the sword of Ares, an object holy and honored among royal Scythians because it was dedicated to the overseer of wars,[48] which had disappeared long ago but was discovered with a bull's help.

Fragment 8 is again to be interrupted. Fragment 10, from Jordanes's Getica, *gives us a more detailed version of the story of the Sword of Ares (rather, in Latin, the Sword of Mars). Unlike fragment 9 above, in which Jordanes seemed to abridge and supplement Priscus's account freely, fragment 10 is likelier to be an omission by Constantine VII's excerptors. Like the story of Zerkon in fragment 11* below, the Sword of Ares story probably fell outside the bounds of Constantine's "On embassies." The excerptors omitted it here and probably placed it in a different collection. We still should not put much trust in Jordanes as a faithful transmitter of Priscus's original words, but it is likely that fragment 10 contains information direct from Priscus.*

FRAGMENT 10

From the *Getica* of Jordanes

Although it was in his [Attila's] nature always to be confident in his greatness, when the sword of Mars was discovered, an object always held sacred among Scythian kings, it nevertheless gave him additional confidence. Priscus the historian reports that it was found under the following circumstances, saying: When a certain shepherd saw a cow from his flock limping and could find no cause of such a wound, he anxiously followed the traces of blood and finally came to a sword which the cow had accidentally stepped on while grazing. The shepherd dug it up and immediately brought it to Attila. Attila rejoiced at the gift and, since he was majestic, he thought he had been appointed ruler of the whole world and the sword of Mars had granted him omnipotence in war.

FRAGMENT 8 (CONTINUED)

From the *Excerpts on Romans' Embassies to Foreigners* of Constantine VII Porphyrogennetos

(147) Each of us wanted to say something about the situation, but when Onegesios came out, we went to him and tried to learn about any major developments. As soon as he finished talking with some barbarians, he told me to ask Maximinos which man of consular rank the Romans were sending as an ambassador to Attila. (148) I returned to the tent, delivered the message and discussed with Maximinos what we ought to say in response to the barbarian. I then went back to Onegesios and said that the Romans were willing to discuss the disputed issues, if he went to them, but if he did not, the emperor would send whomever he wanted as ambassador. (149) Immediately he ordered that I get Maximinos. When he arrived, he led him to Attila and, returning a short while later, Maximinos said that the barbarian wished Nomos, Anatolios or Senator to come as ambassador and that he could accept no one other than the men he named. (150) Maximinos said he had responded that he ought not to make the emperor suspicious of these

men by naming them for the embassy, but Attila said that, unless they chose to do what he wanted, the disputes would be resolved with weapons.

(151) When we went back to the tent, Tatoulos, Orestes's father, arrived with the message that Attila was inviting both of us to his banquet, which would take place around the ninth hour of the day. (152) We watched for the right time and arrived at the dinner as invited guests. We and the Western Roman ambassadors stood on the threshold opposite Attila. (153) The cupbearers gave out a cup[49] according to the local custom so that we could pray before being seated. When this was done, we sipped from the cup and moved to the chairs, where we had to dine while sitting.

(154) All the chairs were placed along the walls of the house, on each side. Attila was seated on a couch in the middle. There was another couch behind him, beyond which some steps led up to his bed, which was veiled with fine linens and intricate drapes, hung as adornments, just as the Greeks and Romans arrange for newlyweds. (155) I thought the first rank of diners was on Attila's right, and the second rank on his left, where we were, although Berichos, a well-born Scythian man, was seated ahead of us. (156) But Onegesios was seated on a chair to the right of the king's couch, and opposite Onegesios two of Attila's children were sitting on a chair. The eldest was seated on Attila's couch, not near him but at the edge, looking at the ground out of respect for his father.

(157) Once everyone was sitting in order, a cupbearer came in and gave Attila a wooden cup of wine. He took it and welcomed the man first in order. (158) After Attila so honored him, the man rose, and it was not right for him to sit until he sipped from the wooden cup or drank it down and gave it back to the cupbearer. (159) As he remained seated, everyone present honored him in the <same> way:

receiving their cups, offering a greeting and taking a sip. For each diner, there was one cupbearer, who had to enter in a line when Attila's cupbearer departed. (160) After the second man and the rest were honored in turn, Attila greeted us in like manner according to the order of our seats. When everyone had been honored by this greeting, the cupbearers withdrew and, after Attila's, tables were set up, with three or four men or even more per table. Each man was able to partake of the dishes set out by the cook so long as he did not disrupt the order of the chairs.

(161) First Attila's servant came in carrying a platter full of meat. After him everyone's waiters placed bread and cooked food on the tables. For the other barbarians and for us lavish meals had been prepared, placed on silver trays, but for Attila there was nothing more than meat on a wooden platter. (162) He showed himself moderate in everything else too. Gold and silver goblets were given to the feasters, but his own cup was wooden. (163) His clothing too was frugal, since it cultivated no quality except cleanliness. Neither his sword, hanging beside him, nor the fastenings of his barbarian shoes nor his horse's bit, like the other Scythians', was adorned with gold or jewels or anything else that marks honor. (164) After the first course was finished, everyone rose. After we stood, no one went back to his seat until each man, in the same order as before, prayed that Attila be safe and drank the cup of wine which had been handed to him. (165) After so honoring him, we sat down and a second platter was placed on each table with other foods. (166) Once everyone partook of this too, we stood up again in the same manner, again drank and sat down.

(167) As evening came, torches were lit. Two barbarians, taking up places opposite Attila, performed original songs, singing of his victories and his excellent military qualities,

while the feasters watched them. (168) Some were enjoying the poems, others, recalling the wars, were aroused in their spirits, and still others were weeping, their bodies grown weak with the passing of time, their courage forced into repose.

(169) After the songs, a certain deranged Scythian came in. He brought everyone to laughter with his meaningless and insane babbling. In the midst of all this, Zerkon the Maurousian[50] slipped in.

The final interruption of fragment 8 brings in a passage from the Byzantine encyclopedia Suda *that seems to fit this context perfectly. The* Suda *does not name Priscus as its source (hence fragment 11* is marked with the conjectural asterisk). Nevertheless, it seems very likely that, like fragment 10 above, fragment 11* is a passage omitted by Constantine VII's excerptors because it fell outside the bounds of their "On embassies" collection. The fragment mentions that Zerkon had been given as a gift to Aspar Ardabourios in Libya. Aspar was the general commanding the Eastern Roman army sent to resist the Vandals in 431. Zerkon's story thus spans about 18 years. (Aspar's father and son were both named Ardabourios, but his own full name is attested as Flavius Ardabourios Aspar. See* PLRE *II 164–69 [Fl. Ardabur Aspar].) Zerkon is said to have been captured by Bleda when the Huns were attacking Thrace. This must have been the campaign against Margos in 441 or against Naissos and other cities in 442.*

FRAGMENT 11*
From the *Suda*

Zerkon, called a Scythian, but a Maurousian by race. The deformity of his body caused laughter, as did his lisp and appearance. He was short and hunchbacked, his feet were twisted, and his nose was visible only as nostrils because of its excessive snubness. He had been given as a gift to Aspar Ardabourios while he was in Libya. He was captured when the barbarians attacked Thrace and he was brought to the royal Scythians. Attila could not bear the sight of him, but Bleda very much enjoyed not just his hilarious remarks, but especially the way he walked and the extraordinary way he moved his body. He was with him when he feasted and when he deployed, putting on a panoply made for laughter during their excursions. For that reason, considering Zerkon's presence desirable even after he had fled with the Roman prisoners of war, Bleda overlooked the other fugitives and commanded that all diligence be given to seeking him. When he saw him captured and led to him in chains, he laughed. Having let go of his anger, he asked the reason for his flight, and why he considered the Romans' situation better than theirs. He answered that the flight was a mistake. He had, he said, a reason for his mistake, namely that his wife had not been given to him. Bleda, moved to laughter even more, gave him a well-born woman, one of the queen's servants, one who was no longer waiting on her on account of some harmful act. In this way he continued in Bleda's company for all time. After Bleda's death, however, Attila gave Zerkon as a gift to Aetius, the Western Roman general, who sent him back to Aspar.

FRAGMENT 8 (CONTINUED)
From the *Excerpts on Romans' Embassies to Foreigners* of Constantine VII Porphyrogennetos

Edekon had cajoled him [Zerkon] into coming to Attila in order to get his wife back through Attila's efforts. He had received her in the barbarians' country because Bleda had desired his presence, but he had left her in Scythia when Attila sent him as a gift to Aetius. He had failed, however, to obtain the object of his hope because Attila grew angry that he had actually returned to his country. (170) Exploiting the opportunity of the feast to enter just then, he put everyone in a good humor and moved everyone to unquenchable laughter with his appearance, his clothes, his voice and words that poured out indiscriminately from him (for he was jumbling up Hunnic and Gothic with Ausonian[51])—everyone except Attila. (171) He himself remained unmoved and unaltered in appearance, and he looked like he was not saying or doing anything resembling laughter, except that he pulled the youngest of his children closer by his cheek (his name was Ernach). He had come in and was standing nearby, and Attila looked at him with serene eyes. (172) I was amazed that he might be slighting his other children by paying attention to that son, but the barbarian sitting next to me, who understood Ausonian and told me to repeat nothing of what he was going to tell me, said that prophets had predicted to Attila that his nation would fall but that it would rise again under this son. (173) As the banquet was dragging on, we departed because we did not want to become drunk.

(174) When day came, we went to Onegesios and said that we must be dismissed and not waste our time. He said Attila was willing to send us away. (175) After a short while,

Negotiating with Attila

he consulted with his advisers about what Attila wanted and composed the letter to be delivered to the emperor. His secretaries were present, but it was Roustikios, a man who set out from Upper Mysia[52] but was captured in the war, who improved the barbarian's excellence in letter writing with his own words.

(176) As he stood up from the meeting, we asked him for the release of Sullos's wife and her children, who were taken during the fall of Ratiaria. He did not forbid their release, but he set a very high price for their ransom. (177) After we begged him to ponder their former happiness and pity them their misfortune, he went to Attila and released the woman for five hundred gold coins, and he sent the children as a gift to the emperor.

(178) At this time, Kreka, Attila's wife, invited us to dinner at the house of Adames, the man who oversaw her affairs. We joined him along with some of the nation's leading men, and there we found cordiality. (179) He greeted us with soothing words and prepared food. Each of those present, with Scythian generosity, arose and gave us each a full cup and then, after embracing and kissing the one who was drinking, received it back. After dinner, we went back to our tent and went to sleep.

(180) On the next day, Attila summoned us again to a banquet and in the same way as before we joined him and feasted. It happened that his older son was not sitting with him on his couch, but Oebarsios, his uncle on his father's side, was there. (181) During the entire banquet, his words were friendly. He was telling us to ask the emperor to give Constantius, whom Aetius had sent to him as a secretary, the wife whom he had promised. (182) Constantius, along with the ambassadors sent by Attila, had visited Emperor Theodosius and said that he was prepared to preserve the peace between the Romans and Scythians for a long time, if

he gave him a rich wife. The emperor agreed and said that he would give him the daughter of Satornilos, a man graced with wealth and lineage (but Satornilos had been killed by Athenaïs, also known as Eudocia—she was called by both names).[53] However, Zeno, a man of consular rank who led a large force of Isaurians, with which he had been entrusted to guard Constantinople during the war, denied that a promise had been made to that effect. (183) In fact, Zeno, the master of soldiers in the East, carried the girl out of the fortress and betrothed her to a certain Rufus, one of his advisers. (184) Since she had been taken away, Constantius asked the barbarian not to ignore the outrages he had suffered, and to give him either the woman stolen from him or another wife who would provide as great a dowry. (185) During the dinner, the barbarian ordered Maximinos to tell the emperor that Constantius must not fail to obtain from him the object of his hope, for lying was not fit for an emperor. (186) Attila gave these orders and Constantius promised he would pay him money if one of the wealthiest women of the Roman Empire were betrothed to him. (187) We left the banquet at the end of the night and, three days later, having been honored with proper gifts, we departed.

(188) Attila sent Berichos with us. He was the man who had been sitting ahead of us at the banquet, one of the select leaders who ruled many villages in Scythia. Attila now sent him to be ambassador to the emperor, but really so that he too received <gifts> from the Romans as an ambassador. (189) While we were lodging at some village during our journey, a Scythian man was captured. He had crossed from Roman territory into barbarian country to spy. Attila ordered him to be crucified. (190) The next day, as we traveled through other villages, two men enslaved by the Scythians were being transported, bound with their hands behind their backs, because they had killed their masters

during the war. They crucified them by putting both their heads on stakes with two projecting beams.

(191) As long as we were in Scythia, Berichos shared the road with us and seemed a quiet and friendly companion, but when we crossed the Istros, he became as if an enemy to us, alleging some stale excuses collected from servants. First, he took back the horse which he had given to Maximinos. (192) Attila had commanded that all his retainers treat Maximinos kindly with gifts and each had sent a horse to him, including Berichos. (193) Accepting a few, Maximinos sent away the others, eager to demonstrate his moderation by his measured behavior. (194) This horse Berichos took back, and he no longer tolerated sharing the journey or a feast with us. Although he had been our guide in the barbarians' country, our relationship came to this. From there, we traveled through Philippoupolis to Hadrianople. Resting there a while, we spoke with Berichos and reproached him for his silence. We told him that he was angry with men who had done nothing wrong. (195) So then, after we conciliated him and invited him to a feast, we set out again. On the road, we met Bigilas as he was returning to Scythia. After we told him Attila's responses to our embassy, we held fast to our journey home.

(196) As we approached Constantinople, we thought Berichos had changed his temper. He did not forget his wild nature, though; instead, he began disputes and accused Maximinos of saying in Scythia that the generals Areobindos and Aspar had no respect for the emperor and accused him of belittling their deeds and exposing them as inconsequential barbarians.

The following passage picks up immediately after the long fragment 8. It is marked in the preserved text as the beginning of Priscus's Book 4. The scene shifts back to Attila's camp, where Bigilas arrives carrying the gold he intends to pay to Edekon to carry out the assassination of Attila. But Attila is prepared for him.

FRAGMENT 8.1

From the *Excerpts on Romans' Embassies to Foreigners* of Constantine VII Porphyrogennetos

Book 4

(1) As soon as Bigilas crossed into Scythia and reached Attila's location, he was encircled and held by barbarians who had been readied for this encounter. They seized the money that he was carrying to Edekon. (2) When they led him to Attila, he was asked why he was carrying so much gold. He said that he was planning ahead for himself and his attendants, lest their embassy lose speed through lack of provisions or a scarcity of horses or the exhaustion of their pack-animals on the long road. Also, he said, many Romans were begging him to ransom their relatives and so he was prepared to purchase prisoners of war.

(3) Attila said, "You worthless beast"—meaning Bigilas—"you will not weasel your way out of justice, nor will any excuse be good enough for you to escape your punishment. You have more money than you need to acquire provisions, to buy horses and pack-animals and to ransom prisoners of war, which I forbade you to do when you were here with Maximinos." (4) Finished speaking, he ordered that Bigilas's son (who was then for the first time accompanying Bigilas to the barbarians' country) be struck down with a sword unless Bigilas first said for whom and for what reason he was carrying the money.

(5) When he saw the boy being led to his death, he fell to tears and laments and shouted out that justice should

bring the sword against him, not the innocent boy. Without hesitation, begging nonstop that he himself be killed and his son be released, he described the plans devised by Edekon, the eunuch, the emperor and himself. (6) Knowing from Edekon's report that Bigilas was telling the whole truth, Attila ordered him to be bound in chains and threatened that he would not release him until his son went back and brought another fifty pounds of gold to him for their ransom. (7) He was bound, and his son returned to Roman territory. Attila also sent Orestes and Eslas to Constantinople.

The next fragment comes from a different collection of Constantine VII, but (after the excerptor's introductory words) immediately follows the previous passage.

FRAGMENT 12

From the *Excerpts on Foreigners' Embassies to the Romans* of Constantine VII Porphyrogennetos

(1) After he seized Bigilas, who had been detected plotting against him, and the one hundred pounds of gold, which were sent by Chrysaphius the eunuch, Attila straightaway sent Orestes and Eslas to Constantinople. He instructed Orestes to go to the emperor wearing around his neck the purse in which Bigilas placed the gold that was to be given to Edekon. He was to display it to the emperor and the eunuch and to ask if they recognized it. (2) And he instructed Eslas to say aloud: while Theodosius was a child of a well-born father, Attila too, being well-born and the successor to his father Moundiouchos, carefully guarded his good breeding. Theodosius, however, had fallen away from his good breeding and so was a slave to him insofar as he had consented to the payment of tribute. (3) He

was therefore not acting justly when he, like a worthless servant, secretly attacked his better and a man whom fortune had revealed to him as his master. (4) He said that he would therefore not revoke the charge against those who committed offenses against him, unless Theodosius should send the eunuch to be punished. These are the reasons they went to Constantinople.

Attila's demand for Chrysaphius was not the eunuch's only trouble. Maximinos reported to Theodosius the affair of Constantius, mentioned in fragment 8 §181–186 (p. 77–78, above), an affair that brings Chrysaphius also into conflict with the general Zeno. This Zeno—not the same man as would become Eastern emperor in 474—was a general from Isauria, a province on the mainland opposite Cyprus. With his Isaurian troops, he had defended Constantinople when the Huns approached in 447 and had served as consul in 448.

FRAGMENT 12.1

From the *Excerpts on Foreigners' Embassies to the Romans* of Constantine VII Porphyrogennetos

(1) It happened that Chrysaphius was also demanded by Zeno. Maximinos reported that Attila said the emperor must fulfill his promise and give Constantius the woman whose betrothal to another man could not have happened contrary to the emperor's wishes. Either, he said, the audacious man would have paid the price, or the emperor's power was such that he did not even rule his own servants, against whom, if he would like, he was ready to provide an alliance. (2) Theodosius, bitten in his heart, confiscated the girl's property.

Theodosius had promised to join in marriage Constantius, an Italian man working as one of Attila's secretaries (but different from Constantius, the secretary traveling with the Western Roman ambassadors in fragment 8 §75–76 [p. 58, above]), and the wealthy daughter of Satornilos (or Saturninus), whose name we do not know. But Zeno had undermined the emperor's plans by marrying the woman to his own retainer. Probably the marriage of Satornilos's daughter was a symptom of a larger dispute between Zeno and Chrysaphius, although it is not possible to reconstruct the details.

FRAGMENT 13

From the *Excerpts on Romans' Embassies to Foreigners* of Constantine VII Porphyrogennetos

(1) Demanded by both men, Attila and Zeno, Chrysaphius was in anguish. Although everyone was offering him their kindness and their efforts on his behalf, he decided to send Anatolios and Nomos as ambassadors to Attila, Anatolios because he led the emperor's personal troops and negotiated his peace treaties, Nomos because he held the office of *magister* and, like Anatolios, was counted among the patricians, men who outrank all the other magistrates. (2) Nomos was sent with Anatolios not only because of his high rank but also because he was well-disposed toward Chrysaphius and would outdo the barbarian in spending; for he was not one to spare money when he was eager to arrange affairs. (3) They were dispatched, first, to abate Attila's anger and to persuade him to preserve the peace according to their agreements, and, second, to say that a woman not inferior in family and wealth to Satornilos's daughter would

be betrothed to Constantius. Satornilos's daughter, they were to say, had not wanted to marry Constantius. She married a different man lawfully, since it was not sanctioned among the Romans for a woman to be betrothed to a man unwillingly. (4) The eunuch also sent gold to the barbarian so that he would be appeased and his fury abated.

This embassy took place in early 450. Anatolios and Nomos were two of the former consuls Attila had named as acceptable ambassadors (fragment 8 §149 [p. 71, above]). Anatolios had already negotiated with Attila twice, once on the occasion of the siege of Asemos (fragment 5 [p. 37, above]) and again in 448, probably the occasion on which Bigilas served as the translator. Accompanying Anatolios and Nomos was Bigilas's son, bringing the gold Attila had demanded to ransom his father.

FRAGMENT 14

From the *Excerpts on Romans' Embassies to Foreigners* of Constantine VII Porphyrogennetos

(1) Anatolios and Nomos's party, after they crossed the Istros, proceeded into Scythia as far as the river called Drenkon.[54] Attila met them there, out of respect for the men, that they would not be worn out by the long journey. (2) Although he began the discussion insolently, he was won over by the abundance of gifts and, softened by their gentle words, he swore to keep the peace according to the same agreements, to withdraw from Roman territory along the Istros and to stop badgering the emperor about the fugitives so long as the Romans would not take in new fugitives from him. (3) He also released Bigilas after receiving the fifty pounds

of gold brought to him by Bigilas's son, who had come to Scythia with the ambassadors, and he released numerous prisoners of war without ransom as a favor to Anatolios and Nomos. (4) He also gave them horses and animal hides, with which the royal Scythians adorned themselves, and then sent them away, sending Constantius with them so that the emperor would keep his promise to him.

(5) When the ambassadors returned and reviewed in detail everything said between the barbarian and themselves, a woman, the former wife of Armatos, son of Plinthas, the Roman general and former consul, was betrothed to Constantius. (6) Armatos had gone to Libya for a battle against the Ausoriani. He was successful in the war but had fallen ill and died. Now the emperor persuaded his wife, distinguished in family and wealth, to marry Constantius.

(7) When the differences with Attila were resolved in this way, Theodosius feared that Zeno would usurp the throne.

Matters between Attila and Theodosius were thus settled in terms not wholly unfavorable to the Romans. Attila withdrew to the far side of the Danube. The affairs of Bigilas and Constantius were brought to conclusion. And, while tribute payments were expected to continue, it does not seem that the amount was increased. It seems that, in the early months of 450, both Attila and Theodosius had their attentions drawn elsewhere: Theodosius to internal usurpation, Attila to more westerly opportunities.

NOTES

1. The 447 date for the fragments that follow is not without controversy. Some scholars place these negotiations in 443. For the 447 date, see Blockley 1981, 168–69; Heather 2006, 307–8.

2. A town on the Danube, near modern Archar in northwestern Bulgaria, approximately 175 km southeast of Viminakion and Margos, the Huns' previous crossing point. Pleiades ID: 207376.
3. Maenchen-Helfen 1973, 118–119.
4. Senator's route took him up the western shore of the Black Sea to Odessos, modern Varna, Bulgaria. Pleiades ID: 216904.
5. Also spelled *Asamos*, modern Muselievo, Bulgaria, just upriver from where the Osam River empties into the Danube, a little over 150 km east of Ratiaria. Pleiades ID: 216715.
6. The Greek translates the Latin title *magister utriusque militiae per Thracias*, the chief military officer along the lower Danube.
7. This Roman general, the father of Anagastes, is called Ornigisklos in fragment 38 (p. 151, below) and Arnegisklos in fragment 78* (p. 163, below). For his career, see *PLRE* II 151 (Arnegisclus).
8. Ratiaria: see fr. 3 §3 (p. 36, above). Naisos, also spelled Naissos: see fr. 1b §1 (p. 14, above). Philippoupolis: modern Plovdiv, Bulgaria; Pleiades ID: 216927. Arkadioupolis, a.k.a. Bergoule or Bergule: modern Lüleburgaz, Turkey, about 150 km northwest of Constantinople; Pleiades ID: 511185. Constantia: presumably the fortress mentioned in fr. 1.1 §2 (p. 10, above) as opposite Margos, and not the other fortress named Constantia on the Upper Danube near Szentendre, Hungary (Pleiades ID: 197564). In either case, Constantia stands out of geographical order. Ratiaria, Naisos, Philippoupolis and Arkadioupolis trace a northwest-to-southeast route from the Danube toward Constantinople.
9. The Pontos is the Black Sea. The sea near Kallipolis and Sestos is either the Sea of Marmara or the northeastern Aegean Sea. Both Kallipolis (modern Gallipoli, Turkey; Pleiades ID: 501450) and Sestos (near modern Yalova, Turkey; Pleiades ID: 501609) lie on the Gallipoli peninsula, the north shore of the Dardanelles.
10. Hadrianople: modern Edirne, Turkey, about 75 km northeast of Arkadioupolis; Pleiades ID: 501428. Herakleia / Peirinthos: modern Marmara Ereğlisi, Turkey, on the north shore of the Sea of Marmara; Pleiades ID: 511357. Athyras: modern Büyükçekmece, Turkey, 55 km east of Herakleia / Peirinthos and 33 km west of Constantinople; Pleiades ID: 511172. Attila thus, according to Theophanes, overran all the Roman territory and settlements from Belgrade, Serbia (near Margos), through Bulgaria, into northwestern Turkey (except Hadrianople and Herakleia, probably because these major cities were too well fortified) and came within 33 km of the walls of Constantinople.
11. John of Antioch and other ancient authorities testify to the relationship between the Hun Edekon and Odovacer, but some

scholars, including Maenchen-Helfen, have been skeptical. For references, see *PLRE* II 385–86 (Edeco); the *PLRE* article accepts the identification.

12. Just as Priscus calls the province Moesia "Mysia" (fragment 1.1 [p. 10, above]), he follows the example of other classicizing writers in calling the province Pannonia "Paionia." The ancient Paionians were a people of the Macedonian region known to Homer (*Iliad* 16.291, 17.350) and Herodotus (5.1, etc.).

13. Novae is the site of modern Svishtov in north central Bulgaria (Pleiades ID: 216899). Even starting from Sirmium (modern Sremska Mitrovica, Serbia) near the eastern edge of Pannonia Secunda, the Danube (a.k.a. Istros) runs approximately 650 km from Pannonia to Novae. But the concessions made by Aetius probably extended much further west, and so we should imagine that Attila demanded the Romans abandon a still larger expanse of territory.

14. Modern Sofia, Bulgaria. Serdica, like Naissos, had already been sacked (fr. 8 §4 [p. 48]), but unlike Naissos (fr. 8 §13 [p. 49]) it was still populated.

15. My translation reflects the syntactic confusion of the original: nominative singular participles with a plural main verb. The confusion perhaps results from the excerpter's attempt to summarize an omitted passage.

16. i.e., *magister officiorum*, Master of Offices. Priscus transliterates the Latin title into Greek.

17. There is a minor textual discrepancy here. Some manuscripts read "he sent back to him"; others have "he sent back to you." Most editors have assumed that the text changes here to a direct quotation of the letter and they have emended the text to read "I sent back to you." Carolla, the most recent editor, has instead emended the text to read "they sent back," without an indirect object. My translation follows Carolla's text and assumes that there is no direct quotation; it thus remains closest to the reading of the first group of manuscripts. In any case, the meaning is clear.

18. Literally, "Indian stones." On the identification as pearls, see Thompson 1947, 62.

19. Priscus translates into Greek *magister militum per Illyrcium*.

20. Something has dropped out of this clause, and various editors have filled the lacuna in various ways. I translate Carolla's conjecture, though without much confidence that it is precisely right. It does seem to capture the necessary meaning. Blockley emends the text and translates: "he claimed that Edeco [i.e., Edekon] supported him in this." This is the least intrusive of editors emendations, but

it seems wrong that Bigilas would have emphasized his intimate connection with Edekon aloud since they were already under the suspicion resulting from Orestes's remark at Serdica. Bigilas's purpose was to make a private visit to the Hunnic leaders, under the pretense of speaking with Attila but in fact to speak privately with Edekon.

21. The proposal that Onegesios travel to the emperor to mediate the disputes was one of the emperor's original proposals (fr. 8 §4). Skottas would be interested in this because Onegesios was his brother.

22. I translate the emendation preferred by most editors, a first-person plural verb, although Carolla writes a first-person singular form. (The manuscripts give the verb as an impossible third-person singular.) The only indication in the paragraph whether Priscus represents himself as speaking for the entire embassy or on his own initiative is the first-person plural "us" that stands as the object of "support" above.

23. I translate Carolla's emendation (*hapantas tous apontas*). The manuscripts have "they went through absent men" (*apontas*), which previous editors have emended to "they went through them all" (*hapantas*).

24. Editors have recognized that the manuscripts' sentence is missing a necessary negative.

25. Fragment 68* (p. 115, below) reports his name as Ellac.

26. The Istros is the Danube. The other rivers cannot be identified with certainty.

27. Priscus transliterates the Latin title *comes*. The following two titles, though, are Greek translations of Latin terms, perhaps *praeses Norici ripensis* and *comes rei militaris* or *dux*. (See *PLRE* II 926 [Promotus 1] and *PLRE* II 946–47 [Romanus 2].)

28. Patavion (usually spelled Poetavio in Latin) is modern Ptuj, Slovenia. Pleiades ID: 197446. There is much textual confusion in this passage. A few words have almost certainly dropped out of the text. Carolla suggests that "from Patavion" means that Orestes journeyed after the wedding from Patavion to Hunnic Pannonia. Cf. fr. 7 §1 (p. 44) on Orestes's Pannonian home. (We should note that the Greek cannot mean simply that Romulus's daughter was "from Patavion," i.e., that she was born in Patavion.) Other editors have placed a period after "married Romulus's daughter" and marked a lacuna, before taking "from Patavion" with the following sentence. Thus, Blockley translates, "Orestes had married a daughter of Romulus....[*sic*] They were making this embassy from Patavio, a city in Noricum." This reading, though, is impossible. As Carolla

points out, the Greek word order guarantees that "from Patavion" belongs to the sentence in §76.

29. "Galatians" is Priscus's archaizing name for the Gauls. "Eastern Galatians" would refer to central Asia Minor.

30. Modern Sremska Mitrovica, Serbia on the Sava River. Pleiades ID: 207447. Sirmium was the capital of the Illyrian Prefecture and of Pannonia Secunda province. As before, Priscus uses the archaic name Paionia for the Roman province Pannonia.

31. Blockley argues for retaining the majority manuscript reading *Skuthikôn* (the Scythians) instead of the emendation *sunthêkôn* (the agreements) adopted by editors since Niebuhr in 1829. The manuscripts, however, are likely wrong. Nowhere else does Priscus use the form *Skuthikoi* to refer collectively to the Scythians; he exclusively uses the shorter form *Skuthai*. *Skuthikos* appears in only two contexts: (1) written by itself in the feminine singular, it refers to Scythia, the territory; (2) as an adjective modifying a noun.

32. This insertion seems necessary, as in §50 above. Surprisingly, Carolla does not include it. The emendation was first suggested by Bekker and has appeared in most subsequent editions.

33. A textually difficult sentence. I translate the received text as best as possible. It requires: (1) understanding *ei* ("if") to mean "since," a possible if unusual meaning (cf. LSJ s.v. εἰ VI: "in citing a fact as a ground of argument or appeal, *as surely as, since*"); (2) either assuming that a preposition has dropped out before *prophaseôs* ("explanation")—some editors have in fact inserted *meta* ("with") here—or understanding *eulabeia* to govern both *prophaseôs* and *tou theiou* ("religion") and have two slightly different meanings, a figure speech known as zeugma; (3) understanding the participle *paraitoumenos* to mean "intercede for," another rare but not impossible meaning.

34. Although *Italia* is the normal classical word for Italy, used frequently by Thucydides and many others, Priscus here uses *Ausonia*, more common in classical poetry. The language of the Ausonians is thus Latin. Later (§135), Priscus does use *Italia*.

35. A bold metaphor. He speaks of success in Greek business as clothing to be removed and cast aside.

36. The text briefly changes from indirect statement (reporting what the Greek was saying) to direct quotation.

37. I follow Blockley's interpretation of this obscure clause. Cf. Blockley 1983, 385–86 n. 59.

38. I translate this sentence as emended by Niebuhr and printed by most editors, though not Carolla, who more closely follows the received manuscript. Her version means something like, "One will not grant

a decision to a wronged man who comes into court, unless he puts down some money for the judge and the judge's assistants."

39. With different punctuation, this clause may state that the farmers mentioned at the end of §105 were to pay the provision-tax.
40. Or with Thompson's emendation: "in the hope that they might abstain from base things and pursue what is considered noble, and they recall them to their senses when they err."
41. That is, the Black Sea.
42. I translate most editors' text *dokôn* ("beams") rather than Carolla's *dorôn* ("hides"). The manuscript reading is the impossible *logôn* ("words"). Others have suggested *lithôn* ("stones") and *lugôn* ("chaste-tree withes").
43. i.e., Persia. As Herodotus records, the Medes were a nation conquered by Cyrus the Great's Persians. In classical Greek literature "Mede" and "Persian" became virtually synonymous.
44. Today, the Sea of Azov.
45. It is unclear what this refers to. Marquart, cited by Thompson who is cited by Blockley 1983, 386–87, thought it was the oilfields of Baku in Azerbaijan, but that is far distant from the route Priscus describes.
46. Translating Niebuhr's emendation *anagkasein* for the received text *anagkasas*, which is printed by Carolla but only possible if Priscus switches to a direct quotation mid-sentence.
47. It is unclear who "that man" is, but it is likely Valentinian III, the Western Roman emperor. Priscus attributes these remarks to Constantiolus, who is from Pannonia, in the West, and specifically that part of Pannonia ceded to Attila. Given that Pannonia was granted to Attila by Aetius, it is possible that "that man's generals" refers obliquely to Aetius.
48. I read, along with most editors and some manuscripts, *polemôn* for *polemiôn* ("enemies"), which is printed by Carolla.
49. Translation of a conjecture from a nonsensical manuscript reading.
50. A Maurousian, in classical Greek, is someone from northwestern Africa, which the Romans called Mauretania. *Mauri*, the Latin term for the people, gives rise to the common English translation "Moor."
51. As in fragment 8 §94 above, Priscus uses "Ausonian" to signify "Italian." Thus, Zerkon and the Hun below are speaking Latin.
52. That is, the province of Moesia Superior, where Margos and Viminakion were located. This Roustikios is not the same man as the translator introduced earlier, who traveled with Priscus to Attila's camp.
53. On Satornilos, see *PLRE* II 979–80 (Saturninus 3). He had been

comes domesticorum before his death in 444, assassinated on the order of the empress Eudocia. On Eudocia, see *PLRE* II 408–9 (Aelia Eudocia (Athenais) 2). She had been born a pagan in Athens, but was baptized a Christian when she became engaged to Theodosius. She married him in 421 and was proclaimed Augusta, or empress, in 423. Some of her poetry has survived.

54. Presumably the same as the Drekon River mentioned at fr. 8 §64 (p. 56 above) and the Dricca mentioned by Jordanes in fr. 9 (p. 60, above). Exact location unknown.

ATTILA IN THE WEST

FRAGMENT 62*

A fragment of John of Antioch, preserved in the *Excerpts on Plots* of Constantine VII Porphyrogennetos

Theodosius the Younger was growing angry with Zeno. He was afraid that he would aim at usurpation, if seizing the throne could be done without danger to himself, a fact which troubled him very much. Even while he easily pardoned all mere errors, he was harsh and unmovable not only toward anyone preparing for usurpation but also toward anyone considered worthy of the emperorship. He tried every means possible to remove them. In addition to the aforementioned people, he expelled Baudon and Danielos on the pretext that they were aiming at usurpation. Eager, therefore, to use the same policy to defend himself against Zeno, he stuck to his earlier plan: Maximinos crossed into Isauropolis[1] and overpowered the lands there first; he then sent a force to the east by sea to bring Zeno to terms. Now, he did not abandon his decisions, but he delayed the plan when he became troubled by a greater fear.

A messenger arrived with the news that Attila was attacking the imperial court at Rome because Honoria, the sister of Valentinian, had summoned him to her aid. Honoria, who herself possessed the ornaments of royal power, was caught having a secret affair with a certain Eugenios, who managed her affairs. He was killed for the crime but she was driven from power and betrothed to Herkoulanos, a former consul and a man of such fine habits that he was not suspected of working toward imperial authority nor revolution. She made the matter worse and terribly grievous by sending a eunuch named Hyakinthos to Attila and offering him money to avenge her marriage. She also sent a ring, thus promising herself to the barbarian. He prepared himself to go after the Western crown, but considered how he might overpower Aetius first, for he believed that he could not realize his hope other than by removing the man.

When Theodosius learned all this, he sent Valentinian the advice to release Honoria to Attila. Valentinian, though, arrested Hyakinthos and examined the whole situation. He ordered that his body should suffer many outrages and his head should be cut off. He gave Honoria, the sister of Valentinian, as a gift to his mother, who had often asked for her. And so Honoria at that time escaped [...]².

Theodosius did not live to see how events transpired. He died by falling off a horse on July 28, 450 at age 49 with no sons and without naming an heir. A month later, Marcian was proclaimed emperor, apparently with the support of Zeno, Aspar and Theodosius's sister Pulcheria, who married Marcian. Marcian had been almost unknown before his accession, a low-level aide among Aspar's troops. He was born in 392 and served as a common soldier in the army. He fought in the campaign against Persia in 421–22, possibly having attained the rank of tribune. We do not have any indication that he ever progressed beyond this low-level command post before he was proclaimed emperor. His rise from among Aspar's men suggests a simultaneous resurrection for Aspar himself, who had fallen into some discredit in the later years of Theodosius's reign. (Priscus hints at this at fragment 8 §196 [p. 79, above].) Below we will see Aspar's son Ardabourios commanding troops on Marcian's behalf *and Aspar himself advising Marcian's successor Leo. As for Zeno and Pulcheria, we see their influence in the condemnation of Chrysaphius. (Pulcheria's role was mentioned in fragment 52* [p. 23, above].) For his support in Marcian's accession, Zeno was named patrician by the new emperor, but died soon thereafter.*

As with the stories of Theodosius's early life, Priscus may have narrated Marcian's younger years in a flashback digression. (Evagrius, who supplies the next fragment, does exactly this.) Thanks to Marcian's obscure origins, fantastic stories grew up about his youth. Priscus's conjectural fragments preserve two such tales. The first story concerns Marcian's enrollment in the military, presumably sometime in the 410s.

FRAGMENT 63*

From the *Ecclesiastical History* of Evagrius

Accordingly, Marcian, as it is recorded by Priscus the orator and many others as well, was Thracian by birth, son of a military man. Eager to follow in his father's footsteps, he set out toward Philippoupolis where he could join the military formations. He saw by the road a recently slain body that had been tossed on the ground. Standing beside it (even beyond all his other virtues he was very philanthropic), he felt pity at what had happened and delayed his journey for a long time to pay suitable respects.

When some people saw this, they reported it to the magistrates in Philippoupolis. The magistrates detained Marcian and interrogated him about the circumstances surrounding the murder. Guesswork and probability carried more weight than the truth he told. Though he denied the murder, he was about to pay the murderer's penalty when some divine hand suddenly tipped the scale and handed over the murderer. As that man suffered capital punishment for the act, Marcian was welcome to retain his own head. And so, unexpectedly saved, he arrived at one of the military stations there, where he wished to report the news. They were impressed with him and, estimating that he would be great and probably very noteworthy, they received him with the greatest pleasure. They enlisted him in their ranks, not at the lowest degree, as the military law dictates, but at the degree of a man who had just died, Augustus by name.

So they recorded "Marcian, i.e. Augustus" in the record, so that his name anticipated the appellation of our emperors, who put on the name Augustus as they put on the purple robe. Just as the name did not dare to remain on him apart from the rank, so the rank did not seek out another name for boasting; authority and the surname were established at the same time, indicated through a single naming, ranking and appellation.

In the second story, Marcian has traveled to North Africa in Aspar's campaign against Geiseric and the Vandals. Evagrius preserves a version of the story, immediately following his narrative of Marcian's military enrollment. He cites as his source Procopius, whose version is printed here. The tale takes place after the Vandals' siege of Hippo Regius in 432.

FRAGMENT 56*

From the *Vandalic War* of Procopius

Thus the Vandals took Libya away from the Romans and held it. Whichever enemies they took alive they considered equivalent to prisoners of war and so they imprisoned them. It happened that among them was Marcian, who would become emperor after Theodosius's death. At that time, Geiseric summoned the prisoners to the king's court, so that he could know, by examining them, to which master each of them should be enslaved without neglecting each one's own merit. Since they were gathered under a clear sky around the middle of a spring day, they sat oppressed by the sun. Marcian was sleeping unnoticed among them, somewhere or other. An eagle flew overhead, its wings spread, as they say. Always remaining in the same spot in the air, it cast a shadow on Marcian alone.

Geiseric, a very shrewd man, saw from the upper rooms what was happening. He suspected that the event was godly and so summoned the man to ask him who in the world he was. He said he was Aspar's confidant; the Romans call such a man *domesticus* in their language. It became clear to Geiseric, as soon as he heard his answer and added in, first, the bird's deed and, second, how powerful Aspar was in Byzantium, that <the> man would become <emperor>. Reckoning on the one hand that if he made him disappear from among men, it would be abundantly clear that the bird's action would have amounted to nothing (since he would not shield from the sun an emperor who was about to die) and so he would be killing him for no reason, but reckoning on the other hand that if the man was destined to become emperor at a later time, the man would never suffer death at his hands, he judged it wrong to kill him, for the designs of God's mind may not be hindered by a man's decision. He bound Marcian with oaths that he would never march against the Vandals if ever the decision rested on him. In this way Marcian was released, came to Byzantium and, upon Theodosius's death later, received the emperorship. He became a good emperor in everything except Libyan affairs, to which he paid no attention. But this happened at a later time.

With Marcian in place on the Eastern throne in 450, Attila faced a choice whether to renew his attacks on the Eastern Empire or to turn to the West. Both empires were rejecting his demands.

FRAGMENT 15

From the *Excerpts on Foreigners' Embassies to the Romans* of Constantine VII Porphyrogennetos

(1) When it was announced to Attila that Marcian had succeeded to the Eastern Roman imperial throne after the death of Theodosius and when it was announced to him what had happened concerning Honoria, he sent representatives to the Western Roman ruler to argue that no harm should come to Honoria, whom he had betrothed to himself. He would avenge her, he said, unless she received the ornaments of power. He also sent representatives to the Eastern Romans to collect the arranged tribute. Both sets of ambassadors returned unsuccessful.

(2) The Western Romans replied that Honoria could not marry him because she had already been given to another man, and that the scepter was not owed to her since the rule of the Roman Empire belonged not to females but to males. The Eastern Romans said they would not consent to the payment of the tribute Theodosius arranged. If Attila remained peaceful, they said, they would give him gifts; if he threatened war, they would lead against him arms and men not inferior to his force.

(3) Attila's mind was divided and he was unsure which side he would attack first. He decided it was best for now to

turn his attention toward the bigger war and march against the West, in order to fight not only the Italians but also the Goths and Franks—the Italians to get Honoria and her money, the Goths to establish favor with Geiseric.

Attila's decision to march westward was settled by the end of 450. The next fragment discusses his motivations. All of our sources focus on Honoria's scandalous affair. Attila probably had other political and especially economic motivations for wanting to attack the West, and the request from Honoria served as a convenient pretext. Various reasons have been suggested, all of which probably contributed to the decision. The Balkans had been plundered dry and so Attila needed to seek wealth elsewhere to sure up his power among the barbarians. The affair concerning the banker Silvanos had been a personal affront to him. The final sentence in the previous fragment hints tantalizingly at a collusion between Attila and Geiseric, a partnership that the sixth-century historian Jordanes also reports. The next fragment notes Attila's desire to intervene in Frankish affairs and so gain influence over those powerful people, in opposition to Aetius. But even when the sources mention these other casus belli, *they return to the court scandal.*

FRAGMENT 16

From the *Excerpts on Foreigners' Embassies to the Romans* of Constantine VII Porphyrogennetos

(1) As a pretext for war against the Franks, Attila used the death of their king and the king's sons' disagreement about their realm. The elder son was determined to ally

himself with Attila, the younger son with Aetius. We saw the younger son going as an ambassador to Rome, when he was still smooth-faced, with blond hair that poured around his shoulders to a great length. (2) Aetius had adopted him and given him numerous gifts, and then together with the emperor sent him away in friendship and alliance.

(3) For these reasons, Attila, while preparing his expedition, again sent men from his court to Italy, demanding that they hand over Honoria. He said that she had promised to join herself to him in marriage. The proof, he believed, was the ring she sent, which he enclosed so that it could be exhibited. He said Valentinian was to yield half of the empire to him because Honoria had succeeded to her father's rule but it had been stolen from her through her brother's greed. (4) When the Western Romans held fast to their earlier opinion and acquiesced in none of his demands, he held fast all the more to his war preparations by stirring up the whole host of warriors.

Attila marched the Huns and his other subject peoples from the Hungarian Plain across Europe, north of the Alps. Jordanes reports that there were a half million people with him. They crossed the Rhine in the spring of 451 and began plundering Gaul as they had plundered the Balkans.

Few details about the Gallic campaign survive. The Huns seem to have ransacked and plundered numerous towns in northeast Gaul. There is no evidence about further politicking with the Franks. One source reports that Attila had told Valentinian that he was marching West in order to attack Theoderic's Visigoths, who had been settled around Toulouse since 418, but the horde never moved toward the southwest. The Paschal Chronicle, *which here presents Priscan material at best secondhand, gives us a few badly confused lines about the Huns in Gaul. In this next fragment, it is necessary to read Marcian for Theodosius and Theoderic for Alaric. (Alaric was the Visigothic king who sacked Rome in 410.)*

FRAGMENT 64*
From the *Paschal Chronicle*

While Theodosius and Valentinian, the Augusti, were emperors, Attila, from the race of the Gepid Huns, marched against Rome and Constantinople with a multitude of many tens of thousands. He notified Valentinian, the emperor of Rome, through a Gothic ambassador, "Attila, my master and yours, orders you through me to make ready the palace for him." He gave the same notice to Theodosius, the emperor in Constantinople, through a Gothic ambassador. Aetius, the first man of senatorial rank of Rome, heard the excessive daring of Attila's desperate response and went off to Alaric in Gaul, who was an enemy of Rome because of Honorius. He urged him to join him in standing against Attila, since he had destroyed many Roman cities. They unexpectedly launched themselves against him as he was bivouacked near the Danoubios River, and cut down his many thousands. Alaric, wounded by a *sagitta*[3] in the engagement, died.

Attila died similarly, carried off by a nasal hemorrhage while he slept at night with his Hunnic concubine. It was suspected that this girl killed him. The very wise Priscus the Thracian wrote about this war.[4]

The Chronicle *author misnames the Eastern emperor and the Visigothic king. He also loses track of his geography, moving the decisive battle back to the*

Danube (which he calls Danoubios, not Priscus's usual Istros). And he loses track of his chronology, putting the Gallic campaign in 450 instead of 451. Perhaps worst of all, he kills off Attila too soon. But he does give us one key piece of correct information: Aetius, the man who once habitually hired the Huns as allied mercenaries, now fought against the Huns to protect the West. Aetius's movement against the Huns is confirmed, among other sources, by another conjectural Priscus fragment, from Theophanes.

FRAGMENT 65*

From the *Chronicle* of Theophanes

Attila rose up against the emperors [...] Valentinian of Rome, because he did not give him his sister Honoria as a wife. Proceeding to the city of Aurelia,[5] he engaged with Aetius, the Roman general. After his defeat, having lost his force, he turned back to the Ligus River,[6] dishonored.

Theophanes gives us a correct location: Aurelia, modern-day Orléans. From these hints and from other, better sources, the events can be reconstructed. While ravaging northeastern Gaul, Attila decided to besiege Orléans. As Aetius's forces, including Theoderic's Visigoths, approached, Attila lifted the siege, moved eastward and prepared for battle. The exact location of the battle cannot now be determined. It is variously called the Catalaunian Fields or the campus Mauriacus. *The most detailed narrative is to be found in Jordanes (chapters XXXVIII.197–XLI.217), complete with a stirring battlefield exhortation by Attila: "What is war but your usual custom? Or what is sweeter for a brave man than to seek revenge with his own hand? It is a right of nature to glut the soul with vengeance. Let us then attack the foe eagerly; for they are ever the bolder who make the attack" (Jordanes XXXIX.203–204; trans. Mierow). The Huns and their allies fought so fiercely that the Visigothic king Theoderic was killed. But when the fighting ceased, Aetius's Romans were victorious. The Huns retreated. They left Gaul and followed the Danube back to their base in the Hungarian plain.*

Priscus tells us that during the ensuing winter (451/ 452), Attila renewed his tribute demands on Marcian and the Eastern Empire. His demands were not well received.[7]

FRAGMENT 18

From the *Excerpts on Romans' Embassies to Foreigners* of Constantine VII Porphyrogennetos

(1) When Attila sought the tribute arranged by Theodosius or else threatened war, the Romans replied that they were sending ambassadors to him, and so Apollonios was sent. His brother had married Satornilos's daughter, the one whom Theodosius wanted to betroth to Constantius but whom Zeno had married off to Rufus. But that person died at the time.[8]

(2) Apollonios, then, being one of Zeno's advisers and holding the office of general, was sent to Attila as an ambassador. He crossed the Istros, but did not gain access to the barbarian. Attila was angry that he had not brought the tribute which, he said, had been arranged for him by better, more kingly men. So he did not even receive the ambassador because he scorned him who sent him.

(3) At this point, Apollonios clearly accomplished a

man's deed. Because Attila was not letting his embassy depart and was not willing to speak with him but was demanding that he deliver the gifts he was carrying from the emperor and threatening death unless he handed them over, he said that it was not fitting for the Scythians to ask for what they could take, whether gifts or war spoils. He meant that they would get gifts if they received him as an ambassador, but spoils if they killed him and took them. (4) He thus returned home without accomplishment.

After regrouping during the winter, Attila set out again for the West in 452. This time, he invaded Italy. As in the previous year's campaign, Attila's exact aims are unknown, but his tactics are familiar: plunder small towns and besiege fortified cities.

FRAGMENT 66A*

From the *Getica* of Jordanes

Attila saw an opportunity in the Visigoths' retreat[9] and he recognized what he had often wished for, his enemies divided. Now fearlessly aiming at the overthrow of the Romans, he mobilized his troops. On his first invasion he besieged Aquileia,[10] the metropolis of Venetia located on the tip, or tongue, of the Adriatic Sea. The Natissa[11] River, flowing down from Mount Piccis, laps its eastern walls. He was making no progress there after a long-lasting siege because the powerful Roman soldiers were putting up a strong resistance inside while his own army was already complaining and wishing to retreat.

Walking around the walls to deliberate whether to break camp or linger still longer, Attila noticed that some white birds, namely storks, which had built their nests in the gables of houses, were moving their chicks out of the city and, contrary to their usual behavior, were carrying them outdoors through the countryside. As he was a very shrewd investigator, he understood the omen and said to his men: "Look at the birds preparing for the future. They desert a city soon to perish and they abandon citadels soon to fall. They see that danger is near. This is not an empty belief, nor uncertain. Fear of what is yet to come alters the habits of those who foresee them."

What more did he need say? He rekindled the troops' desire to sack Aquileia. War machines were built, all sorts of engines brought near. Without delay, they entered the city, ransacked, divided and so cruelly vanquished it that scarcely any trace remained to be seen. Then, bolder and not yet satiated with Roman blood, the Huns raged like Bacchants through the remaining Venetian cities.

Procopius read Priscus and retold the story too. (His opening sentences are incorrect. Aetius is not yet dead in 452 nor were the emperors paying Attila any tribute.)

FRAGMENT 66B*

From the *Vandalic War* of Procopius

After Aetius died, no one stood opposed to Attila. He therefore plundered all Europe with no effort and exacted payment of tribute from both empires. He collected an annual tribute from the emperors. They say the following great stroke of luck happened to Attila as he was besieging the large, populous city of Aquileia, located beside the sea but far from the Ionian Bay. He was tired of the siege, they say, which had already lasted a very long time, because he was unable to seize the place by force or in any other way. He ordered his entire army to prepare for an immediate withdrawal, with the aim that they would all break camp on the next day at sunrise.

On the following day around daybreak, they say, the barbarians lifted the siege and were already beginning their departure, when a single stork, whose nest was on a tower of the city wall and who was feeding its chicks there, all of a sudden flew up with its children. The father stork flew and the chicks, since they were not yet fully fledged, some flew with him, others were carried on the back of their father, and in this way they flew very far away from the city. When Attila saw this (he was very clever at putting everything together and interpreting it), he ordered the army to remain in place, explaining afterwards the unlikelihood that the bird would have flown away from there with his young unless he had divined that something bad would happen there in the near future. Thus, they say, the barbarian army re-established itself for the siege, and not much later the portion of the city wall which had held the bird's nest fell down suddenly without cause. The enemy, they say, gained access into the city and so Aquileia was captured by force. In some such way did the events at Aquileia take place.

From other sources, we learn that the Huns marched across northern Italy looting every town they came to, without resistance: Concordia (modern Concordia Sagittaria), Antinum (Quarto D'Altino), Patavium (Padua or, in Italian, Padova), Vicetia (Vicenza), Verona (still called Verona), Brixia (Brescia) and Bergomum (Bergamo). Jordanes, citing Priscus, continues the story from where he left off in fragment 66a* (p. 104, above).

FRAGMENT 17
From the *Getica* of Jordanes

Continuing on their course, they also sacked Mediolanum, the chief city of Liguria and once a royal city, and also consigned Ticinum to the same fate.[12] In their rage, they turned against neighboring cities and devastated almost all of Italy. When his mind turned to approaching Rome, as Priscus the historian reports, his own men dissuaded him, not out of regard for the city to which they were hostile, but because they remembered the example of Alaric, the onetime king of the Visigoths. They felt anxiety for the fortune of their own king because, after Alaric had crushed Rome, he did not survive very long but soon departed from human affairs.

So while his mind swayed back and forth, whether to go or not go, and his deliberations caused a delay, an embassy arrived from Rome that pleased him.[13] Pope Leo approached by himself, in the district of Ambuleium in Venetia, where the Mincius River is frequently forded.[14] Soon, the anger of the army was soothed and Leo returned to where he had come from. Peace was promised and so Attila again departed beyond the Danube, but not before he announced the peace in public and threateningly resolved to bring greater trouble upon Italy if they did not send him Honoria, the sister of Emperor Valentinian and daughter of the Augusta Placidia, with the portion of the imperial wealth owed to him.

Attila's movement was along the Roman roads from east to west. Only at Mediolanum did he finally turn southward toward Ticinum. At Ticinum, though, instead of crossing the Apennines and moving down the west coast of Italy toward Rome, he turned eastward toward

Mantua and then returned to the east. In Jordanes's Priscan account, we see some fanciful guesswork about why Attila did not continue in Italy. The Visigoth Alaric sacked Rome in August 410 but was dead by the end of the year. The embassy of Pope Leo is justly famous, but it is hard to see why the non-Christian Attila would be persuaded by the pontiff. The embassy is probably historical, but other forces come into play. One source mentions a famine occurring in Italy in 452. The Huns certainly would not have had a sufficient supply train to feed the soldiers as they crossed Europe. They were dependent on what they could plunder. It is also reported that the Eastern emperor Marcian took advantage of Attila's absence. He ordered trans-Danubian raids to harass the Huns who had remained behind. Despite his military successes, Attila was faced with a lack of food and a threat to his base. He left Italy and never returned.

Back in the East, Priscus tells us that he resumed his familiar demands.

FRAGMENT 19

From the *Excerpts on Foreigners' Embassies to the Romans* of Constantine VII Porphyrogennetos

After enslaving Italy, Attila returned to his own lands and proclaimed to the Eastern Roman rulers war and enslavement of their country because the tribute arranged by Theodosius had not been sent.

NOTES

1. Presumably a city in Isauria, the region of south central Asia Minor from which Zeno hailed, possibly to be identified with modern Bozkır, Turkey (Pleiades ID: 648652).

2. At least one word has dropped out here. Carolla suggests "justice," Bury suggested "punishment." The story of Honoria is picked up again in fragment 15 (p. 98), below.
3. Latin: "arrow."
4. This paragraph is printed by Carolla and other editors as part of fragment 3a, but it belongs to the present context. See note on 3a (p. 26). A fuller version of Attila's death is preserved in fragment 23 (p. 112).
5. Modern-day Orléans, France. It had been called Cenabum until its destruction by Julius Caesar. It was rebuilt and renamed by the emperor Aurelian. Its full name was Civitas Aurelianorum. Pleiades ID: 138281.
6. The Loire, on which Orléans is situated.
7. Blockley places fragment 18 in 452 or 453, after Attila's second western campaign, but see Zuckerman 1994, 174–6.
8. The identity (and even the gender) of the person who died is unclear from the Greek. Zuckerman argues that it refers to Zeno, who does in fact disappear from our records at this time.
9. Jordanes conflates the campaigns of 451 and 452 by placing the siege of Aquileia immediately after the Battle of the Catalaunian Plains.
10. Still called Aquileia today, in Italy. Pleiades ID: 187290. The city was an important crossroads between the West and the East, and frequent imperial residence.
11. Usually spelled Natiso in Latin but still called Natissa today (and not to be confused with the nearby Natisone).
12. Mediolanum is modern Milan, Italy; Pleiades ID: 383706. Ticinum is modern Pavia, a city just south of Milan; Pleiades ID: 383798.
13. I translate Carolla's reading *placita*, which follows the most recent edition of Jordanes (Giunta-Grillone). It is the minority manuscript reading. Most editors of Jordanes print the majority reading, *placida*. This gives, in Blockley's translation, "a peace mission came to him from Rome."
14. The Mincius is today called the Mincio River, flowing between Lake Garda and the Po River, although some reports suggest that it once flowed westward to the Adriatic Sea. Ambuleium cannot be located with certainty. Mantua is the most significant city along the course of the Mincio.

THE DEATH OF ATTILA

From this point on, the remnants of Priscus's history become disjointed. From the period of the 430s and 440s, we have very little material not related to the Huns. Evidently Priscus used the Hunnic threat and especially the person of Attila to focus his story into a single narrative thread. After Attila's invasion of Italy, Priscus's narrative moves among multiple locations: Syria, Egypt, Libya, Italy, Scythia, Persia and Constantinople. To judge from the order of the fragments in Constantine VII's collections, Priscus maintained a generally but not strictly chronological organization of his material. (For example, fragment 19 belongs between fragments 20 and 21 chronologically, but Priscus evidently concluded the narrative of Attila's Italian campaign of 452 before telling of Maximinos's diplomatic missions to Syria and Egypt in 451 and 452.) In arranging the rest of the fragments, I have similarly tried to tell coherent narratives even if it involves slight shifts in chronology, without any pretension that I have reconstructed Priscus's original narrative order. First, we will finish off the story of Attila (none of which survives in Constantine VII's collections) and then move on to other events of the 450s.

Despite Attila's demands upon his return from Italy, Marcian never sent tribute to Attila. Perhaps Attila in revenge would have struck the Eastern Romans in the next campaign season. But, in 453, he died before he got the chance. The Romans must have rejoiced at his most inglorious end. Priscus's account of Attila's death is transmitted via one of Jordanes's most vivid passages.

FRAGMENT 23

From the *Getica* of Jordanes

At the time of his death, as Priscus the historian reports, Attila married an exceedingly beautiful girl, Ildico by name, the last of his innumerable wives, as was the custom of that nation. Unwound by the excessive partying at his wedding and weighed down by wine and sleep, he was lying on his back. He often had nosebleeds, but his blood now flowed backward, since it was prevented from following its accustomed course, and spilled down a deadly journey into his throat, killing him. Thus intoxication brought a shameful death to a king glorious in war.

Late the following day, royal courtiers, suspecting something sorrowful, broke through the great doors and discovered Attila's unwounded corpse. They saw that the death had been caused by a hemorrhage, and they found the girl crying under a cover, her face turned down. Then, as is the custom of that nation, they cut their hair and befouled their faces with deep wounds so that the distinguished warrior might be mourned not with feminine lamentations and tears, but with manly blood.

At that time, a wondrous event occurred: a divinity stood above the Eastern emperor Marcian in his sleep. He had been suffering anxiety because of his fierce enemy. The dream showed him that the bow of Attila had been broken that very night, as if because the Huns relied so much upon that weapon. Priscus the historian says he received a true testimonial and so accepts this story. For Attila was considered so frightful to great empires that the gods revealed his death to rulers as a gift.

We will not fail to say a few words about the many ways his shade was honored by his people. The corpse was laid out in the middle of a field, inside silk tents—a solemn and wondrous sight to behold. Cavalrymen chosen from the whole Hunnic nation paraded in a circle, like chariot racers, in the place where he had been laid. They recounted his deeds in a funereal song like this: "Distinguished king of the Huns, Attila, son of his father Mundiucus, lord of the strongest nations, who with a power previously unknown alone controlled the Scythian and Germanic kingdoms, who terrified both Roman empires and captured many of their cities, who was appeased by supplications and accepted an annual tribute lest the remaining cities be subjected to plundering: and since he accomplished all this by the success of good fortune, taking pleasure not in wounding his enemies nor in deceiving his people but in a nation safe among its joys, he passed away without any feeling of grief. Who therefore would consider this event, something where no one sees an obligation for vengeance, a death?"

After the mournful lament, they performed with a tremendous revel over his tomb the rite they call *strava*. By comingling and alternating contrary emotions, they displayed funereal grief mixed with joy, and in the solitude of night they buried his body. His coffins they reinforced, the first with gold, the second with silver, the third with strong iron, making it known that those elements suit an all-powerful king: iron, because he subdued nations; gold and silver, because he received prestige from both empires. They also attached weapons stripped from slaughtered enemies, medallions lavish with their kaleidoscopically shining gemstones and various other insignia by which princely dignity is refined. To protect these riches from curious human hands, they massacred the men hired for the work, paying them an execrable wage. Thus a quick death came to both the buriers and the buried.

After Attila's death in 453, the fragility of the Hunnic Empire was exposed. Jordanes continues the story, as the sons of Attila battle against each other and against his former subjects at the Battle of the River Nedao (location unknown) in 454. Blockley, probably rightly, considers there to be little Priscus-derived material here.

FRAGMENT 68*

From the *Getica* of Jordanes

After the rites were finished, since young minds are usually excited by the chance to snatch power, the heirs of Attila began contesting the kingship. All desiring to rule autonomously, they all destroyed the empire simultaneously. Thus an abundance of heirs often burdens kingdoms more than a lack of them. Attila's sons, who were nearly a people unto themselves thanks to his freewheeling libido, demanded that the subject nations be divided among them by equal lot in order that, as with household property, warlike kings and their people might be distributed by lot. When Adaricus, the king of the Gepids, learned of this, he was mortified that so many nations were being treated like lowly slaves. He became the first to revolt against the sons of Attila. He erased the shame of slavery that had been inflicted on him and happiness followed. By his revolt, he freed not only his own nation but also others who were equally oppressed. All people find it easy to follow when someone acts for the common good.

And so they were armed for mutual destruction. War was waged in Pannonia, next to a river called Nedao. Various nations Attila had held in his sway came into combat there. Kingdoms and their peoples are divided, from a single body distinct limbs are formed, not such limbs as have compassion at the suffering of the single whole, but limbs that are reciprocally insensate when the head is cut off, that never find equals to themselves unless they themselves injure themselves with mutual wounds—and thereby the strongest nations destroyed themselves.[1] I think the scene there must cause wonderment, where it was possible to see a Goth fighting with pikes, a Gepid raging with a sword, a Rugian breaking off spears from his wound, possible to picture a Suavian with a stone[2], a Hun with an arrow, possible to construct an Alanic rank with heavy armor, a Herulean rank with light armor.

After many grim clashes, an unexpected victory fell to the Gepids. Ardaricus's sword and unity annihilated nearly 30,000 men from the Huns and their allied nations. In the battle Attila's eldest son Ellac was killed, whom his father was said to have loved so much beyond his other children that he placed him first among all the various children in the kingdom. His fortune, however, was not in harmony with his father's desire. For it is undisputed that, after slaughtering many enemies, he was killed so heroically that his father, if he had outlived him, would have wished to die so gloriously. After his death, his remaining full brothers were scattered near the shore of the Pontic Sea,[3] where (as we wrote) the Goths had earlier dwelled. And so yielded the Huns to whom the whole world was once thought to yield: their disintegration was so calamitous that a nation which, with their forces united, used to terrify, when divided, tumbled down. This was the reason Ardaricus, the Gepid king, happily ran to the various nations which were unwillingly enslaved to Hunnic hegemony and lifted their minds, afflicted for so very long, to the joyfulness of a coveted freedom. Many of them, by sending embassies, came to Roman land and were welcomed by the emperor

Marcian with the greatest pleasure, and he distributed settlements for them to inhabit.

NOTES

1. The syntax of this highly complex sentence is delightful in its ambiguity. Halfway through the third relative clause, at the word "equals," the reader discovers that the clause's antecedent cannot be "limbs," because the adjective's gender has changed from neuter to feminine, but there is no indication what the new subject is until the final two words of the sentence, *fortissimae nationes*, "strongest nations," and thus the metaphor of the divided body at last yields to the literal political reality with which the sentence began. I have tried to replicate the effect with the verb tenses and the dash.
2. "With a stone" is Haupt's emendation of Jordanes's text. See Giunta and Grillone 1991, ad §261. The manuscripts and other editors read "on foot," but the emendation creates a parallelism typical of the passage.
3. i.e., the Black Sea.

DIPLOMACY IN THE EAST

While the West was preoccupied with Attila, Marcian could turn his attention to threats on his eastern and southern borders. Maximinos reappears on the scene. He had served Theodosius on at least two missions: the embassy to Attila and a military raid against Zeno and the Isaurians (fragment 62* [p. 93, above]). In 451, Marcian sent him to Syria to intervene in a war between the Romans and the Saracens, i.e. the Arabs. The war effort was being led by Ardabourios, the son of the general Aspar whom we have seen commanding troops against the Vandals and the Huns. Notice that Priscus reports that he himself remained in Maximinos's company. Unlike in previous Constantinian excerpts, this report is in the third person, an indication that the excerptor has probably rephrased Priscus's original text.

FRAGMENT 20

From the *Excerpts on Foreigners' Embassies to the Romans* of Constantine VII Porphyrogennetos

Ardabourios, son of Aspar, was fighting a war against the Saracens around Damascus[1] and, when Maximinos the general and Priscus the historian arrived there, they found him in discussions with the Saracen ambassadors concerning peace.

Maximinos moved on to Egypt to arbitrate a dispute between the Blemmyes and Noubades, two nomadic

peoples dwelling south of the Roman provincial border.

FRAGMENT 21

From the *Excerpts on Foreigners' Embassies to the Romans* of Constantine VII Porphyrogennetos

(1) After the Blemmyes and Noubades were defeated by the Romans, both nations sent ambassadors to Maximinos, wishing to make a peace treaty. They promised to maintain the peace so long as Maximinos remained in Theban territory.[2] If he would not accept a treaty of that length, they agreed not to take up arms during his lifetime. (2) Since he also disapproved of the ambassadors' second proposal, he made a hundred-year treaty which stipulated the release of the Roman prisoners of war without ransom, whether captured during that incursion or another; the return of cattle captured at the time and reimbursement for those consumed; the transfer of well-born hostages to them as sureties of the treaty;[3] and their unhindered crossing to the temple of Isis according to the ancient custom, with the Egyptians having charge of the river boat in which the image of the goddess is placed and ferried across. (3) (At a specified time the barbarians carry the statue into their own land and, after they receive its oracular pronouncements, bring it back safely to the island.)

(4) Maximinos decided that the treaty was to be ratified in the temple <at> Philae.[4] Certain of his advisers[5] were sent, and the Blemmyes and Noubades who negotiated the treaty on the island were also present. (5) After the agreements were recorded and hostages transferred (the hostages were children and grandchildren of the rulers, a thing that had never before happened in this war, since

children of the Noubades and Blemmyes had never served as hostages to the Romans), it happened that Maximinos fell into precarious health and died. (6) When they learned of the death of Maximinos, the barbarians took back the hostages by force and overran the country.

During his time in Egypt, Priscus witnessed riots caused by the removal of the Alexandrian Christian patriarch Dioskoros. Dioskoros had been removed by the Council of Chalcedon in 451 for Christological heresy, among other reasons. Evagrius, who preserves Priscus's account, places the riots immediately after the Council, but Maximinos's death is, for other reasons, dated to early 453. The chronology of these Egyptian scenes is highly disputed and much of it turns on a textual corruption. See note 8 below.

FRAGMENT 22

From the *Ecclesiastical History* of Evagrius

Then Dioskoros was condemned to live in Gangra in Paphlagonia,[6] and Proterios was elected bishop by unanimous vote of the Alexandrian synod. When he took up his seat, a great and irresistible tumult arose among the people as they surged toward different viewpoints. Some longed for Dioskoros, as is likely to happen at such times, and others very vigorously cleaved to Proterios, so that many irreversible things were accelerating.

Now, Priscus the orator records that at that time he came to Alexandria[7] from the Theban district[8] and saw the people coming together against the commanders. When the military force tried to curb the disturbance, they pelted them with rocks. The troops turned and ran up to the ancient temple of Sarapis, but the people besieged them and burned them alive. When the emperor learned of these events, Priscus says, he dispatched two thousand recruits. They sailed with such a good wind that they landed at the great city of Alexandria on the sixth day. Then, as soldiers were abusing the Alexandrians' wives and daughters, troubles much worse than before were accelerating. Later, the people came together in the hippodrome and begged Florus, the commander of the military brigades and a civic magistrate, to restore to them the grain allowance he had taken away from them, as well as the baths, the spectacles and whatever had been eliminated because of their disorder. And so, Priscus reports, Florus, taking his[9] advice, appeared to the people, promised these things and quickly dissolved the disturbance.

Sarapis is the Greek form of the Egyptian divinity Osiris-Apis, which named the shared essence of the god Osiris and Apis, the sacred bull of Egyptian cult. The Macedonian rulers of Egypt, the Ptolemies, used Sarapis to legitimize their rule over conquered Egypt. The following conjectural fragment may preserve Priscus's explanation of Sarapis's origin.

FRAGMENT 67*

From the *Ecclesiastical History* of Nikephoros Kallistos Xanthopoulos

Serapis is Zeus, or the Nile, or a certain Apis, a man from the city of Memphis[10] who when a famine was taking place assisted the Alexandrians from his own stores. At his death, they dedicated a temple and a monument to him at the spot where a cow with a certain distinguishing mark was reared, transformed, it seems, into a symbol of agriculture. They also called the cow Apis from the name of its master. Because they carried[11] the coffin (*soros*) of that man Apis into the temple, they called his monument "Sorapis", or even "Serapis" through a change of the letters. His temple was very beautiful and his statue, made from various materials, was very large and fearful, as it touched one wall with one hand and the other wall with the other. In the middle of the statue, there was another temple that ranged about, in which was suspended another image, which was brazen and not large. They entwined iron in its head and inserted a magnetic stone perpendicularly in the coffered work of the ceiling, thereby positioning it in the middle of the air, touching neither the earth nor the ceiling.

After Maximinios's death, Priscus joined the staff of Euphemios, Marcian's Master of Offices. In 456, Euphemios served as an arbiter in a dispute over the throne of the Lazi, currently held by King Gobazes, who wished to rule jointly with his son. The territory of the Lazi, called Lazike in Greek, was the coastal plain region on the eastern shore of the Black Sea, a strategically important area for its border with the Persian Empire. Gobazes was a client king to the Roman Empire, but as fragment 25 hints, he was attempting to shift his loyalty to the Persians.

FRAGMENT 25

From the *Excerpts on Romans' Embassies to Foreigners* of Constantine VII Porphyrogennetos

(1) After the Romans went to Kolchis[12] and fought the Lazi, the Roman army returned to their stations and the emperor's

retainers began preparing for another campaign. They debated whether they would initiate the war by taking the same road or the road through Armenia that borders Persia, if they could first prevail upon the Parthian[13] monarch with an embassy. They thought it was completely impracticable to sail along the difficult coast since Kolchis lacks a harbor. (2) Gobazes himself sent ambassadors to the Parthians, and also sent ambassadors to the Roman emperor. The Parthian monarch, since he was fighting a war against the so-called Kidarite Huns, turned away the Lazi who were fleeing to him.

FRAGMENT 26

From the *Excerpts on Foreigners' Embassies to the Romans* of Constantine VII Porphyrogennetos

(1) Gobazes sent ambassadors to the Romans. The Romans replied to the ambassadors sent by Gobazes that they would refrain from war if Gobazes himself gave up his power or at least if he deprived his son of the kingship. (2) It violated longstanding law, they said, for both men to govern the land. So Euphemios, who held the office of *magister*, proposed that one of them rule Kolchis, Gobazes or his son, and that the war be resolved like that. Euphemios, who was admired for his intelligence and rhetorical excellence, managed Emperor Marcian's affairs and guided him through many good deliberations. He also took Priscus the historian to share in the concerns of his office.[14]

(3) Given the choice, Gobazes chose to hand over the kingship to his son, and give up the symbols of his power. He sent messengers to the Roman ruler to ask that, now that only one Kolchian was governing, he no longer take up arms in anger against him. The emperor ordered him to cross into Roman territory and to give an account of

his decisions. He did not refuse the meeting, but he asked him to give Dionysios, the man long ago sent to Kolchis to negotiate with Gobazes, as a pledge that he would do nothing irreversible. (4) Therefore Dionysios was sent to Kolchis and they came to terms over the disputes.

Marcian's ability to send his major ambassadors to minor hotspots perhaps indicates the sense of relief the Romans experienced after the death of Attila. With the Hunnic Empire quickly dissolving, attention could be turned elsewhere. The same was true in the West. There, though, instead of focusing on the many pressing problems such as the Franks' continuing immigration or the Vandals' hold on North Africa, attention turned inward and became dissension.

NOTES

1. The same as modern Damascus, Syria. Pleiades ID: 678106.
2. Egyptian Thebes, not Greek; modern-day Luxor, Egypt; Pleiades ID: 786017.
3. Reading Classen's emendation *didosthai pisteôn heneka tôn spondôn* for the received text *didosthai hôste hôn heneka tôn spondôn*, which is printed by Carolla but makes little sense.
4. Philae is an island in what is now Lake Nasser, the lake created by the construction of the Aswan Dam on the Nile. Its temple complex has been moved to Agilkia Island nearby. Pleiades ID: 786089.
5. There is almost certainly a textual problem here, perhaps caused by incomplete excerption. The sentence lacks a connecting particle, a very unusual syntactic feature in Priscus. The word translated "advisers" is *epitêdeionôn*, a word otherwise unattested in ancient Greek but apparently a variant of *epitêdeiôn* ("close associates"). Editors are divided as to what to print. About half print what I have here translated. Others print the manuscript reading *epitêdeion on* and include these words in the previous sentence. Thus Blockley, but he omits the words in his translation. I feel some confidence that I have at least represented the sense accurately.
6. Gangra is modern Çankırı, Turkey, about 400 km east of Constantinople. Pleiades ID: 844926.

7. Alexandria, Egypt retains its ancient name today. Pleiades ID: 727070.
8. The received text does not make sense. Emendations disagree whether Priscus was coming to Alexandria after the conclusion of Maximinos's negotiations in the Theban district or he was on his way there. I translate what most of the editors, including Carolla and Blockley, print, but without much confidence. Whitby (2000, 76–77 notes 73–75) provides a good summary of the problem and its ramifications.
9. Thought not certain, the pronoun's antecedent is likely Priscus.
10. A major ancient city, the site is uninhabited today. It is located near the town of Mit Rahina, Egypt, about 20 km south of Cairo, on the west bank of the Nile River. Pleiades ID: 736963.
11. I read the nominative plural participle *metagagontes*, as printed in Migne's edition of Nikephoros Kallistos (accessed via the online TLG [http://www.tlg.uci.edu/]) for the genitive singular *metagagontos*, printed by both Blockley and Carolla, even though Blockley seems to translate the nominative.
12. Kolchis is a classicizing term for Lazike. Pleiades ID: 863770.
13. That is, Persian.
14. Presumably the excerptor has replaced a first-person pronoun (as Priscus used throughout our fragment 8) with the author's name.

TURMOIL IN THE WEST

Aetius had driven his former friends the Huns out of the West. With the ineffective Valentinian III still on the throne in 454, Aetius was the man who truly controlled the empire's affairs. He was powerful enough to keep Valentinian from entering on the fool's mission of traveling to Constantinople to claim the Eastern throne when Theodosius died. He was also negotiating a marriage alliance between his son and Valentinian's daughter. But success breeds resentment. In a series of fragments from John of Antioch, almost certainly derived from Priscus, assassinations pile up. New players on the stage include Petronius Maximus (called simply Maximus here), a former urban prefect, praetorian prefect and consul, and Herakleios, the primicerius *of Valentinian's bedchamber, that is, the second-ranked eunuch chamberlain.*

FRAGMENT 69*

A fragment of John of Antioch, preserved in the *Excerpts on Plots* of Constantine VII Porphyrogennetos

The affairs of the Western Romans were in disarray. A certain Maximus, a well-born and powerful man who had served twice as consul, was antagonistic toward Aetius, the general of the legions in Italy, because he knew that Herakleios (he was a eunuch and carried the greatest weight with the emperor) was also hostile to Aetius on the same pretext: both men were attempting to substitute their own power for Aetius's. The two men entered into a conspiracy and persuaded the emperor that unless he killed Aetius first, and quickly, he would be killed by him.

Valentinian, fated to fare badly by tearing down the wall of his own rule, accepted the words of Maximus and Herakleios and prepared death for Aetius while Aetius was in the palace ready to share his advice with the ruler, trying to throw in his two cents' worth of insight.[1] As Aetius explained revenue projections and calculated the tax receipts, Valentinian all at once sprang up from his seat with a cry and said that he would no longer bear being the victim of so many drunken depravities. By holding him responsible for the troubles, he said, Aetius wanted to deprive him of power in the West just as he had deprived him of the Eastern Empire, insinuating that it was Aetius's fault he did not go and expel Marcian from office.[2] As Aetius was marveling at this unexpected outburst and was trying to divert him from his irrational change, Valentinian drew his sword from his sheath and rushed at him with Herakleios, who was also already carrying a ready knife under his cloak, as he was *primicerius* of the chambers. Both men repeatedly struck Aetius's head and killed this man who had accomplished many manly deeds in both domestic and foreign wars. He had acted as regent for Valentinian's mother Placidia and for her son when he was young by forming an alliance with the barbarians. He outgeneraled Boniface as he was crossing from Libya with a great force, so that Boniface died from an anxiety-induced disease, and Aetius became master of his wife and his wealth. He also used trickery to kill Felix, with whom he served as general, since he knew that Felix was planning his murder at Placidia's instigation. He also prevailed against the Goths in Western Galatia when they kept intruding onto Roman territory, and he brought to terms the Aimorichiani when they were rebelling against the Romans. To put it briefly, he established such a powerful force that not only emperors but also neighboring nations yielded to his commands.

The Suda *preserves an anecdote about Aetius's death, possibly derived from Priscus. It admittedly does not sound much like Priscus, but most editors include it in their collections.*

FRAGMENT 70*
From the *Suda*

Then <the eunuch> induced Valens's mystic initiates—"I call the women's apartments a phalanx <of eunuchs," said Valens>[3]—who are always the hidden sparks of bad acts, to accuse Aetius of plotting against the emperor so that he might usurp his power. They struggled to persuade the emperor. The weight of the promised money was heavy, as it rubbed their innards.[4] They were clever at weaving plots when money was promised. For the race is insatiable. They always stand agape in view of greed, and everything bad in the palace is attributable to their peevishness. The emperor was persuaded by their sycophancies and, moved to murder Aetius, he killed him in a flash.[5] Reckoning that his deed was a boon to him, he said to someone capable of guessing riddles: "Did I not perform the killing of Aetius well, my man?" The other replied: "Whether well or not, I do not know. But know that you cut off your right hand with your left."

John of Antioch, drawing on Priscus, continues the story in a fragment that spans the period from September 454, when Aetius was murdered, to June 455. Valentinian's next victim was Boethius, the grandfather of the future philosopher of the same name.

FRAGMENT 71*

A fragment of John of Antioch, preserved in the *Excerpts on Plots* of Constantine VII Porphyrogennetos[6]

After the murder of Aetius, Valentinian also killed Boethius, a prefect, although he was as pleasing to him as anyone. After he laid them out unburied in the forum, he immediately summoned the Senate and accused the men of many crimes, since he feared the senators might dare a revolt because of Aetius's death.

Maximus visited Valentinian after Aetius's murder, to be promoted to consul. Failing in this, he wanted to become a patrician, but Herakleios did not grant him this rank either. Herakleios was pursuing the same course of action as Maximus and did not want to have any power counterbalanced to his own. So he beat back Maximus's efforts by convincing Valentinian, who was now free from Aetius's influence, that he did not need to transfer Aetius's power to others.

Consequently, Maximus grew angry because of his failure to obtain both ranks. He summoned Optelas and Thraustelas, Scythian men who were excellent in war, who had fought alongside Aetius and who kept company with Valentinian. After discussing the situation and exchanging pledges with them, he blamed the emperor for murdering Aetius and he explained why it was a good idea to stalk him: they would reap the greatest rewards, he said, if with justice they exacted revenge when the opportunity arose.

Not many days later, Valentinian decided to ride his horse on the Field of Ares,[7] together with a few bodyguards and Optelas's and Thraustelas's men. As soon as he dismounted and was preparing to practice archery, Optelas and his men attacked. Drawing the swords hanging at their sides, they advanced. Optelas struck Valentinian on the side of the head and, as Valentinian turned to see who had assaulted him, Optelas struck a second blow, against his eye, and felled him. Thraustelas took down Herakleios. Taking the emperor's diadem and horse, both men ran off to Maximus. Their attack proved innocuous to them, either due to their unexpected boldness, or perhaps because the others present were terrified of their reputation in war.

Something divine happened at the death of Valentinian. A swarm of bees appeared and drew up the blood flowing from his body into the earth. They sucked up all of it. And so Valentinian died at the age of thirty-seven.[8]

Rome was in tumult and confusion. The military was divided, some wanting to elevate Maximus into office, others eager to elect Maximianos (the son of Domninos, an Egyptian businessman who had found success in Italy), who administered household business for Aetius. But Valentinian's wife Eudoxia was eager for Majorian. Maximus's bribes, nevertheless, surpassed all and so he won the palace. Thinking to make his rule secure, he forced Eudoxia to marry him by threatening death. And so in this way Maximus came to rule the Romans.

Geiseric, the ruler of the Vandals, learned of the murders of Aetius and Valentinian and decided it was time to attack Italy, seeing that the peace was void now that those who had made the treaty were dead, that the man coming into power did not possess a noteworthy force and that, some also say, Valentinian's wife Eudoxia summoned him secretly out of grief over her husband's murder and her forced marriage. With a great expedition and with the nation under him, then, he proceeded from Africa to Rome. When Maximus learned that Geiseric's army was positioned at Azestos[9] (this was a place near Rome), he became very fearful. He mounted his horse and fled. The imperial bodyguards and the freemen whom he used to trust the most deserted him; when they saw him riding away, they mocked him and berated his cowardice. Just as he was about to leave the city, someone threw a stone at the side of his head and killed him. Arriving at the scene, a mob tore his corpse to pieces and, carrying his limbs on a pole, they sang songs of victory. And so he met the end of life in this way, after three months as a usurper.

Meanwhile, Geiseric entered Rome.

Among Maximus's first acts as emperor, he married his son to Eudocia, the daughter of Valentinian, and he sent to Gaul Avitus, a semi-retired former praetorian prefect in Gaul who had assisted Aetius in persuading Theoderic's Goths to join the fight against Attila. His mission was to win support for Maximus's rule from the Goths, now under the rule of King Theoderic II, son of the Theoderic killed fighting against the Huns. Both actions backfired.

Eudocia had long been betrothed to Huneric, the son of Geiseric, though the marriage had never taken place. By breaking the engagement, Maximus handed Geiseric a pretense for invading Italy. From his base in North Africa, Geiseric was now able to assert himself into imperial politics at a level he had probably desired but not been able to achieve. The Vandal army crossed the Mediterranean, marched up Italy and sacked Rome, inflicting damage upon the city much worse than the Goths in 410. They captured Eudocia, her sister Placidia and Eudoxia, their mother and Valentinian's widow. Eudocia was at last married to Huneric.

Maximus's desire for the Goths' support marked a radical change in Roman policy. Since the Goths entered the empire in 376, emperors had worked to limit their influence and keep them geographically contained. This was a policy successfully executed by Aetius, until he needed their help against the Huns. Maximus turned the Goths into power brokers. When Avitus learned of Maximus's assassination, he was still negotiating with the Goths, and he turned to them for his next move. The Goths proclaimed Avitus emperor, which the Roman senators in Gaul ratified in July 455.

FRAGMENT 24

From the *Excerpts on Romans' Embassies to Foreigners* of Constantine VII Porphyrogennetos

(1) After Geiseric ravaged Rome and Avitus became emperor, Marcian, the Eastern Roman emperor, sent ambassadors to Geiseric, ruler of the Vandals, to tell him to keep out of Italy and send back the royal women who had been taken as prisoners of war, namely Valentinian's wife and her daughters. (2) The ambassadors returned to the East without accomplishment. Geiseric heeded none of Marcian's ambassadors and truly did not want to release the women.

(3) Marcian sent him more letters and also sent Bleda to be ambassador. (He was a bishop of Geiseric's sect.[10] The Vandals too adhered to the Christian religion.) When he reached him and saw that he did not heed his embassy, he chose bolder words, saying that he would not be well served if in his present prosperity he was preparing for the Eastern Roman emperor to wage war against him instead of releasing the royal women. (4) But neither the reasonableness of the earlier embassy's words nor the threatened terror made Geiseric think sensibly. He sent Bleda away without accomplishment and, dispatching a force back to Sicily and the part of Italy across from it, caused devastation everywhere.

(5) The Western Roman emperor Avitus also himself sent ambassadors to Geiseric, to remind him that if he chose not to honor the longstanding treaty he too would prepare for war, reliant upon his own forces and the aid of his allies. He also sent word to Ricimer to move into Sicily with his army.

*Ricimer was a mid-level commander (*comes*) who had served under Aetius. He was, like Aspar in the East, of barbarian heritage but a well-established Roman officer. (Aspar was an Alan; Ricimer was half-Goth and half-Sueve.) And like Aspar, he became a strong force behind the throne but never sought it for himself. On his mission in 456, he had success against Vandals who, after departing the Italian peninsula, continued to make raids in Sicily and Corsica. Presumably at Avitus's initiative, Ricimer was promoted to* magister militum, Master of Soldiers.

Avitus returned to Italy in 456 with a Gothic bodyguard. It did not sit well with the Romans.

FRAGMENT 72*

A fragment of John of Antioch, preserved in the *Excerpts on Plots* of Constantine VII Porphyrogennetos

During the reign of Avitus, there was a famine and the people, holding Avitus responsible, forced him to remove from Rome the allies who had come in with him from Galatia. He also sent away the Goths, whom he had brought in for his personal guard. He paid them by selling off the bronze from public works of art, since there was no gold in the imperial treasury. His action roused the Romans to revolt because the city's beauty had been lost.

Turmoil in the West

Now that they were free from their fear of the Goths, both Majorian and Ricimer openly revolted. Avitus, disquieted partly by the domestic turmoil, partly by the Vandalic wars, retreated from Rome and held fast to the road to Gaul. Majorian and Ricimer attacked him on the road and forced him to flee to a sacred precinct, where he abdicated his rule and removed his imperial attire. No sooner had Majorian's men lifted the siege than Avitus's life ended in starvation, after eight months on the throne. Others say that he was strangled. And such was the end of the life and emperorship of Avitus.

After Avitus was deposed, the Western throne was empty for over a year, until Majorian acceded in December 457. Majorian had revolted with Ricimer, but was not his certain ally. Before accepting the purple, he worked carefully to sure up his rule not only with Ricimer but also with two other significant men.

First, he won the support of Marcellinus, a general who had rebelled when Valentinian was assassinated. In 457, he had set himself up as the independent ruler of Dalmatia, the province on the eastern shore of the Adriatic Sea.

Second, he was recognized as emperor by the new Eastern emperor Leo I. Marcian died in January 457. As in 450, a low-ranking military officer was tapped by Aspar to be the new emperor. Aspar evidently expected Leo to be his puppet, but Leo would prove to be not so easily controlled.

With this support, Majorian donned the purple at the end of 457. He spent the first few years of his reign repairing relations between the Romans and the Goths who had favored Avitus. He also, with the Goths' help, secured the imperial rule in Spain and, under the command of Marcellinus, he dispatched forces to Sicily to protect it from further Vandal raids. From Spain, he himself intended to launch an assault on Vandal Africa in 460.

FRAGMENT 27

From the *Excerpts on Foreigners' Embassies to the Romans* of Constantine VII Porphyrogennetos

(1) When the Goths in Galatia agreed to an alliance with him, the Western Roman emperor Majorian overpowered the nations that bordered his dominion, some with weapons, others with words. Having gathered a fleet about three hundred strong, he tried to cross to Libya with this great force. (2) The Vandal leader sent ambassadors to him first, wishing to resolve their differences with words. When he did not convince him, he ravaged the entire land of the Maurousians, where Majorian's men would have to march on their way from Iberia. He also befouled the water.

Majorian never made it to Africa. His fleet was destroyed before the crossing when the Vandals attacked it in port. Another fragment, through the filter of John of Antioch, repeats the first sentence and a half, with slight variations, and then completes the story.

FRAGMENT 73*

A fragment of John of Antioch, preserved in the *Excerpts on Plots* of Constantine VII Porphyrogennetos

When the Goths in Galatia agreed to an alliance with him, the Western Roman emperor Majorian overpowered the nations that bordered his dominion, some with words, others with weapons. Having gathered a fleet about three hundred strong, he tried to cross to Libya with this great force, but he retreated after ending the war by shameful treaties. Now, as he was crossing to Italy, Ricimer plotted death for him. Majorian dismissed his allies after the retreat and returned to Rome with his own men. Ricimer's men, though, arrested him and removed his purple robe and his diadem. They struck him and decapitated him. This was the end of the life of Majorian.

Majorian was killed in 461. The Vandals' success in preventing him even from crossing into Africa emboldened their aggressiveness against the Western Empire for the next decade. Domestically, after killing Majorian, Ricimer installed on the throne a senator named Libius Severus, who is not even mentioned in our extant Priscus. He was put in place so that Ricimer could be the de facto *ruler, but the rest of the Roman world did not take kindly to the arrangement. Leo I in Constantinople refused to recognize his legitimacy.*

Leo was busy dealing with a war waged by a resurgent group of eastern Goths and their king Valamer. Valamer had loosely united various bands of Goths in and around Pannonia (who would later be called the Ostrogoths) and led them in breaking away from the Huns as their empire collapsed. Once free, some sources say that Marcian settled the future Ostrogoths in Pannonia, though others argue that they entered the Empire of their own initiative, like the Goths now living around Toulouse who had fought at Hadrianople eighty years earlier (and who would become the Visigoths).

FRAGMENT 28

From the *Excerpts on Romans' Embassies to Foreigners*
of Constantine VII Porphyrogennetos

After Valamer the Scythian violated the treaty and ravaged many Roman cities and lands, the Romans sent ambassadors to him. They censured him for his revolt and, since he told them that a lack of necessities had caused his people to rouse themselves to war, they arranged to pay to him three hundred pounds of gold each year so that he would not overrun the land again.

Valamer employed Attila's tactic of extracting tribute from the Romans and, like the Huns, he returned to non-Roman territory for the time being.

Leo I's non-recognition of Libius Severus was a problem for the new Western regime. More pressing, though, were challenges closer to home. Marcellinus, still in Sicily, decided to rebel. So too did Aigidios, a commander in Gaul. And the Vandals were not to miss an opportunity to exploit the turmoil.

FRAGMENT 29

From the *Excerpts on Romans' Embassies to Foreigners*
of Constantine VII Porphyrogennetos

(1) No longer abiding by the treaty with Majorian, Geiseric sent a host of Vandals and Maurousians to ravage Italy and Sicily. Marcellinus had already withdrawn from the island because Ricimer, wishing to deprive him of his force, bribed the Scythians who were the majority of his followers. They deserted Marcellinus and turned toward <Ricimer, while Marcellinus>[11], fearful of the plot (for he could not rival

Ricimer's wealth), left Sicily for home. (2) Embassies were therefore sent to Geiseric, one from Ricimer to say that he ought not to disregard the treaty, the other from the Eastern Roman ruler, instructing him to keep away from Sicily and Italy and to release the royal women.

(3) Even after many ambassadors were sent to him at different times, Geiseric did not release the women until he married the older of Valentinian's daughters (her name was Eudocia) to his own son Huneric. Then he also released Theodosius's daughter Eudoxia[12] along with Placidia, her other daughter, whom Olybrius had married. (4) Geiseric did not shrink from devastating Italy and Sicily, but pillaged them all the more since he wanted Olybrius to rule the Western Romans after Majorian because of their kinship through marriage.

John of Antioch adds one more sentence to the passage.

FRAGMENT 74*

A Fragment of John of Antioch, preserved in the *Excerpts on Plots* of Constantine VII Porphyrogennetos

Geiseric ransacked Italy because he wanted Olybrius to rule the West because of their kinship through marriage. But he did not make it clear that the cause of the war was that Olybrius had not yet entered the Western palace; instead, he claimed that it was because the wealth of Valentinian and Aetius had not been given to him, partly in the name of Eudocia, who was married to his son, and partly because the boy Gaudentios was spending time with him.

Gaudentios was the son of the late Aetius. He had been betrothed to Valentinian's daughter Placidia before

Geiseric married her to Olybrius. Geiseric, as the next fragment explains, was alleging Gaudentios's claim to power as a pretense for his aggression.

In the early 460s, then, the West faced the extraordinary situation of the Roman general Ricimer vying against the Vandal king Geiseric to decide which puppet would be the emperor of Rome, while two other generals—Marcellinus, now reestablishing himself in Dalmatia, and Aigidios in Gaul—led revolts. Leo I in the East wanted nothing to do with it. As Priscus mentions below, Leo's court was willing to mediate conflicts between the West and their antagonists but they so strenuously shunned military involvement that they concluded a treaty with Geiseric.

FRAGMENT 30

From the *Excerpts on Foreigners' Embassies to the Romans* of Constantine VII Porphyrogennetos

(1) The Western Romans feared that Marcellinus and his growing force would wage war against them too. At the same time, they were being harassed, on one side by the Vandals, on the other by Aigidios, a man from western Galatia who had served with Majorian and who now possessed a sizeable force and was incensed at the murder of the emperor. (For a time the campaign against the Goths in Galatia had taken him away from the war against his Italian foes; contending with them over the borderland, he fought valiantly and displayed great manly deeds in that war.) Faced with these problems, the Western Romans sent ambassadors to the Eastern Romans, so that they could be reconciled with both Marcellinus and the Vandals.

(2) Phylarchos[13] was sent to Marcellinus. He persuaded

him not to take up arms against Romans. Crossing to the Vandals, however, he departed without accomplishment since Geiseric threatened he would not end the war unless the property of Valentinian and Aetius was given to him. (3) In fact, he had taken from the Eastern Romans a portion of Valentinian's property, namely Eudocia, Huneric's wife.

Each year, therefore, at the beginning of spring, he alleged this pretense of war and set out with his fleet against Sicily and Italy. The cities in which there was an Italian fighting force he did not recklessly attack, but seizing the lands in which there was no oppositional force, he ravaged them and enslaved the populations. (4) The Italians were unable to defend all the places where the Vandals were landing. They were overpowered because of the enemy numbers and their lack of a naval force. Although they had sought naval forces from the Easterners, their request failed due to the Eastern treaty with Geiseric. The empire's division caused Western Roman fortunes to worsen all the more.

(5) At that time embassies were sent to the Eastern Romans by the Saragouri, Ourogi and Onogouri, nations that had emigrated from their own abodes. The Sabiri had attacked them after they were driven out by the Avars, who had themselves been displaced by the nations inhabiting the coastal headland. So too the Saragouri, driven to search for land, came near the Akateri Huns and after repeatedly engaging them in battle, prevailed against the tribe and reached the Romans, whose kindness they wished to obtain. (6) The emperor and his courtiers showed them favor and gave them gifts before sending them away.

NOTES

1. Literally: "trying to introduce a small gold coin of insight." Blockley, understanding *pronoia* as a concrete noun and the infinitive

2. Blockley, following de Boor, has offered the best emendation and interpretation of this difficult sentence. I follow his lead in translating it.
3. Supplied from the *Suda* article on women's apartments (*gynaikônitis*) (Suid. Γ 500). Some have suggested that Valens is a mistake for Valentinian. This is to misunderstand the point of the sentence. The author cites a quip by Valens that had become proverbial (and that is quoted elsewhere in the *Suda*)—that the women's quarters are a phalanx of eunuchs—in order to indicate the identity of the conspirators, namely the palace eunuchs.
4. An obscure sentence. Suda Online reports an emendation by Kuster which makes the final clause read, "which caused their innards to smolder" (http://www.stoa.org/sol/, accessed 2 December 2013).
5. Literally: "more quickly than speech." The same phrase appears in fr. 75* (p. 146, below), though with a synonym of "more quickly."
6. This fragment immediately follows fr. 69* in the preserved text of John of Antioch.
7. That is, the Campus Martius.
8. This is incorrect. He was 35.
9. Location unknown.
10. That is, the Vandals were Arians, a heretical sect of Christianity which professed that Jesus was created, not always existent, and therefore subordinate to God the Father.
11. Editors mark a lacuna here. I translate Blockley's sensible insertion.
12. Valentinian's widow and mother of Eudocia and Placidia.
13. Phylarchos is the ambassador sent by Leo in response to the Western court's request for meditation.

HUNS, PERSIANS, GOTHS AND VANDALS

With the mention of Geiseric's treaty with Eastern Emperor Leo I in the previous fragment (fragment 30), Priscus shifts his attention back to the East. The rest of Priscus's history will focus primarily but not exclusively on foreign affairs at Constantinople. Whether this is the true character of Priscus's later books or is an accident of the transmission through Constantine VII's "On embassies" collections cannot be known. The narrative is much more condensed than the expansive descriptions of Attila's Huns, but Priscus's clarity and vividness continue to be evident. To judge from the transmitted order of the fragments, Priscus still maintains a basically chronological order, but (cf. his "at that time" at the beginning of fragment 30's last paragraph) there is no indication that, even in this complex series of events around the Empires, he tried to mark chronology precisely.

Little is known about the peoples named in the last paragraph of fragment 30. The Avars, who would become a major antagonist to the Byzantine Empire in the sixth century and beyond, make one of their first appearances in the historical record here. The Saragouri, Ourogi and Onogouri, though, are little attested. Nevertheless, the passage does provide insight into the turmoil taking place in the Hungarian Plain and Scythia in the 450s and 460s, after the collapse of the Hunnic Empire. Various peoples fought for dominance, allying with and rebelling against one another in a frenzy of warfare. The Saragouri emerged as one of the stronger nations (cf. fragment 37 [p. 150, below]). Their defeat of the Akateri Huns stands out. The Akateri, as Priscus wrote in fragment 8 §56–61 (p. 55, above), were a powerful Scythian tribe to whom Attila had given his eldest son Ellac as king after bungled Romans diplomatic efforts to win them over.

The beginning of the next fragment implies that the negotiations with the Saragouri, Ourogi and Onogouri broke down and fighting broke out. It then turns to the Persians, who were dealing with incursions from the north by a band of Huns, called Kidarites, who had not been under Attila's lordship. The negotiations with the Persians can be dated to 464.

FRAGMENT 31

From the *Excerpts on Foreigners' Embassies to the Romans* of Constantine VII Porphyrogennetos

(1) While the fugitive nations feuded against the Eastern Romans, an embassy arrived from Italy, saying that they could no longer resist unless the Easterners reconciled them to the Vandals. An embassy also arrived from the Persian monarch on behalf of Persian fugitives dwelling in the Roman Empire and on behalf of Magi who dwelled in Roman land from ancient times. The ambassadors charged the Romans with wishing to keep these people from practicing their ancestral customs, laws and religious practices,[1] and so harassing them and not permitting them to perpetually kindle the fire they call unquenchable, as the law required. (2) The embassy also stated that the Romans must provide money and show concern for the fortress

Iouroeipaach,[2] which lies at the Caspian Gates, or at least to send soldiers to guard it. The Persians, they said, should not be alone in bearing the expense and the protection of the place. For if they should fail, the neighboring nations' violence would readily strike not only the Persians but also the Romans. (3) They also said that they must, like allies, supply funds for the war against the so-called Kidarite Huns. If the Persians should succeed, the Romans would benefit from the nation not being permitted to cross into the Roman Empire.

(4) Regarding all these demands, the Romans answered that they would send someone to negotiate with the Parthian monarch.[3] They said that there were no fugitives among them, nor were they harassing the Magi about their religious worship; furthermore, they were not justified in demanding money for garrisoning the fortress Iouroeipaach and for the war against the Huns since the Persians had taken up these activities on their own behalf.

(5) Tatianos, a man enrolled at the rank of patrician, was sent as ambassador to the Vandals on behalf of Italy. Constantius,[4] who had attained the consulship three times and had reached the rank of patrician as well as consul, was sent to the Persians.

Fragments 31 and 32 are overlapping fragments that come from different Constantinian collections.

FRAGMENT 32

From the *Excerpts on Romans' Embassies to Foreigners* of Constantine VII Porphyrogennetos

(1) In the time of the Roman emperor Leo, Tatianos, a man enrolled at the rank of patrician, was sent as ambassador to

the Vandals on behalf of Italy. Constantius, who had taken the consulship three times and had reached the rank of patrician as well as consul, was sent to the Persians.

(2) Tatianos returned from the Vandals immediately, without accomplishment, his words unacknowledged by Geiseric. Constantius, though, remained in Edesa,[5] a Roman city bordering Persia, because the Parthian monarch delayed his reception for a long time.

Priscus uses the occasion of the Persian embassy to tell a story of royal deception worthy of Herodotus. In fact, Herodotus tells a very similar story at the beginning of his third book, when the Egyptian Amasis tries to deceive the Persian Cambyses and thus precipitates a war. Here the Persian king Peroz (in Greek, Peirozes; reigned 459–484) attempts to deceive the Hunnic king Kounchas. The similarity to Herodotus is no accident. Just as when Priscus inflected the siege of Naissos narrative with echoes of Thucydides and Dexippus (see Introduction pp. xix–xx and fragment 1b [p. 14]), here he expects his readers to notice the resemblance to Herodotus and to interpret his story in the classical context. It is a fine example of Priscus's classicizing historiography.

FRAGMENT 33

From the *Excerpts on Romans' Embassies to Foreigners* of Constantine VII Porphyrogennetos

(1) The Persian monarch then received into his land the ambassador Constantius, who had remained in Edesa for a time, as I said about his embassy. He ordered him to come while he was occupied not in the cities, but on the border

between his cities and the Kedarite[6] Huns. He was engaged in <a war> caused by the Huns' refusal to take the tribute that past Persian and Parthian kings had agreed upon.[7] (2) His father, having refused to pay the tribute, took up the war and then bequeathed it and the kingdom to his son. Because they kept suffering defeat in battle, the Persians wished to solve the Hunnic problem by deception.

(3) And so, it was said,[8] Peirozes (this was the Persian king's name at the time) sent messages to Kounchas, the Hunnic leader, stating that, hoping for peace with them, he wanted to agree to an alliance and to offer his sister in marriage; for he happened to be very young and not yet the father of children. (4) Kounchas, it was said, accepted the proposal, but married not Peirozes's sister, but another woman decked out in royal fashion, whom the Persian monarch sent off after informing her that if she revealed nothing of the deception, she would share in kingship and happiness, but if she revealed the theatrics, she would suffer death as a penalty since the Kedarite ruler would not endure a servile wife in place of a well-born woman.

(5) The treaty thus negotiated, Peirozes did not enjoy his deception against the Hunnic leader very long. Because the woman was concerned that the nation's ruler would learn of her situation from others and would cruelly subject her to death, she revealed what had been perpetrated. (6) Kounchas praised the woman for her truthfulness and kept her as his wife. He wished to punish Peirozes for his trickery, and so he pretended that he was having a war against neighboring peoples, and that he needed men, not men fit for war (for there were thousands available to him) but men who would be his generals. (7) Peirozes sent him three hundred elite men. The Kidarite ruler killed some, and others he maimed and sent back to Peirozes to report that he had paid this penalty for his deceit.

(8) Thus the war was rekindled and they fought violently. Peirozes accordingly received Constantius in Gorga[9] (this was the name of the place where the Persians were encamped). After treating him kindly for several days, he sent him away with no auspicious response to his embassy.

Despite the Romans' refusal to help resist the Kidarites, the Persians succeeded in routing the Huns and securing their border in the Caucasus.

Evagrius preserves a possibly Priscus-derived account of the Great Fire of Constantinople in 465.

FRAGMENT 75*

From the *Ecclesiastical History* of Evagrius

Events like these or even worse happened at Constantinople. The disaster began in the part of the city beside the sea, which they call the Bosporus. It is reported that at the hour when lamps are lit some mischievous, murderous demon in the form of a woman, or even in truth a needy woman enraged by a demon (both things are said) carried a lamp to a bazaar to sell some of her worn things. After she set the lamp down, she went away, but her flame seized some flax and stirred up a conflagration. In a flash it ignited the house; from it, everything nearby simply disappeared as the fire encompassed not only flammable materials, but even stone dwellings. It lasted until the fourth day and overcame every defense, so that the entire center of the city, from north to south, was consumed, an area five stades long and fourteen stades wide. The reports say that nothing survived, whether in public buildings or private, not pillars, not stone crypts, but every type of dry material burned like something flammable. The disaster took place in the northern quarter of the city, where the city's dockyards are also located, from the Bosporus to the ancient temple of Apollo, in the southern quarter from the Harbor of Julian to houses not far from the oratory of the church called Concord, and in the very middle of the city from the Forum of Constantine to the so-called Square of Taurus. It was a sight pitiful and hateful to all. However many beautiful works graced the city, either adorned for magnificence and incomparability, or for common or private purposes, they were all at once haphazardly turned into hills and mountains, impassable, impenetrable, packed with miscellaneous materials, jumbling earlier appearances. Not even the inhabitants could be relied on to know the place, what something used to be or where it had been.

Priscus briefly returns to the story of the Lazikan king Gobazes, which began in fragments 25 and 26 (pp. 121 and 122, above). Back in 456, Gobazes traveled to Constantinople in the company of the Roman ambassador Dionysios to negotiate a peace treaty. Now, in 465 or 466, he comes again with Dionysios.

FRAGMENT 34

From the *Excerpts on Foreigners' Embassies to the Romans* of Constantine VII Porphyrogennetos

After the city was burned in the time of Leo, Gobazes came with Dionysios to Constantinople wearing Persian dress and attended by bodyguards in the Median manner. When the courtiers received him, at first they censured his rebellion, but then sent him away cordially because he captivated them with his flattering words and by wearing Christian tokens.

Gobazes's Persian dress is significant. As Priscus hinted earlier, the Lazi had rebelled against their status as a Roman client kingdom and had handed themselves over to the Persians. The Persians refused at first, but, perhaps buoyed by their success against the Kidarite Huns, they later accepted the Lazi into their own sphere of influence, thus giving themselves access to the Black Sea and a firm control of the entire Caucasus region.

The scene shifts back to the Danube frontier, where we find the Eastern Romans mediating a dispute between the Skiri and the Valamer's Goths. According to Jordanes, the Skiri had killed Valamer in battle. The Goths wanted revenge.

FRAGMENT 35

From the *Excerpts on Foreigners' Embassies to the Romans* of Constantine VII Porphyrogennetos

(1) The Skiri and Goths began battling but then separated and prepared to summon their allies. Both sides came to the Eastern Romans, among others. Aspar believed they should remain neutral, but Emperor Leo wanted to aid the Skiri. (2) And so he sent a letter to his general in Illyria, enjoining him to send whatever aid he had against the Goths.

This mediation, in about 466, is notable for the disagreement between Emperor Leo and the general Aspar, who put Leo on the throne. Leo prevailed in this debate and he would continue to dominate his patron.

Even with backing from the Romans, the Skiri could not resist the Pannonian Goths. Jordanes records that the Goths fought against a combined force of Skiri, Sueves, Sarmatians, Gepids and Rugi. (He mentions that, among the Skiri, there was a leader named Edica. If he is the same man as Attila's commander Edekon, this is probably where he met his end.) The battle was a massive victory for the Goths, who were quickly emerging as the most dominant power in the former Hunnic Empire—dominant, but by no means the sole power. The Huns were still around. Attila's sons, thirteen years removed from their father's death and holding onto the last remnants of their power, turned to the Romans for help.

FRAGMENT 36

From the *Excerpts on Foreigners' Embassies to the Romans* of Constantine VII Porphyrogennetos

(1) During this time, an embassy from the sons of Attila came to Emperor Leo. They dismissed the causes of the earlier dispute and said they ought to sign a peace treaty. According to their old custom, they said, they ought to meet the Romans at the Istros, set up a market and trade whatever they happened to need. Their embassy accomplished nothing and so they returned home. (2) The emperor decided that the Huns should not participate in transactions with Romans since they had devastated their land so many times. (3) When the sons of Attila received the response from the embassy, they were in disagreement among themselves. Dengizich wanted to wage war against the Romans because the ambassadors came away without accomplishment; Ernach forbade this preparation because he was already distracted by wars in his own country.

Meanwhile, the Persians too were drawn into the trans-Danubian turmoil when the Saragouri, who in fragments

30–31 (pp. 138–144, above) defeated the Akateri Huns and feuded with the Romans, turned eastward. The Iberia mentioned below is not the southwestern European peninsula but a semi-independent kingdom, like Lazike and Armenia, southeast of the Black Sea.

FRAGMENT 37

From the *Excerpts on Foreigners' Embassies to the Romans* of Constantine VII Porphyrogennetos

(1) The Saragouri marched against the Persians after they attacked the Akateri and other nations. When they reached the Caspian Gates and found the Persian fortress there, they turned to another road. When they came to the Iberians, they ravaged their country and also overran Armenian lands. As a result, the Persians, who feared this incursion would be added to the war against the Kidarites which they had been fighting for a long time, sent ambassadors to the Romans and asked them to give money or men for garrisoning the fortress called Iouroeipaach. They said what they often said on these embassies: because they were submitting to battles and not allowing the looming barbarian nations to pass through, the Romans' territory remained unravaged. (2) The Romans responded that each man must protect his own property by fighting on behalf of his own land, and so they went back without accomplishment.

In 467,[10] the Eastern Romans suffered the destruction wrought by a powerful earthquake, as we learn in a Priscan fragment from Evagrius.

FRAGMENT 43

From the *Ecclesiastical History* of Evagrius

During the same years, as the Scythian war against the Eastern Romans was being contested, Thrace and the Hellespont were shaken by an earthquake along with Ionia and the islands called Cyclades, so that much of Knidos[11] and Crete were leveled. Priscus records that extraordinary thunderstorms took place in Constantinople and Bithynia, water falling from the sky like a river for three and four days. Mountains fell to the plains, he said, villages were inundated and destroyed, and even islands appeared in Lake Boane, not far from Nikomedeia,[12] because of all the rubbish that was channeled into it. But these events took place later.

Attila's son Dengizich decided to wage war against the Romans without his brother. He was opposed by Anagastes, a Roman general of Gothic heritage. But this time, Dengizich's demands of Leo are met with a more welcoming response.

FRAGMENT 38

From the *Excerpts on Foreigners' Embassies to the Romans* of Constantine VII Porphyrogennetos

(1) When Anagastes the son of Ornigisklos learned that Dengizich was embarking on war against the Romans and was holding his position firmly on the bank of the Istros (for Anagastes himself commanded the river's garrison in the Thracian region), he sent some of his men and asked why they were preparing for battle. (2) Scornful of Anagastes, Dengizich dismissed the emissaries before they accomplished anything, and he sent the emperor

messengers to say that unless he gave him and his attendant army land and money, he would declare war. (3) When his ambassadors arrived at the palace and repeated what they were instructed to say, the emperor replied that he was ready to do everything if they came to him and offered him obedience. He took pleasure, he said, in nations which came seeking alliances.

Dengizich and his Huns made a temporary peace with Leo, but it was short-lived.

Around the same time (467), the Romans were contending against a mixed band of Goths and Huns in Thrace. Maenchen-Helfen, the specialist in the Huns, suggests that these are Dengizich's Huns, already acting in violation of the peace settlement (Maenchen-Helfen 1973, 168). It is not precisely clear who the Goths are, whether they are an offshoot of the Pannonian Goths—who do not otherwise move into the Empire en masse until 473—or a band who lived in or near Thrace. Of particular note are the Roman commanders working against the Huns and Goths. One commander is Chelchal, whom Priscus names as a Hun. Two others are Anagastes and Ostrys, both of whom were of Gothic heritage.

FRAGMENT 39

From the *Excerpts on Foreigners' Embassies to the Romans* of Constantine VII Porphyrogennetos

(1) Anagastes, Basiliscus, Ostrys and some other Roman generals shut the Goths into a valley and besieged them. The Scythians were oppressed by hunger and a lack of necessities [. . .][13] to send an embassy to the Romans to

say that, if they were to surrender and be allotted land, they would obey the Romans in whatever they wanted.

(2) The Romans responded that they would bring the embassy's message to the emperor. The barbarians replied that they wanted to come to accommodations concerning their hunger but they could not make long truces. The Roman commanders, after deliberation, promised to provide sustenance for them, until the emperor's decision was returned, if they apportioned themselves into units the same way the Roman army was divided. In this way, they said, they would easily tend to them, since the generals would compete for their units' provisions with an eye to generosity, and so could see to their own allotted units without having to be concerned for everyone.

(3) The ambassadors reported the instructions to the Scythians, who arranged themselves into as many segments as Aspar and the Romans formed. Chelchal, a man of the Hunnic race and a subordinate of Aspar's commanders, went to the barbarian segment assigned to them. He summoned the leading men of the Goths (they were in the majority) and began saying that the emperor would give them land, not for their own use but for the Huns among them. (4) Due to their neglect of farming, he said, the Huns used to attack them and snatch their provisions like wolves. As a result, the Goths occupied a position of servitude and could not provide their own sustenance, although the Gothic race had long persisted without a treaty with the Huns, even from the time of their forefathers who swore they would escape their alliance with them. At this point, besides being deprived of their own possessions they were also belittling their ancestors' oaths. (5) As for himself, Chelchal said, even though he boasted of his Hunnic heritage, it was out of a desire for justice that he told them this news and counseled them on what needed to be done.

(6) Perturbed by his words but believing that Chelchal had spoken benevolently, the Goths banded together and slew the Huns among them. A violent battle arose on both sides, as if they were obeying a circulating password, <so that not only Aspar's commanders>[14] but also in fact the other unit commanders, who were standing marshaled with their men, killed whichever of the barbarians they met. When the Scythians figured out the trickery and deceit, they called themselves together and placed themselves in the Romans' hands.

(7) But Aspar's men had destroyed the segment assigned to them, and the battle was not without danger for the other generals, as the barbarians fought so violently that their survivors cut through the Roman lines and in this way escaped the siege.

By 469, Dengizich was again at arms. He was killed in battle by Anagastes and his head was put on public display in Constantinople. His brother Ernach, who had favored peaceful relations with the Romans, does not reappear in the historical record.

Also in 467, Constantinople was involved in a complex dispute among the Persians, the Lazi and a people called the Souani, who lived east of Lazike but were under the Lazi's dominion. They had seized some Persian fortresses in the Caucasus. The passage is difficult because of a textual corruption in the second line that obscures the identities of the main players in the dispute (see note 15 below).

FRAGMENT 41

From the *Excerpts on Foreigners' Embassies to the Romans* of Constantine VII Porphyrogennetos

(1) As the Romans' and Lazi's dispute with the Souani was very great and the Souani vehemently fought against [. . .],[15] and as the Persians wished to make war on him because of the fortresses that had been taken away <by> the Souani,[16] he sent an embassy, asking the emperor to send him reinforcements from among the soldiers who were guarding the boundaries of the Armenians who paid tribute to the Romans. Since they were near, he said, he would thereby have ready assistance and not be in peril while anxiously awaiting men coming from afar. Moreover, since they were close, he would not be beset by their expenses if by chance the war were delayed, as had happened before. (2) When Herakleios had come with help against[17] the Persians and the Iberians who were making war on him, he became preoccupied in fighting other nations and dismissed his allies because of the burden of supplying their provisions. So when the Parthians turned their sights toward them,[18] he called in the Romans again.

(3) After they promised to send help and a commander, a Persian embassy also arrived, announcing that they had defeated the Kidarite Huns and had forced their city Balaam to surrender. They publicized the victory and boasted about it in barbarian fashion, wishing to demonstrate how much power they had at the time, but the emperor dismissed them as soon as the news was announced, since he was deep in thought about Sicilian events.

Leo was deep in thought about Sicily because he had decided that it was time to recover Carthage from the

Vandals. Events in the West since Ricimer's installation of Libius Severus in 461 had been dictated by Severus's lack of acceptance around the Roman world.

Aigidios's revolt in Gaul continued for four years. Ricimer had contained him, but not defeated him, by paying the Gallic Goths to harass him. Aigidios was engaged in negotiations with the Vandal Geiseric to join forces against Ricimer and Severus when he was assassinated in 465. Further north in Gaul, the Franks were beginning to emerge as the future power they would be. Further east, Marcellinus had returned to Dalmatia to reconstitute his forces. He was kept in check by Leo, but the threat of him invading Italy always remained. Leo himself never recognized Severus throughout his four year reign. In short, Ricimer and Severus controlled the Italian peninsula and nothing else.

Severus died in November 465. Later writers alleged that Ricimer poisoned him because he had become an obstacle to Ricimer's power, but a contemporary stresses that he died of natural causes. In either case, with Severus gone, Ricimer began negotiating with Leo to find an acceptable candidate for the Western throne. Finally, in April 467, Anthemius was proclaimed emperor. He had been a distinguished military commander under both Marcian and Leo for over 15 years. He was also Marcian's son-in-law. He would not be a man Ricimer could control, but evidently Ricimer and Leo had another goal in mind, one that required their cooperation: an all-out assault on Vandal North Africa.

FRAGMENT 40
From the *Excerpts on Romans' Embassies to Foreigners* of Constantine VII Porphyrogennetos

Emperor Leo sent Phylarchos to Geiseric to announce Anthemius's emperorship and to threaten war unless he should keep away from Italy and the emperorship. He returned with the message that Geiseric was unwilling to submit to the emperor's demands but was preparing for war, since his treaty was violated by the Eastern Romans.

In 461, Geiseric had wanted to install his son-in-law Olybrius as the Western emperor. He invaded Italy to do it, but failed. Olybrius was still alive in 467 and waiting in the wings, as Geiseric continued to threaten the Roman regime. It can come as no surprise that he rejected the accession of Anthemius.

In order to put an end to Geiseric's aspirations, Leo and Anthemius organized a naval assault on Carthage under the command of Leo's brother-in-law Basiliscus. It was launched in 468.

Three authors, Theophanes, Procopius and Evagrius, preserve Priscus's account of the expedition.

FRAGMENT 42
From the *Chronicle* of Theophanes

In this year Emperor Leo equipped a great expedition and sent it off against Geiseric, ruler of the Africans. After the death of Marcian, Geiseric brought about many calamities in Roman territory: plundering and obliterating many war prisoners and cities. For this reason, the emperor, moved by indignation, gathered 1,100 ships from the entire eastern sea, filled them with armies and weapons and deployed them against Geiseric. They say that he spent 130,000 pounds of gold on this expedition. He appointed as general and commander of the expedition Basiliscus, the brother of the Augusta Verina, who had already been consul and had defeated the Scythians in Thrace on many occasions. He gathered a large force, including some from the West. Again and again, he engaged in naval battles with Geiseric's force <and> sank <a great many> of his ships. He could have conquered even Carthage itself, but later, enticed by Geiseric with gifts and lots of money, he willingly gave way and was defeated, as Priscus the Thracian recorded.

FRAGMENT 76*

From the *Vandalic War* of Procopius

For these reasons Emperor Leo wanted to punish the Vandals, and so he raised an army against them, an army which reportedly numbered nearly 100,000. Once his fleet of ships from the Eastern half of the sea was assembled, he demonstrated his considerable generosity to both the soldiers and the sailors, afraid that stinginess might be a hindrance to his eagerness to punish the barbarians. So, they say, he spent 130,000 pounds of gold for nothing. Since the expedition was doomed not to destroy the Vandals, he appointed as commander Basiliscus, the brother of his wife Verina, a man extraordinarily desirous of the throne, which he hoped would come to him without a struggle if he obtained Aspar's friendship. [. . .][19]

Leo had earlier established Anthemius as the Western emperor. He was a senator, wealthy and well-born. He now instructed him to take control of the Vandalic war. Furthermore, Geiseric was asking, even repeatedly beseeching, that the empire be handed over to Olybrius, who was living with Placidia, Valentinian's daughter, and who was well-disposed to him because of their marriage ties. When he failed in his request, he grew even angrier and ravaged the emperor's entire land.

There was a certain Marcellinus in Dalmatia, an acquaintance of Aetius and a respected man, who when Aetius died in the aforementioned way no longer thought it right to obey the emperor. Instead, he revolted and caused all the others to revolt too, so that he himself controlled Dalmatia and no one dared to fight against him. Emperor Leo won over this Marcellinus by intensely appeasing him. He ordered him to go to the island of Sardinia, in the Vandals' domain. Marcellinus drove the Vandals from there and held it with no difficulty.

Herakleios was dispatched from Byzantium to Tripolis in Libya.[20] After defeating the Vandals in battle there, he easily took the cities. He left his ships there and led his army on foot to Carthage. Such was the prelude to the war.

Basiliscus landed his entire fleet at a town no less than 280 stades from Carthage. (A temple of Hermes has stood there since ancient times; from it the place was called Merkourion since that is what the Romans call Hermes.[21]) If Basiliscus had not delayed out of willful cowardice but had attempted to go straight to Carthage, he would have taken it without a blow and would have enslaved the Vandals, who had no defenses. Geiseric dreaded Leo as an unconquerable emperor when he heard that Sardinia and Tripolis had fallen and saw that Basiliscus's fleet was larger than any fleet the Romans were reputed to have ever had. But now the general's delay, whether due to cowardice or treason, prevented the fall of Carthage. Benefitting from Basiliscus's negligence, Geiseric did the following: He armed all his subjects as well as he could and filled his ships while holding in readiness other, empty ships, those which sailed most quickly. He sent ambassadors to Basiliscus to ask him to postpone the war for five days in order that he might take counsel in that time and do what the emperor most wanted. They say that he also, without the knowledge of Basiliscus's army, sent quite a sum of gold and in fact purchased this truce. He acted in the thought—which in fact came true—that a favorable wind would arise during the time of the truce.

Whether he surrendered the occasion freely, as if keeping a promise to Aspar, or he sold it for money, or even that he thought it was better, Basiliscus did the things asked of him. He lingered in camp and awaited the enemy to take advantage of their opportunity. When a favorable wind soon arose, the very thing which they were sitting and waiting for, the Vandals raised their sails and dragged down the boats they had kept ready empty of men, as I said above. They then set sail against the enemy. As they neared the Romans' position, they kindled fire on the boats they were towing. With their sails swelling, they propelled them against the Roman position. Because there was a mass of ships there, wherever these boats made contact fires easily burned and the ships they hit were readily destroyed with them. Thus, as was likely, a confusion gripped the Roman fleet as the fire continued on. The screaming intensified and drowned out the wind and the crackling of the flames. Soldiers were commanding each other, as were sailors, as they used their punting-poles to push the fire-bearing boats away from their own ships, which were then destroying each other because of their disorder. Now the Vandals arrived and began ramming and sinking ships and robbing the escaping soldiers of their arms.

There were some good Roman men in this battle. Chief among them was Ioannes, Basiliscus's officer, who had in no way participated in his treason. Although great chaos encircled his ship, turning this way and that from the deck, he killed a large number of the enemy. When he saw his ship being captured, he leapt in his entire armament from the half-deck into the sea. Geiseric's son Genzon pleaded with him over and over, offering him pledges and showing him the way to safety; he nevertheless plunged his body into the sea, uttering only this: that Ioannes would never live in the hands of dogs.

And so this war came to this end. Herakleios escaped to his home. Marcellinus perished at the deceitful hands of one of his fellow generals.

FRAGMENT 44

From the *Ecclesiastical History* of Evagrius

Anthemius was sent as emperor of Rome thanks to an embassy from the Western Romans. He was married to the daughter of Marcian, the former emperor. The general Basiliscus, the brother of Verina, the wife of Leo, was sent out against Geiseric with armed forces recruited for their merit. Priscus the orator produced these reports very accurately by his labor. He also reported that Leo went around deceitfully, as if he were paying Aspar for promoting him; instead, he killed the man, who had conferred his office on him, and also killed his children Ardabourios and Patrikios, the latter of whom he had earlier made Caesar in order to gain Aspar's good will.

Except for a few miscellaneous fragments to be collected at the end, fragment 44 is the last of Priscus's certain fragments, those which contain his verbatim words or at least cite him by name. Fragment 44's final sentence jumps ahead from 468 to 471, when Aspar and his sons are executed. This, then, is the late dateable event that

Priscus definitely mentioned. Most scholars believe that Priscus's narrative continued for at least a few more years and so they posit that the following conjectural fragments derive from his history. They fill in some of the space between 468 and 471 and take us up to the eve of Rome's final hour.

The fallout from Basiliscus's failure struck both East and West. In Constantinople, the failure left the imperial treasury empty, a situation that Leo could not reverse in the remaining five years of his life. Basiliscus returned in disgrace. He sought refuge in the Church of Saint Sophia until the empress Verina, his sister, interceded on his behalf.

As was stated above, the Eastern Roman army in Thrace did resist a final Hunnic incursion and killed Dengizich in 469, but soon thereafter, perhaps taking advantage of their success and the emperor's failure, the Gothic commanders in the army rebelled. Before the revolt, there seems to have been some infighting among the Goths.

FRAGMENT 77*

A fragment of John of Antioch, preserved in the *Excerpts on Plots* of Constantine VII Porphyrogennetos

In the time of the emperors Anthemius and Leo, Oullibos was killed by Anagastes in Thrace. Both men were Scythians and favored revolt.

By 470, Anagastes was in open revolt and had brought several fortresses under his control. He and the other Goths in the Roman army were closely allied to Aspar;

it is possible to see his hand at work here. Things had not been going well for Aspar in recent years. When Marcian died in 457 and Marcian's son-in-law Anthemius was a leading candidate to succeed him, Aspar successfully opposed him and put his own man, Leo, on the throne. It seems likely that Anthemius's installation on the Western throne was not to Aspar's liking. Moreover, Leo had been relying more and more heavily on Isaurian commanders, especially his son-in-law Zeno, at the expense of Aspar and his favorites. Aspar, though, still had enough power to persuade Leo to marry his daughter to Aspar's son Patrikios and to adopt Patrikios as his Caesar and heir. John of Antioch preserves several anecdotes about these events of 470.

FRAGMENT 78*

A fragment of John of Antioch, preserved in the *Excerpts on Plots* of Constantine VII Porphyrogennetos

After the Isaurians on Rhodes[22] began pillaging and murdering, the soldiers arrested them. They fled by ship to Constantinople with Zeno, the emperor's son-in-law. When they arrived, they harassed the merchants in the market and roused the people to stone them. These events threatened to trigger a civil war, but night settled in and diffused the disturbance.

At this time Anagastes, the chief of the Thracian forces, was stirred to revolt and attacked Roman fortresses. The cause of his dispute, they say, was that Iordanes, the son of Ioannes, whom Anagastes's father Arnegisklos had killed, was assuming the consulship. Anagastes was passed over for the appointment that Iordanes received because he suffered from epileptic seizures and was afraid, he says,[23] that he would earn shame in the Senate because of his illness, if he suffered it there. Others say that he revolted because he needed money. After he caused significant worry, men sent from the royal court finally persuaded him to cease his attack. He revealed Ardabourios, the son of Aspar, as the instigator of the usurpation and sent his letters to the emperor.

Zeno, the emperor's son-in-law and a consul, sent men to remove Indakos from the hill called Papirios's.[24] Once Neon lurked there. After him Papirios and his son Indakos lurked there, overpowering all the local peoples and killing passersby. Help was also sent against the Tzani who were plundering the places around Trapezous.[25]

At that time there was also an uprising among the Goths who dwelled in the Western Galatia and who long ago were called Alaric's. Later, their barbarian multitude settled in Pannonia, led once by Valimer, but after his murder by Thudimer, Valimer's brother.

After Anagastes revealed Ardabourios, the son the Aspar, as the rebellion's instigator, Leo acted against his former patron. Aspar, Ardabourios and Aspar's other son Patrikios were arrested and executed in 471 (cf. fragment 44 [p. 161, above]). The Goths' reacted violently. Anagastes disappears from the historical record, but his fellow general Ostrys (fragment 39 [p. 152, above]) and a Goth named Theoderic Strabo led a new, more widespread revolt. Ostrys too disappears from the record, for reasons unknown, but Theoderic Strabo succeeded in unifying the Goths in Thrace. Theoderic Strabo reconciled with Leo and obtained a generalship. The Pannonian Goths crossed into the Empire in 473 (the fragment above is very confused about the origin of Valamer's Goths). The Thracian Goths contended with them for the emperor's patronage, but eventually united with them, and they traveled together to Italy, in 488–489, where they set up the Ostrogothic Kingdom. But that was to come after Priscus's history ended.

The paragraph above about Indakos is supplemented by a Suda *article that may come from Priscus.*

FRAGMENT 79*

From the *Suda*

Indachos: proper name. He flourished in the time of Leo, the emperor after Marcian; noted for his boldness and his great ability to use his feet; left-handed; he excelled in quickness of feet. He was quicker than Euchidos, Assapos, Chrysomazos, Echion and anyone else celebrated for quickness of feet. In his travels he appeared and disappeared again, like a lightning bolt,[26] resembling not someone running off a cliff but rather someone flying. They testify that he covers on his own feet and without pain a distance that a man with an exchange of horses does not have the strength to cover in a single day. For in the space of one day he went from the citadel Cheris to Antioch,[27] and on the next day was found again in the aforementioned fortress. From this point, not needing rest, he reached Isaurian Neapolis within a day.[28]

The final fragment from the Eastern Empire mentions that the consul Iordanes, whose nomination as consul had precipitated Anagastes's revolt, caused an offense by snooping in Leo's private apartments. We do not know specifically what he was looking for.

FRAGMENT 81*

A fragment of John of Antioch, preserved in the *Excerpts on Plots* of Constantine VII Porphyrogennetos

In the time of Emperor Leo, Iordanes, the general of the East and consul, came to the edge of danger, along with Misael and Kosmas, the palace chamberlains, because they had neglected to guard the palace while the emperor was spending time abroad and thereby had allowed Iordanes to examine what was inside, as he wished.

Leo I died in January 474 and was succeeded by his grandson Leo II at age 6, the son of the Isaurian general Zeno. Leo II promoted his father as co-emperor, but fell ill and died by the end of 474. Except for a twenty-month period (475–476) during which Basiliscus chased Zeno out of Constantinople and usurped the throne, Zeno ruled as sole emperor until his death in 491 of natural causes.

NOTES:

1. There is a break in the syntax here (which I have smoothed over in translation). Some editors have offered emendations, but the sense is not seriously affected.
2. Located in the central Caucasus Mountains, near the southern Russian town of Dzheyrakh, just north of the Georgian border. Pleiades ID:863772.
3. The syntax is again faulty here, with a participle but no main verb, possibly because of the excerpter's condensing.
4. Priscus errs in naming this ambassador. The text should read Constantine. See *PLRE* II 317–18 (Fl. Constantinus 22). He had been the praetorian prefect in charge of rebuilding the walls of Constantinople as the Huns approached after the earthquake of 447.
5. Usually spelled Edessa, this is a city located 83 km east of the Euphrates, modern Şanlıurfa (or simply Urfa), Turkey. Pleiades ID: 658457.
6. The spelling of these Huns' epithet varies between *Kidarite* and *Kêdarite*, even within this passage.

7. Blockley (1983, 396 n. 163) is right that earlier interpreters misunderstood this sentence as meaning that the Huns were refusing to pay tribute. He goes too far, though, in translating the final verb "paid," a common enough meaning for *etheto*, though not one typically used by Priscus. More to the point, it seems likely that the Huns were refusing to receive the current Persian monarch Peirozes's tribute payments, not his ancestors'. The next sentence explicitly states that Peirozes's father refused to pay the tribute. It seems that Peirozes, weary of the war, offered to resume the tribute payments his father had discontinued but the Huns refused.
8. §3–4 is long passage of reported speech, although there is no indication of the speaker.
9. Location unknown.
10. Blockley (1981, 170 n. 64) argues persuasively that the earthquake took place in 467 and that its destruction partially caused Leo to moderate his stance against Dengizch's Huns in the next fragment.
11. There were two ancient cities called Knidos, both of which maintain the name today: one in eastern Cyprus (Pleiades ID: 707539), the other in southwestern Turkey on the Datça peninsula (Pleiades ID: 599575).
12. Nikomedeia (or Nicomedia), modern-day İzmit at the easternmost shore of the Sea of Marmara, about 85 km southeast of Constantinople, had been the eastern Roman capital under Diocletian. Pleiades ID: 511337.
13. There is some syntactic confusion here, presumably either a lacuna in the text of Constantine Porphyrogennetos or the result of the excerptor's selection.
14. Another vexed passage. I translate the preceding participial clause ("as if they were obeying a circulating password") from the manuscript tradition, which Carolla prints, although most other editors accept Bekker's fairly radical emendation to something like "when Aspar learned of it." I also translate Carolla's supplement, in the angle brackets, though with a modification. Where she has "so that not only Aspar," I write "Aspar's commanders," giving credence to Blockley's point that "there is no other indication that Aspar was present himself at these proceedings and, had he been, it is likely that he would have been named amongst the generals at the beginning of the fragment." (Blockley 1983, 397 n. 175.) And so I write "Aspar's commanders" in imitation of §3.
15. The passage is corrupt beyond emendation. No attempt to solve the crux has been satisfactory. The lost passage must have made clear the identity of the "him" in the following clause and the "he" of the main clause; these are not necessarily the same person. See

Blockley 1983, 398 n. 177: the person who sends the embassy to the Romans "would not have been a [Souanian] leader (as Gordon loc. cit.) but the ruler of the Lazi....There is no difficulty with the fact that the Persians were threatening the Lazi because the [Souani] had taken some of their forts, since the [Souani] were regarded as being under the suzerainty of the Lazi." See also Braund 1992.

16. Bekker supplies the preposition so that the clause concludes "by the Souani" instead of "from the Souani."
17. Carolla emends *kai* ("and") to *kata* ("against"). Blockley translates the received text: "For when Heracleius was sent with help and the Persians and Iberians, who were at war with him, were diverted to fighting other peoples, he dismissed the reinforcements since he was worried about supporting them."
18. Some editors have emended to "against him."
19. Not a lacuna in the transmitted text, but an omission of two sections of Procopius's text, which are not believed to derive from Priscus.
20. By *Tripolis*, Procopius refers to the site of modern-day Tripoli, the capital of Libya. Throughout antiquity, though, the city was usually called Oea (Pleiades ID: 344456). With the cities of Sabratha and Lepcis Magna, the region of northern Libya was called Tripolitana (Pleiades ID: 344522). The ancient name *Tripolis* more often refers to modern-day Tripoli, Lebanon (Pleiades ID: 668394).
21. That is, the Roman name of Hermes was Mercury.
22. Large island in the southeastern Aegean. Pleiades ID: 590031.
23. The Greek texts of both Priscus and John of Antioch read "he says (*phêsi*), but Blockley and Roberto (the editor of John) translate "they say," in line with the plurals "they say" and "others say" in the surrounding sentences. That is likely right, but perhaps John is referencing a source not named in the fragment, perhaps even Priscus.
24. A settlement in Isauria, in south central Asia Minor, near Akçaalan, Turkey. Pleiades ID: 648732.
25. Modern Trabzon, Turkey, on the Black Sea. Pleiades ID: 857359.
26. At this point, an entire line has inexplicably dropped out of Carolla's edition. I translate Adler's text from his edition of the *Suda*.
27. Cheris is another name for the hill called Papirios's (see fr. 78*). Antioch, the major city of Roman Syria, was located near modern Antakya in southeastern Turkey. Pleiades ID: 658381. Even a straight line from Cheris to Antioch, which crosses the northeastern corner of the Mediterranean, is 310 km in length.
28. Isaurian Neapolis is probably a settlement near modern-day Kıyakdede, Turkey, on the northeast shore of Lake Beyşehir. Pleiades ID: 639008. A straight line from Cheris to Neapolis measures only (!) 165 km.

THE END OF THE WEST

Two conjectural fragments, about Western events in 472, round out the extant narrative of Priscus. In the first, the stage is set for a confrontation between Anthemius and Ricimer.

FRAGMENT 80*
A fragment of John of Antioch, preserved in the *Excerpts on Plots* of Constantine VII Porphyrogennetos

After the Western emperor Anthemius fell prey to an onerous disease at the hands of magic, he punished many men captured on this charge, especially Romanos, a man who held the office of *magister* and had been enrolled among the patricians. He was also among the close associates of Ricimer. Angry because of him, Ricimer left Rome and called up six thousand men placed under his command for the war against the Vandals.

The conflict between Anthemius and Ricimer sets off a chain reaction of assassinations and accessions over the course of the years 472 to 474. The following fragment is confused about the Burgundian leader Gundobad, whose name is given in two significantly different spellings and who is called both the brother and the cousin of Ricimer. In reality, he was his nephew.

FRAGMENT 82*

A fragment of John of Antioch, preserved in the *Excerpts on Plots* of Constantine VII Porphyrogennetos

Ricimer began a conflict between himself and the Western emperor Anthemius, and moreover, although he was betrothed to Anthemius's daughter Alypia, he instigated a civil war in the city that lasted for five[1] months. The magistrates and the people fought for Anthemius, the mass of domestic barbarians for Ricimer. Also present was Odovacer, a man of the Skirian race. He was the son of Idikon[2] and the brother of Onooulphos, the bodyguard and slayer of Harmatios.

Anthemius lived in the palace, but Ricimer barricaded the locations near the Tiber and plagued those inside with hunger. During an engagement fought by the two sides, much of Anthemius's party fell. Ricimer deceitfully concluded a treaty with the remaining men and then introduced Olybrius as emperor. For five months altogether, a civil war controlled Rome until Anthemius's supporters surrendered to the barbarians and left the emperor naked. Anthemius joined the crowd of beggars and placed himself under the protection of the martyr Chrysogonos. There he was beheaded by Gondoubandos, Ricimer's brother, after a reign of five years, three months, and eighteen days.

Ricimer thought Anthemius worthy of a royal burial, while he introduced Olybrius into the royal court. Within thirty days after Olybrius succeeded to the Roman throne in the way described, Ricimer lost his life by vomiting most of his blood. Then Olybrius died from edema. He survived Ricimer only sixteen days and was numbered among the emperors for six and a half months. Goundoubales slid into Ricimer's place as his cousin and installed Glycerius, the *comes domesticorum*, on the throne. When the Eastern emperor Leo learned of Glycerius's accession, he marshaled an army against him under the command of Nepos, who when he captured Rome subdued Glycerius without a fight. He drove him out of the palace and appointed him bishop of Salon.[3] Glycerius made a mockery of the office for eight months. Nepos was immediately proclaimed emperor and began to rule Rome.

Julius Nepos spent only fourteen months on the throne. The Italian army did not support this ruler imposed by the East. With Attila's former secretary Orestes at their head, they deposed Nepos and he fled back to the East. Orestes proclaimed as emperor his own son Romulus, nicknamed Augustulus, on October 31, 475. Orestes himself was murdered in August 476 and his brother Paulus in September 476. Romulus Augustulus was deposed by the Skirian commander Odovacer. Instead of finding another man to wear the Roman purple, Odovacer took the title king. The Roman Empire in Italy and the West came to an end.

NOTES

1. The manuscripts have "nine months." Some editors have emended the number to agree with the next paragraph, although the discrepancy could result from John's faulty combination of his sources.
2. That is, Edekon the Hun, although there is some doubt about the identification of Odovacer's father with Attila's retainer. See p. 86, n. 11.
3. Presumably the same Dalmatian city referenced in fr. 46 (p. 173, below).

MISCELLANEOUS FRAGMENTS

The few remaining fragments from Priscus's history cannot be placed in the chronological narrative. Except for the final fragment and its odd description of a North Atlantic island, the fragments are primarily single words and sentences and are included here for the sake of completeness.

FRAGMENT 46
From the *Ethnika* of Stephanos of Byzantium

Salona, a city of Illyricum. A native is called a *Salonites*. There is also a Salonai, a city of Delmatia. A native of this place is a *Saloneus*, as Priscus says in his sixth book.[1]

FRAGMENT 47
From the *Suda*

"Reciprocal payment"...oaths were being administered on their reciprocal assurance, not only to them, but also to some of the men who arrived from the palace for discussions with the Romans. From Priscus.

FRAGMENT 48A
From the *Suda*

Priscus says about Charybdis: They sailed along Sicily near Messina down the strait of Italy, where Charybdis was. When turbulent winds overtook these men, they sank.

FRAGMENT 48B
From the *Suda*

When turbulent winds overtook these men, they sank.[2]

FRAGMENT 49
From the *Suda*

The men who were sent did not fail to obtain entrance into the city. From Priscus.

Our final fragment, a conjectural fragment from Procopius, takes us the farthest afield, to the North Atlantic Ocean. Procopius describes Thoule (or Thule) as an island situated far to the north of Britain and ten times its size (Wars 6.15.4–5). To identify it with any actual land is precarious, though Pleiades (ID: 20624) places a very tentative marker in the Shetland Islands.

FRAGMENT 83*
From the *Gothic War* of Procopius

Of the barbarians settled in Thoule, only one nation, who are called Skrithiphini, has a wild way of life. They neither put on clothing nor wear shoes when they walk nor drink wine nor practice agriculture. Neither do the men farm the earth nor do women work in any way on their behalf, but the men's only activity is hunting, and it is always done with the women. The forests, which are extraordinarily large, bring to them a great boon of wild beasts and other animals, as do the mountains that rise up there. They are fattened with meat from captured animals, and they wear their hides; since they have neither linen nor tools for stitching, they bind these hides to each other with the beasts' tendons and thus they cover their whole bodies. Moreover their babies are not nursed in the same ways as other people's. Skrithiphini children are not fed with women's milk nor do they latch onto their mothers' breast, but they are nourished only with the marrow of captured animals. As soon as a woman gives birth, therefore, she immediately wraps the baby in an animal skin and dangles it on a tree. Placing marrow in its mouth, she goes off with her husband to their usual hunt. Since they do everything else in common, they also share this practice. So then, this is how these barbarians live.

NOTES

1. It is not clear that Salona and Salonai were in fact different cities, given that Dalmatia (= Delmatia) is a region of the Illyrian prefecture. Salona was on the Dalmatian site of Solin, Croatia, on the Adriatic coast. Pleiades ID: 197488. There is no Pleiades entry for a Salonai.
2. From a different *Suda* entry than fr. 48a. Priscus is not named as the source of fr. 48b, but the words are identical.

BIBLIOGRAPHY

The following lists contain all the scholarly works cited in the notes as well as a number of important works pertinent to the subject which I did not have occasion to cite.

Works Cited by Abbreviation

CAH XIII: Cameron, Averil and Peter Garnsey. 1998. *The Late Empire, AD 337–425*. Vol. 13 of *The Cambridge Ancient History*. Cambridge: Cambridge University Press.
CAH XIV: Cameron, Averil, Bryan Ward-Perkins and Michael Whitby. 2001. *Late Antiquity: Empire and Successors, AD 425–600*. Vol. 14 of *The Cambridge Ancient History*. Cambridge: Cambridge University Press.
LSJ: Liddel, Henry George and Robert Scott. 1968. *A Greek-English Lexicon*. Revised by Henry Stuart Jones. Oxford: Clarendon Press.
PLRE II: Martindale, J. R. 1980. *The Prosopography of the Later Roman Empire*. Volume 2: *AD 395–527*. Cambridge: Cambridge University Press.

Editions of Priscus and Others, cited by editor's name

Blockley, R. C. 1981. *The Fragmentary Classicising Historians of the Later Roman Empire: Eunapius, Olympiodorus, Priscus and Malchus*. Reprint edition, 2009. Liverpool: Francis Cairns.
————. 1983. *The Fragmentary Classicising Historians of the Later Roman Empire: Eunapius, Olympiodorus, Priscus and Malchus*. Volume 2: *Text, Translation and Historiographical Notes*. Reprint edition, 2007. Liverpool: Francis Cairns.
Bornmann, F. 1979. *Priscus: Fragmenta*. Florence: Le Monnier.
Carolla, Pia. 2008. *Priscus Panita: Excerpta et Fragmenta*. Bibliotheca Scriptorum Graecorum et Romanorum Teubneriana. Berlin and New York: Walter de Gruyter.
de Boor, C. 1903. *Excerpta historica iussu Imp. Constantini Porphyrogeniti confecta*. Vol. 1: *Excerpta de legationibus*. Berlin: Weidmann.
Dindorf, L. 1870. *Historici Graeci Minores*. Vol. 1. Leipzig: Teubner.

Giunta, Francesco and Antonino Grillone. 1991. *Iordanis de origine actibusque Getarum.* Rome: Instituto Palazzo Borromini.
Mariev, Sergei. 2008. *Ioannis Antiocheni fragmenta quae supersunt omnia.* Corpus fontium historiae Byzantinae 47. Berlin and New York: Walter de Gruyter.
Mommsen, Theodor. 1882. *Iordanis Romana et Getica.* Vol. 5, Part 1 of *Monumenta Germaniae Historia*, ed. Societas Aperiendis Fontibus Rerum Germanicarum Medii Aevi. Berlin: Weidmann.
Müller, C. 1868–1870. *Fragmenta hisoricorum graecorum.* Vols. 4–5. Paris: Editore Ambrosio Firmin Didot.
Roberto, Umberto. 2005. *Ioannnis Antiocheni Fragmenta ex Historia chronica.* Berlin and New York: Walter de Gruyter.

Secondary Sources

Adshead, Katherine. 1983. "Thucydides and Agathias." In *History and Historians in Late Antiquity,* ed. Brian Croke and Alanna M. Emmett, 82–87. Sydney: Pergamon Press.
Albini, U. 1984. "Un Burocratismo in Prisco." *Studi italiani di filologia classica* 3rd ser. 2: 246–47.
Allen, Pauline. 1981. *Evagrius Scholasticus: The Church Historian.* Leuven: Spicilegium Sacrum Lovaniense.
——————. 1987. "Some Aspects of Hellenism in the Early Greek Church Historians." *Traditio* 43: 368–81.
Austin, N. J. 1983. "Autobiography and History: Some Later Roman Historians and their Veracity." In *History and Historians in Late Antiquity*, ed. Brian Croke and Alanna M. Emmett, 54–65. Sydney: Pergamon Press.
Baldwin, Barry. 1980. "Priscus of Panium." *Byzantion* 50: 18–61.
Banchich, Thomas M. 1988. "An Identification in the Suda: Eunapius on the Huns." *Classical Philology* 83: 53.
Bayless, William. 1976. "The Treaty with the Huns of 443." *American Journal of Philology* 97: 176–79.
——————. 1979. "The Chronology of Priscus Fragment 6." *Classical Philology* 74: 154–55.
Billerbeck, Margarethe, ed. 2006. *Stephani Byzantii Ethnica.* Vol. 1, A–Γ. Berlin and New York: Walter de Gruyter.
——————. 2008. "Sources et technique de citation chez Etienne de Byzance." *Eikasmos* 19: 301–22.
Bleckmann, Bruno. 2010. "Der salmasische Johannes Antiochenus: ein Versuch zur Bestimmung seines Profils für die Geschichte des Spätantike." In *Historiae Augustae Colloquium Genevense in honorem F. Paschoud septuagenarii: les traditions*

historiographiques de l'Antiquité tardive: idéologie, propagande, fiction, réalité, ed. Lavinia Galli Milić and Nicole Hecquet-Noti, 51–61. Bari: Edipuglia.

Blockley, R. C. 1972. "Dexippus and Priscus and the Thucydidean Account of the Siege of Plataea." *Phoenix* 26: 18–27.

———. 1992. *East Roman Foreign Policy: Formation and Conduct from Diocletian to Anastasius*. Leeds: Francis Cairns.

———. 2003. "The Development of Greek Historiography: Priscus, Malchus, Candidus." In *Greek and Roman Historiography in Late Antiquity: Fourth to Sixth Century AD*, ed. Gabriele Marasco, 289–315. Leiden and Boston: Brill.

Blodgett, Michael. D. 2010. "Attila, flagellum Dei?: Huns and Romans, Conflict and Cooperation in the Late Antique World." PhD diss.: University of California, Santa Barbara.

Bornmann, F. 1974a. "Osservazioni sul testo dei frammenti di Prisco." *Maia* 26: 111–20.

———. 1974b. "Postille a storici bizantini." *Maia* 26: 213–15.

———. 1975. "Note a Prisco." In *Archaeologica: Scritti in onore di Aldo Neppi Modona*, 37–39. Florence: L. S. Olschki.

Braund, David. 1992. "Priscus on the Suani." *Phoenix* 46: 62–65.

Bradley, Dennis R. 1993. "In altum laxare vela compulsus: The 'Getica' of Jordanes." *Hermes* 121: 211–36.

Brodka, Dariusz. 2007. "Attila und Aetius: Zur Priskos-Tradition bei Prokopios von Kaisareia." *Classica Cracoviensia* 11: 149–58.

———. 2008. "Attila, Tyche und die Schlacht auf den Katalaunischen Feldern. Eine Untersuchung zum Geschichtsdenken des Priskos von Panion." *Hermes* 136: 227–45.

———. 2009. "Pragmatismus und Klassizismus im historischen Diskurs des Priskos von Panion." In *Jenseits der Grenzen: Beiträge zur spätantiken und frühmittelalterlichen Geschichtsschreibung*, ed. A. Goltz, H. Leippin and H. Schlange-Schöningen, 11–24. Berlin and New York.

———. 2012. "Wege und Irrwege der byzantinischen historiographie: Quellenkritische Studie zur Priskos-Tradition bei Eustathios von Epiphaneia, Johannes Malalas, Theophanes und Nikephoros Kallistos." *Rheinisches Museum für Philologie* 155: 185–209.

——— and Michal Stachura, eds. 2007. *Continuity and Change: Studies in Late Antique Historiography*. Kraków: Jagiellonian University Press.

Browning, R. 1953. "Where Was Attila's Camp?" *Journal of Hellenic Studies* 73: 143–45.

Buck, D. F. 1992. "Eunapius, Eutropius and the *Suda*." *Rheinisches Museum für Philologie* 135: 365–69.

Burgess, R. W., ed. 2011. *Chronicles, Consuls, and Coins: Historiography and History in the Later Roman Empire*. Farnham and Burlington, VT: Ashgate Variorum.

Burns, Thomas S. 2003. *Rome and the Barbarians: 100 BC – AD 400*. Baltimore: Johns Hopkins University Press.

Büttner-Wobst, Theodor. 1906. "Die Anlage der historischen Encyklopädie des Konstantinos Porphyrogennetos." *Byzantinische Zeitschrift* 15: 88–120.

Caires, Valerie A. 1982. "Evagrius Scholasticus: A Literary Analysis." *Byzantinische Forschungen* 8: 29–50.

Cameron, A. D. E. 1963. "Priscus of Panium and John Malalas in Suidas." *Classical Review* 13: 264.

Cameron, Averil. 1985. *Procopius and the Sixth Century*. Berkeley and Los Angeles: University of California Press.

———. 2012. *The Mediterranean World in Late Antiquity, AD 395–700*. 2nd ed. London and New York: Routledge.

Cataudella, M. R. 2003. "Historiography in the East." In *Greek and Roman Historiography in Late Antiquity: Fourth to Sixth Century AD*, ed. Gabriele Marasco, 391–447. Leiden and Boston: Brill.

Chew, Kathryn. 2006. "Virgins and Eunuchs: Pulcheria, Politics and the Death of Emperor Theodosius II." *Historia* 55: 207–27.

Christensen, Arne Søby. 2002. *Cassiodorus, Jordanes and the History of the Goths: Studies in a Migration Myth*. Copenhagen: Museum Tusculanum Press.

Christie, Neil. 2011. *The Fall of the Western Roman Empire: An Archaeological and Historical Perspective*. London and New York: Bloomsbury Academic.

Constantelos, Demetrios J. 1971. "Kyros Panopolites, Rebuilder of Constantinople." *Greek, Roman and Byzantine Studies* 12: 451–64.

Croke, Brian. 1977. "Evidence for the Hun Invasion of Thrace in AD 422." *Greek, Roman and Byzantine Studies* 18: 347–67.

———. 1981. "Anatolius and Nomus: Envoys to Attila." *Byzantinoslavica* 42: 159–70.

———. 1983. "The Context and Date of Priscus Fragment 6." *Classical Philology* 78: 297–308.

———. 1987. "Cassiodorus and the *Getica* of Jordanes." *Classical Philology* 82: 117–34.

———. 2003. "Latin Historiography and the Barbarian Kingdoms." In *Greek and Roman Historiography in Late Antiquity: Fourth to Sixth Century AD*, ed. Gabrielle Marasco, 349–89. Leiden and Boston: Brill.

———. 2005. "Jordanes and the Immediate Past." *Historia* 54: 473–94.

――― and Alanna M. Emmett, eds. 1983. *History and Historians in Late Antiquity*. Sydney: Pergamon Press.

de Boor, C. 1912. "Suidas und die Konstantinische Excerptsammlung" (Part 1). *Byzantinische Zeitschrift* 21: 381–424.

―――. 1914–1919. "Suidas und die Konstantinische Excerptsammlung" (Part 2). *Byzantinische Zeitschrift* 23: 1–127.

Devillers, Olivier. 1995. "Le conflit entre Romains et Wisigoths en 436–439 d'après les Getica de Jordanès: fortune et infortune de l'abréviateur." *Revue de philologie, de littérature et d'histoire ancienne* 69: 111–26.

Fischer, Andreas. 2008. "Attila, die Franken und die Schlacht auf den Katalaunischen Feldern." In *Hunnen zwischen Asien und Europa: aktuelle Forschungen zur Archäologie und Kultur der Hunnen*, 185–94. Langenweissbach: Beier und Beran.

Flusin, Bernard. 2002. "Les *Excerpta* constantiniens: Logique d'une anti-histoire." In *Fragments d'historiens grecs: Autour de Denys D'Halicarnasse*, ed. Sylvie Pittia, 537–59. Rome: École Française de Rome.

―――. 2004. "Les *Excerpta* constantiniens et la *Chronographie* de Malalas." In *Recherches sur la chronique de Jean Malalas I*, ed. Joëlle Beaucamp et al., 119–36. Paris: Association des Amis du Centre d'Histoire et Civilisation de Byzance.

Gillett, Andrew. 2003. *Envoys and Political Communication in the Late Antique West, 411–533*. Cambridge: Cambridge University Press.

Girotti, Beatrice. 2003. "Per una descrizione dell'opera di Prisco di Panion." *Rivista storia dell'Antichità* 33: 243–46.

―――. 2005. "Spunti per la continuità tra Olimpiodoro di Tebe e Prisco di Panion." *Historia* 54: 355–58.

Goffart, Walter. 1988. *The Narrators of Barbarian History (AD 550–800): Jordanes, Gregory of Tours, Bede, and Paul the Deacon*. Princeton: Princeton University Press.

―――. 2006. *Barbarian Tides: The Migration Age and the Later Roman Empire*. Philadelphia: University of Pennsylvania Press.

Goldsworthy, Adrian. 2009. *How Rome Fell: Death of a Superpower*. New Haven and London: Yale University Press.

Gordon, C. D. 2013. *The Age of Attila: Fifth-Century Byzantium and the Barbarians*. Revised edition, with introduction and notes by David S. Potter. Ann Arbor: University of Michigan Press.

Gračanin, Hrvoje. 2003. "The Western Roman Embassy to the Court of Attila in AD 449." *Byzantinoslavica* 61: 53–74.

Greatrex, Geoffrey. 2001. "Lawyers and Historians in Late Antiquity." In *Law, Society, and Authority in Late Antiquity*, ed. R. W. Mathisen, 148–61. Oxford: Oxford University Press.

——— and Jonathan Bardill. 1996. "Antiochus the Praepositus: A Persian Eunuch at the Court of Theodosius II." *Dumbarton Oaks Papers* 50: 171–97.

Halsall, Guy. 2007. *Barbarian Migrations and the Roman West, 376–568*. Cambridge: Cambridge University Press.

Heather, Peter. 1989. "Cassiodorus and the Rise of the Amals: Genealogy and the Goths under Hun Domination." *Journal of Roman Studies* 74: 103–28.

———. 1991. *Goths and Romans, 332–489*. Oxford: Clarendon Press.

———. 1996. *The Goths*. Cambridge, MA: Blackwell Publishers.

———. 2006. *The Fall of the Roman Empire: A New History of Rome and the Barbarians*. Oxford and New York: Oxford University Press.

Hohlfelder, Robert L. 1984. "Marcian's Gamble: A Reassessment of Eastern Imperial Policy toward Attila, AD 450–453." *American Journal of Ancient History* 9: 54–69.

Holmes, Catherine. 2010. "Byzantine Political Culture and Compilation Literature in the Tenth and Eleventh Centuries: Some Preliminary Inquiries." *Dumbarton Oaks Papers* 64: 55–80.

Hughes, Ian. 2012. *Aetius: Attila's Nemesis*. Barnsley, UK: Pen and Sword.

Huxley, G. L. 1980. "The Scholarship of Constantine Porphyrogenitus." *Proceedings of the Royal Irish Academy* 80: 29–40.

Jeffreys, Elizabeth M. 1979. "The Attitudes of Byzantine Chroniclers towards Ancient History." *Byzantion* 49: 199–238.

———. 2003. "The Beginning of Byzantine Chronography: John Malalas." In *Greek and Roman Historiography in Late Antiquity: Fourth to Sixth Century AD*, ed. Gabriele Marasco, 497–527. Leiden: Brill.

———, Brian Croke and Roger Scott, eds. 1990. *Studies in John Malalas*. Sydney: Australian Association for Byzantine Studies.

———, Michael Jeffreys and Roger Scott, trans. 1986. *The Chronicle of John Malalas: A Translation*. Melbourne: Australian Association for Byzantine Studies.

Jones, A. H. M. 1964. *The Later Roman Empire, 284–602: A Social, Economic and Administrative Survey*. 2 vols. Norman: University of Oklahoma Press.

———. 1971. *The Cities of the Eastern Roman Provinces*. Oxford: Clarendon Press. E-book edition, Sandpiper Books, 1998.

Kaldellis, Anthony. 2004. *Procopius of Caesarea: Tyranny, History, and Philosophy at the End of Antiquity*. Philadelphia: University of Pennsylvania Press.

———. 2012. "The Byzantine Role in the Making of the Corpus of Classical Greek Historiography: A Preliminary Investigation." *Journal of Hellenic Studies* 132: 71–85.

Kelly, Christopher. 2009. *The End of Empire: Attila the Hun and the Fall of Rome*. New York and London: Norton.

———. 2013. *Theodosius II: Rethinking the Roman Empire in Late Antiquity*. Cambridge: Cambridge University Press.

Kim, Hyun Jin. 2013. *The Huns, Rome and The Birth of Europe*. Cambridge and New York: Cambridge University Press.

King, Charles. 1987. "The Veracity of Ammianus Marcellinus' Description of the Huns." *American Journal of Ancient History* 12: 77–95.

Lee, A. D. 2013. *From Rome to Byzantium AD 363 to 565: The Transformation of Ancient Rome*. Edinburgh: Edinburgh University Press.

Lemerle, Paul. 1986. *Byzantine Humanism: The First Phase*. Canberra: Australian Association for Byzantine Studies.

Lenski, Noel. 1999. "Assimilation and Revolt in the Territory of Isauria, from the 1st Century BC to the 6th Century AD." *Journal of the Economic and Social History of the Orient* 42: 413–65.

Maenchen-Helfen, J. Otto. 1973. *The World of the Huns*. Ed. Max Knight. Berkeley, Los Angeles and London: University of California Press.

Maltese, Enrico V. 1977. "Note ed osservazioni sul testo di Prisco di Panion." *Helikon* 17: 263–75.

———. 1979. "A proposito dell'opera storica di Prisco di Panion." *Quaderni di storia* 5: 297–320.

Man, John. 2006. *Attila: The Barbarian King Who Challenged Rome*. New York: T. Dunne Books/St. Martin's Press.

Mango, Cyril, Roger Scott and Geoffrey Greatrex. 1997. *The Chronicle of Theophanes Confessor: Byzantine and Near Eastern History, AD 284–813*. Oxford: Clarendon Press.

Marasco, Gabriele, ed. 2003. *Greek and Roman Historiography in Late Antiquity: Fourth to Sixth Century AD*. Leiden and Boston: Brill.

McEvoy, Meaghan A. 2013. *Child Emperor Rule in the Late Roman West, AD 367–455*. Oxford: Oxford University Press.

Mierow, Charles Christopher, trans. 1915. *The Gothic History of Jordanes*. Reprint edition, 2006. Merchantville, NJ: Evolution Publishing.

Moravcsik, G. 1966. "Klassizismus in der byzantinischen Geschichtsschreibung." In *Polychronion: Festschrift Franz Dölger zum 75, Geburtstag*, 366–77. Heidelberg.

Németh, András. 2010. "Imperial Systematization of the Past: Emperor Constantine VII and His Historical Excerpts." PhD diss., Central European University. Budapest, Hungary. Available online at: www.etd.ceu.hu/2010/mphnea01.pdf

Panteghini, Sebastiano. 2009. "Die *Kirchengeschichte* des Nikepohoros Kallistos Xanthopoulos." *Östkirchliche Studien* 58: 248–66. Available online at: http://www.oeaw.ac.at/byzanz/repository/Panteghini_OST59.pdf

Peretz, Daniel. 2006. "The Roman Interpreter and His Diplomatic and Miltiary Roles." *Historia* 55: 451–70.

Pittia, Sylvie. 2006. "La fiabilité des fragments d'Appien sur l'histoire diplomatique et militaire de Rome aux IVe–IIIe siècles." In *Guerre et diplomatie romaines (IVe–IIIe siècles): pour un réexamen des sources*, ed. Emmanuèle Caire and Sylvie Pittia, 113–35. Aix-en-Provence: Publications de l'Université de Provence.

Rohrbacher, David. 2002. *The Historians of Late Antiquity*. London and New York: Routledge.

Šašel Kos, Marjeta. 1994. "The Embassy of Romulus to Attila: One of the Last Citations of Poetovio in Classical Literature." *Tyche* 9: 99–111.

Schmitt, W. O. 1970. "Zur Biographie des Geschichtsschreibers Priskos bei Raffaele Maffei di Volterra." *Klio* 52: 389–93.

Schreiner, Peter. 1987. "Die Historikerhandschrift Vaticanus Graecus 977: Ein Handexemplar zur Vorbereitung des konstantinischen Excerptwerkes?" *Jahrbuch der Österreichischen Byzantinistik* 37: 1–29.

Scott, Roger. 1981. "The Classical Tradition in Byzantine Historiography." In *Byzantium and the Classical Tradition*, ed. M. Mullett and R. Scott, 61–74. Birmingham.

Ševčenko, Ihor. 1992. "Re-reading Constantine Porphyrogenitus." In *Byzantine Diplomacy: Papers from the Twenty-fourth Spring Symposium of Byzantine Studies, Cambridge, March 1990*, ed. Jonathan Shephard and Simon Franklin, 167–95. Aldershot: Variorum.

Thompson, E. A. 1945a. "The Camp of Attila." *Journal of Hellenic Studies* 65: 112–15.

———. 1945b. "Priscus of Panium, Fragment 1b." *Classical Quarterly* 39: 92–94.

———. 1947. "Notes on Priscus Panites." *Classical Quarterly* 41: 61–65.

———. 1950. "The Foreign Policies of Theodosius II and Marcian." *Hermathena* 76: 58–75.

———. 1996. *The Huns*. Revised edition, with an afterword by Peter Heather. Originally published as *A History of Attila and the Huns*, 1948. Oxford: Blackwell Publishers.

Thurn, Ioannes. 2000. *Ioannis Malalae Chronographia*. Berlin and New York: Walter de Gruyter.

Toynbee, Arnold. 1973. *Constantine Porphyrogenitus and His World*. London and New York: Oxford University Press.

Treadgold, Warren. 2007a. *The Early Byzantine Historians*. Basingstoke and New York: Palgrave Macmillan.

———. 2007b. "The Byzantine World Histories of John Malalas and Eusthathius of Epiphania." *International History Review* 29: 709–45.

Velkov, Velizar. 1977. *Cities in Thrace and Dacia in Late Antiquity (Studies and Materials)*. Amsterdam: Adolf M. Hakkert.

Wagner, Norbert. 2008. "Der Name der 'Schrittfinnen'." *Historische Sprachforschung* 121: 241–44.

Ward-Perkins, Bryan. 2005. *The Fall of Rome and the End of Civilization*. Oxford: Oxford University Press.

Wescher, C. 1868. "Fragments inédits de l'historien grec Priscus relatifs au siège de Noviodunum et à la prise de Naïssos." *Revue archeologique* n.s. 18: 86–98.

Whitby, Michael, trans. 2000. *The Ecclesiastical History of Evagrius Scholasticus*. Liverpool: Liverpool University Press.

——— and Mary Whitby, trans. 1989. *Chronicon Paschale, 284–628 AD*. Liverpool: Liverpool University Press.

Whittow, Mark. 2009. Review of Mariev 2008. *Bryn Mawr Classical Review* 2009.12.06. Available online at: http://bmcr.brynmawr.edu/2009/2009-12-06.html.

Williams, Stephen and Gerard Friell. 1999. *The Rome That Did Not Fall: The Survival of the East in the Fifth Century*. London and New York: Routledge.

Zuckerman, Constantin. 1994. "L'Empire d'Orient et les Huns: Notes sur Priscus." *Travaux et Mémoires byzantines* 12: 159–82.

INDEX

Adames, Hunnic courtier 77
Adaricus, Gepid king 114–115
Aetius, Western general 94, 132, 137, 139; antagonism with Huns 59, 99–103, 130–131; death of xxx, 105, 125–129, 159; cooperation with Huns 7, 28–31, 43–44, 52, 54, 58, 75–77, 87 n. 13, 90 n. 47; dispute with Boniface and Felix 28–31
Africa, North xxxii, 7, 10, 28–32, 96, 123, 130, 134–135, 156–161; *see also* Libya
Agathias, historian xiii, xvii, xxiv, xli n. 8
Agintheos, Eastern general 49
Aigidios, Western general 136, 138, 156
Aimorichiani 126
Akateri 55–56, 63, 67, 139, 142, 150
Alans 6, 10, 28, 115, 132
Alaric, Gothic king 101, 107–108, 164
Alcildzuri *see* Amilzouri
Alexandria xii, xxxi, xxxv, 119–120
Alypia, daughter of Anthemius 170
Ambrose, bishop of Milan 6
Amilzouri (*also* Alcildzuri) 8–9
Ammianus Marcellinus 5–6, 8
Anagastes, son of Arnegisklos 86 n. 7, 151–152, 154, 162–165
Anatolios, Eastern general and ambassador 25–26, 37, 39, 44, 51, 53, 71, 83–85
Anthemius, Western emperor xvi, 156–159, 161–163, 169–170
Antiochos, Eastern courtier 23–24
Apollonios, Eastern ambassador 103–104
Aquileia, siege of 104–106
Arcadius, Eastern emperor 19, 24

Ardabourios, son of Aspar, Eastern general 74, 94, 117, 161, 164
Areobindos, Eastern general 41, 79
Argagisklos *see* Arnegisklos
Armenia 122, 150, 155
Arnegisklos (*also* Argagisklos, Ornigisklos) Eastern general 41, 151, 163
Asemos, Thracian fortress 39, 84
Aspar, Eastern general: ethnicity 132; and Vandals 30–31, 74–75, 96; and Huns 32, 41, 79; and Goths 153–154, 167 n. 14; and Valentinian III 20; and Marcian 94; and Leo I 95, 133, 148, 162–164; and Basiliscus 158, 160–161
Athenaïs *see* Eudocia
Athyras, Thracian fortress 41
Attila, Hunnic king: as part of Priscus's structure xiv–xvii, xix, xxvii, xxxi, xxxvi, 3, 26, 47, 111, 141; Hunnic royal succession 10, 35, 41; praised as a god or divinely favored 48, 54, 70–71; life among the Huns xi–xii, 56, 59–62, 67, 72–77; campaigns and threats against the Eastern Empire 3, 10–11, 17 n. 12, 35–39, 41, 50, 81–84, 104, 108, 111 (*see also* tribute); his ambassadors to the Romans 41–47, 66–67, 77–79, 81–82; receiving ambassadors 36, 50–55, 61, 67, 71–72, 76–77, 84–85, 103–104; attempt to assassinate 21, 43, 45–47, 51, 53–55, 79–81, 84–85, 88 n. 20 (*see also* Bigilas, Edekon); engagement to Honoria 93–94, 98–99, 102; campaigns and threats against the Western Empire xxxii, 3, 58–59, 68–69, 93–94,

98–108, 117, 130; meets Pope Leo 107–108; and Persians 68–69; and Vandals 99; and other non-Roman peoples 11, 55–56, 61, 142; death and funeral xiv, 101–102, 111–113; aftermath of his death 11–12, 76, 114–115, 123, 136, 149, 151
Aurelia (Orléans), Gallic city 102–103
Avars 139, 141
Avitus, Western emperor 130–133

Bahram V *see* Vararanes
Basich, Hunnic royal 68–69
Basiliscus, Eastern general xvi, xxxii, 152, 157–162, 166
Bdellas *see* Bleda
Belisarius, Eastern general xxviii, 32
Berichos, Hunnic ambassador 72, 78–79
Bigilas, Eastern translator 44–49, 51–56, 79–81, 84–85
bishops, anonymous: of Margos 13–14; of Sirmium 58–59; of Smyrna 27; *see also* Dioskoros; Leo, Pope; Proterios
Black Sea (*also* Pontos) xi, xix, 6, 33 n. 1, 36, 41, 67, 115, 121, 148, 150
Bleda (*also* Bdellas) Hunnic king xxix, 10–11, 35, 57–59, 74–76
Bleda, Eastern ambassador and bishop 131
Blemmyes 117–119
Boethius, Western official 127–128
Boïski (*also* Boisci) 8, 10
Boniface, Western general 28–31, 126
Britain 28, 174
Byzantium *see* Constantinople

Carthage 31–32, 155, 157–159
Cassiodorus, historian of the Goths xxvi, xliii n. 27
Catalaunian Fields, battle of 102
Caucasus Mountains 6, 146, 148, 154
Charaton, Hunnic king 7
Chelchal, Eastern commander 152–154

Christianity and Christians xi, xviii, xxx, xxxiv, 7, 23–25, 91 n. 53, 107–108, 119, 131, 140 n. 10, 147
Chrysaphius, Eastern courtier 21–23, 44–47, 51, 54, 81–84, 95
Constantia, Danubian fortress 10, 41
Constantia, Pannonian fortress 86 n. 8
Constantine I the Great, Roman emperor xi, xxiv, 14, 21, 27, 147
Constantine VII Porphyrogennetos, Byzantine emperor xx–xxv, xxix, xxxi, xxxvi; his excerptors' techniques xxii, xxvii, 16 n. 6, 47, 70, 74, 81, 111, 117, 124 n. 14, 167 n. 13
Constantine, Eastern ambassador, misnamed as Constantius 143–146, 166 n. 4
Constantinople (*also* Byzantium) xxvi, xxxiii, xxxv, 7, 14, 17 n. 7, 20, 24, 26–27, 28, 35, 37, 42–44, 78–79, 82, 86 n. 8, 97, 101, 125, 141, 146–147, 151, 154, 159, 163, 166
Constantiolus, Pannonian traveler to Attila 68–69
Constantius, Attila's Gallic secretary 58–59
Constantius, Attila's Italian secretary 52, 58, 68, 77–79, 82–85, 103
Constantius, Eastern ambassador *see* Constantine, Eastern ambassador
Constantius, Flavius, brother-in-law of Honorius 19
Cyrus *see* Kyros

Dalmatia 133, 138, 156, 159, 173
Damascus xii, 117
Danube River *see* Istros
Dengizich, son of Attila 149, 151–152, 154, 162
Dexippus, historian xix–xx, xxiv, 17 n. 19, 144
Diocletian, Roman emperor xxxi
Dionysios, Eastern ambassador to Huns 8

INDEX

Dionysios, Eastern ambassador to Lazi 123, 147
Dioskoros, Alexandrian patriarch 119

Edekon (*also* Idikon) Hunnic ambassador 43–51, 55–56, 58, 76, 80–81, 86 n. 11, 149, 170
Edesa (*also* Edessa) 144
Egypt xvii, xxxv, 117–120
Ellac, son of Attila, ruler of Akateri 55, 61, 67, 72, 115, 142
Epigenes, Eastern ambassador 10
Ernach, son of Attila 76, 149, 154
Eslas, Hunnic ambassador 8, 54, 56, 81
Ethiopians 42
Eudocia (*also* Athenaïs) Eastern empress, wife of Theodosius II 22, 78, 91 n. 53
Eudocia, daughter of Valentinian III, wife of Huneric 32, 125, 130–131, 137, 139
Eudoxia, Licinia, Western empress, wife of Valentinian III 20, 129–131, 137
Eugenios, lover of Honoria 93
Eugenius, Roman usurper 6
Eunapius, historian xi, xvii, xxiv–xxv, xli n. 7
eunuchs xxix–xxx, 20–23, 127; *see also* Antiochos, Chrysaphius, Herakleios, Hyakinthos
Euphemia, daughter of Marcian xli n. 3, 161
Euphemios, Eastern official xii, 121–122
Eusebius, historian xviii
Eustathius of Epiphaneia, historian xxxiii, xxxv
Evagrius, historian xiii, xxx–xxxii, xxxv, 95–96

Felix, Western general 28–30, 126
Florus, Eastern commander 120

foreign (non-Greek and non-Latin) words in the *History*: *kamon* 57; *medos* 57; *strava* 113; *see also* Latin words in the *History*
Franks 99–100, 123, 156
fugitives, used as bargaining chips 7, 11–13, 35–39, 42, 44, 47, 49, 53, 55–56, 84, 142–143

Galatians: as name for Gauls 58, 132
Galla Placidia *see* Placidia
Gaudentios, son of Aetius 125, 137–138
Gaul 6, 28–29, 100–103, 125, 130–131, 133, 136, 138, 156
Geiseric, Vandal king xviii, 29–33, 41, 96–97, 99, 129–132, 136–139, 141, 144, 156–161
Genzon, son of Geiseric 32, 161
Gepids 101, 114–115, 148
Glycerius, Western emperor 170–171
Gobazes, Lazic king xvii, 121–123, 147
Gondoubandos *see* Gundobad
Goths 5–6, 9, 115, 132, 152–154, 162; Eastern Goths or Ostrogoths 135, 148–149, 164–165; Western Goths or Visigoths 28, 99–104, 126, 130–135, 138, 156, 164; as name for Vandals 29
Goundoubales *see* Gundobad
Greece xxiv, 14, 40
Gundobad (*also* Gondoubandos *and* Goundoubales) nephew of Ricimer 169–171

Hadrianople 6, 28, 41, 79, 135
Helion, Eastern ambassador 25
Herakleia (*also* Peirinthos) 41
Herakleios, Eastern general 155, 159, 161
Herakleios, Western courtier 125–129
Herkoulanos, Western official 93
Herodotus, historian xvii, xix, xxiv, xli n. 8, 144
Heruli 115

Hippo Regius 30, 96
Honoria, sister of Valentinian III 93–94, 98–100, 102, 107
Honorius, Western emperor 19–20, 101
Huneric, son of Geiseric 31–32, 130, 137, 139
Huns xix, 11–12, 66; origins 5, 8–10; royal succession 6– 7, 10, 35; embassies from 8, 42, 44–46, 68, 78–79, 81–82, 98, 100–101, 149, 152; embassies to 10–11, 13, 36, 41, 47–81, 83–85, 103–104, 107; invasions of Eastern Empire xx, xxxii–xxxiii, 6–8, 12–16, 25, 31–32, 36–40, 82, 136, 152–154, 162; invasions of Persia 68–69; invasions of Western Empire 6, 100–103, 104–108, 130; dissolution of their empire 114–115, 123, 135, 141, 149; *see also* Aetius, relations with Huns; Akateri; Gepids; Kidarites; Scythians
Hyakinthos, Western courtier 94

Iberia (Asian) 150, 155
Iberia (European) 134
Idikon *see* Edekon
Ildico, wife of Attila 101, 112
Illyria (*also* Illyricum) 10, 12–14, 39, 45, 49, 62, 148, 173
Indachos (*also* Indakos) Isaurian rebel xxx, 164–165
Ioannes, Eastern commander (*PLRE* II Ioannes 25) 160–161
Ioannes, Eastern general (*PLRE* Ioannes the Vandal 13) 163
Iordanes, Eastern official 163, 165–166
Iouroeipaach, Persian fortress 142–143, 150
Isaurians xxx, 42, 82, 163
Isauropolis 93
Isdigerdes (Yazdgard I), Persian king 24–26
Isdigerdes (Yazdgard II), Persian king 25

Istros River (*also* Danube River) xx, xxxvii 5–8, 10–14, 16, 31–32, 35, 44–45, 49–50, 62, 79, 84–85, 103, 107–108, 148–149, 151
Italy 28–31, 68, 100, 104–108, 129–132, 135–139, 142–144, 156–157, 165, 171
Itimari 8, 9

John of Antioch, historian xxiv–xxvi, xxviii, xxx, 86 n. 11
John, Western usurper 20, 28
Jordanes, Gothic historian xxvi–xxviii, xxxvii, 11, 99, 102–103
Justinian, Byzantine emperor xxviii, xxxii

Karpileon, son of Aetius 54
Kidarites (*also* Kedarites) Hunnic tribe 122, 142–146, 148, 150, 155
Kolchis, as name for Lazike 121–123
Kounchas, Kidarite Hun king 144–145
Kouridachos, Akateri king 56
Kreka, wife of Attila 67, 77
Kurisch, Hunnic royal 68–69
Kyros (*also* Cyrus) Eastern official 26–27, 34 n. 5

Latin words in the *History* xviii–xix, xxxv; *comes* 58; *comes domesticorum* 171; *cubicularius* 24; *domesticus* 97; *magister* 46, 47, 83, 122, 169; *praepositus* 23, 24; *primicerius* 126; *quaestor* 10; *sagitta* 101; *see also* foreign (non-Greek and non-Latin) words in the *History*
Lazi xvii, 121–122, 147–148, 154–155
Leo I, Eastern emperor: accession 133; and Aspar 95, 133, 148, 161, 163–164; and Goths 135, 162, 164; and his courtiers 165–166; and Huns 149, 151–152; and Isaurians 163, 165; and Lazi 147; and Scythian tribes 139, 148; and

Vandals 138–139, 141, 143–144, 155–162; and Western empire 135–136, 138, 156, 159, 171; death xvi, 166
Leo II, Eastern emperor xxxiii, 166
Leo, Pope 107–108
Libius Severus *see* Severus, Libius
Libya 29, 31–33, 75, 85, 96–97, 126, 134–135, 159; *see also* Africa, North
Licinia Eudoxia *see* Eudoxia

Maeotis Lake (*also* Maiotis) Sea of Azov 9, 16 n. 2, 69
Majorian, Western emperor 129, 133–135, 137–138
Malalas, John, historian xiii, xxiv, xxxii–xxxv
Malchus, historian xiii, xvi–xvii, xxiv
Marcellinus, Western general 133–134, 136–139, 156, 159, 161
Marcian, Eastern emperor xi–xii, 21, 121, 156, 161; early life and accession xviii, xxxi, 23, 94–98; and Egypt 120; and Goths 135; and Huns 98, 101, 103, 108, 111–112, 116, 123; and Lazi 122; and Syria 117; and Vandals xviii, 97–98, 131, 157; and Western empire 126; death 133, 157, 163
Margos, Thracian city 10, 12–14, 16, 74
Martialos, Eastern official 46–47
Maurousians (*also* Moors) 74–75, 90 n. 50, 134, 136
Maximianos, Western official 129
Maximinos, Eastern ambassador xii, xli n. 1; and the Huns 46–48, 52–54, 61–62, 66–67, 71, 78–80, 82; and the Isaurians 93; and the Saracens 117; and the Egyptians 117–119
Maximus, Petronius, usurper against Valentinian III 125–126, 128–130
Maximus, usurper against Theodosius I 6

Medes: as name for Persians, 68–69, 147
Mediolanum (Milan) 107
Memphis, Egypt 120
Moors *see* Maurousians
Mysia: as name for Moesia 10, 13, 62, 77

Naissos xix–xx, 14–15, 32, 41, 45, 49, 74, 144
Nedao River 114
Nepos, Julius, Western emperor 43, 171
Nikephoros Kallistos, historian xxxv
Nomos, Eastern ambassador 71, 83–85
Noubades 117–119
Novidounon (*also* Noviodunum) 11–12

Octar, Hunnic king 7
Odessos, Thracian town 36, 86 n. 4
Odovacer, king of Italy 34, 170–171
Olybrius, Western emperor 137–138, 157–158, 170
Olympiodorus, historian xvii, 7
omens and dreams xviii, 8–10, 49, 70–71, 96–98, 104–106, 112, 129
Onegesios, Hunnic ambassador 48, 52, 55–56, 60–63, 65–68, 71–72, 76–77
Onogouri 139, 141–142
Optelas, assassin of Valentinian III 128–129
Orestes, secretary to Attila, father of Romulus Augustulus 43–45, 48–51, 58, 72, 81, 171
Orléans *see* Aurelia
Ornigisklos *see* Arnegisklos
Ostrogoths *see* Goths, Eastern
Ostrys, Eastern commander 152, 164
Oullibos, Eastern commander 162
Ourogi 139, 141–142

Paionia *see* Pannonia
Panion, Thracian city xi, 3, 4 n. 1

Pannonia (*also* Paionia) 43–44, 58, 60, 114, 135, 164
Papirios, Isaurian rebel 164, 168 n. 27
Parthians: as name for Persians xix, 42, 69, 122, 143–145, 155; *see also* Persians
Paschal Chronicle xxxiii–xxxiv, 4 n. 1
Patavion (*also* Poetavio) 58
Patrikios, son of Aspar 161, 163–164
Paulinos, Eastern official, tutor to Theodosius II 21–22
Peirinthos *see* Herakleia
Peirozes (*also* Peroz), Persian king 142–146, 167 n. 7
Persians xix, xxxii, 6–7, 24–26, 68–69, 94, 121–122, 142–150, 154–155; *see also* Medes *and* Parthians
Petronius Maximus *see* Maximus, Petronius
Philippoupolis xix, 41, 79, 95
Phylarchos, Eastern ambassador 138–139, 157
Placidia, daughter of Valentinian III 130–131, 137, 159
Placidia, Galla, Western empress, mother of Valentinian III 19–20, 28–30, 94, 107, 126
Plakitos, Eastern official, tutor to Theodosius II 21
Plataea, battle of, as literary model xix–xx
Plinthas, Eastern ambassador 8, 10, 85
Poetavio *see* Patavion
Pontos *see* Black Sea.
Priscus, as a character in his *History*: on embassy to Attila 47–48, 52–54, 60, 62–68, 71–72, 76; in Rome 100; in Syria 117; in Egypt 119–120; in Lazike 122
Priscus, historian: biographical data, xi–xiv; structure of his *History* xiv–xvii, 7, 19–20, 79, 95, 111, 141, 161–162; his classicism xvii–xx, 144; sources for his text xx–xxxv

prisoners of war 11, 32, 37, 39–41, 55, 58, 60, 75, 80, 85, 97, 118; Priscus's conversation with 62–65
Procopius, historian xiii, xvii–xviii, xxiv–xxv, xxviii–xxix, xxx–xxxi, xli n. 8
Promoutos, Western ambassador xxxvi, 58, 68, 72
Proterios, Alexandrian bishop 119
Pulcheria, Eastern empress 23, 94–95

Ratiaria 36, 41, 77
Ravenna 20
Ricimer, Western general 132–133, 135–138, 156, 169–170
Romanos, Western ambassador (*PLRE* II Romanus 2) xxxvi, 58, 68, 72
Romanos, Western official (*PLRE* II Romanus 4) 169
Rome xii, 58, 68, 93, 100–101, 107, 128–133, 169, 171
Romulus Augustulus, Western emperor 43, 169
Romulus, Western ambassador xxxvi, 58, 68–69, 72
Roua, Hunnic king xv, xvi, 7, 8, 10
Roubi 11–12
Roustikios, Eastern translator 52, 68
Roustikios, secretary to Attila's secretary 77
Rufus, adviser to Zeno 78, 103
Rugi 11, 115, 148

Sabiri 139
Salonae (*also* Salona *and* Salon) Illyrian city xxxv, 171, 173
Saracens 42, 117
Saragouri 139, 141–142, 149–150
Sarapis *see* Serapis
Satornilos (*also* Saturninus) Eastern official 78, 83–84, 103
Scythians 9–11, 55, 68, 113, 136, 151, 158; as name for Goths xix, 8, 136, 152–154, 162; as name for Huns xix, 3, 10–11, 13–14, 35, 38–41, 44–45, 48, 50–51, 53–54, 56–58, 60–63, 66, 70, 73, 75, 77–79, 85,

104; Priscus's Greek terms for 89 n. 31
Sebastian, Western general 22, 31
Senate and senators: Eastern 10, 24, 38, 158, 163–164; Western 101, 128, 131, 135
Senator, Eastern ambassador 36, 71
Sengilachos, Eastern ambassador 8
Serapis (*also* Sarapis) Egyptian god xxxv, 120–121
Serdica 14, 45, 48, 51, 54
Severus, Libius, Western emperor 135–136, 138, 156
Sicily 31, 41, 131–132, 134, 136–137, 139, 155–156, 173
Silvanos, Roman banker 58–59, 68, 99
Singidunum 16
Sirmium 16, 58, 60, 87 n. 13
Skiri 6, 148–149
Skottas, Hunnic ambassador 37–38, 50, 52–53
Skrithiphini 174–175
Socrates, historian xi, xiii, xxiv
Souani 154–155
Sozomen, historian xi, xiii
Spain 28, 133–134
Stephanos of Byzantium xxxv
Stilicho, Roman general 6
Suda xiii–xv, xxix–xxx
Sueves 28, 132, 148
sword of Ares / Mars 70–71
Syria 117

Tatianos, Eastern ambassador 143–144
Tatoulos, father of Orestes 43, 58, 72
Thebes, Egypt 118–119
Theoderic II, Western Gothic king 130
Theoderic Strabo, Eastern general 164
Theoderic, Western Gothic king 100–103, 130
Theodoret, historian xi

Theodorus, son of Geiseric 32
Theodosius I, Roman emperor xi, 6, 19
Theodosius II, Eastern emperor xi, xvi, 3, 27, 117; birth and accession 19; and his courtiers xxix, xxxiii, 20–24; and Persians xxxii, 7, 24–26; and Western Empire 20, 94; and Vandals 31, 41; and Huns and their tribute 7, 10, 25, 35–37, 41, 98, 101, 103, 108; receives Hunnic ambassadors 42–45; and the attempted assassination of Attila 46–47, 81–82; his ambassadors to Attila 48, 51, 53–55, 60, 62, 66, 69, 71, 79; giving a wife to Constantius 77–78, 82–83, 85, 103; and Zeno 85, 93; death 94, 97–98, 125
Theodoulos, Eastern general 36, 39
Theophanes, historian xxxi–xxxii, 4 n. 1
Theophylact Simocatta, historian xiii, xvii, xxiv
Thoule 174–175
Thrace xi, xxxii, 4 n. 1, 7, 14, 35–41, 44, 62, 74–75, 95, 151–152, 158, 162, 164
Thraustelas, assassin of Valentinian III 128–129
Thucydides, historian xvii, xix–xx, xxiv, xli n. 8, 17 n. 19, 144
Thudimer, Eastern Gothic king 164
Tounsoures (*also* Tuncarsi) 8, 9
treaties: Blemmyes and Noubades 118; Eastern Romans and Goths 136; Eastern Romans and Huns 10–11, 13, 16, 35, 37–38, 41–42, 47, 53, 83–84, 149, 152; Eastern Romans and Persians 25; Eastern Romans and Roubi 12; Eastern Romans and Vandals 41, 138–139, 141,157; Western Romans and Vandals 31–32, 129, 132, 135–137; in Western civil conflict 170

tribute 63; Armenians to Eastern Romans 155; Eastern Romans to Goths 136; Eastern Romans to Huns 11, 16, 35–38, 41, 69, 81, 85, 98, 103, 105, 108, 111, 113; Persians to Kidarite Huns 145, 167 n. 7; Vandals to Western Romans 31; Western Romans to Huns 105; Western Romans to Vandals 33

Tuncarsi *see* Tounsoures

Uldin, Hunnic king 6–7

Valamer (*also* Valimer) Eastern Gothic king 135–136, 148, 164
Valens, Roman emperor 28, 126, 140 n. 3
Valentinian III, Western emperor: birth and accession 19–20, 28–29; and Vandals 31–32; and Huns 59, 90 n. 47, 93–94, 100–102, 107; desirous of Eastern throne 125–126; murder of Aetius xxx, 126–127; murder of Boethius 127–128; death 128–129; aftermath of his death 133, 137, 139; treatment of wife and daughters after his death 129–131, 137–138, 159 (*see also* Eudocia, Eudoxia, Placidia)
Valips, Roubi leader 11–12
Vandals: entry into the Roman Empire 28; attacked by Aspar's and Boniface's forces 7, 10, 29–30, 74, 96–97; treaties with Romans 31–32; control of North Africa 31–33, 42, 123; invade Italy and Sicily 129–134, 136–139, 142; prevent Majorian's invasion 134–135; receive ambassadors from Eastern Romans 143–144; attacked by Basiliscus's forces xxxii, 155–161; threatened by Ricimer 169

Vararanes (*also* Bahram V), Persian king 24–26
Verina, Eastern empress, wife of Leo I 158, 161–162
Viminakion 13–14, 16, 62
Visigoths *see* Goths, Western
Vithimir, Gothic king 6

Women, anonymous: Boniface's wife 126; Constantinople fire-starter 146; Constantius's wife 85; Eskam's daughter 56; Kounchas's wife 145; Leo's daughter 163; Onegesios's wife 61; Romulus's daughter 58; Satornilos's daughter 78, 82–84, 103; Scythian queen / Bleda's widow 57–58; Sullos's wife 77; Zerkon's wife 75–76

Xenophon, historian xix, xxiv

Yazdgard *see* Isdigerdes

Zeno, Eastern emperor (*PLRE* II Fl. Zenon 7) 82, 163–164, 166
Zeno, Isaurian general (*PLRE* II Fr. Zenon 6) 78, 82–83, 85, 93–95, 103, 109 n. 8
Zerkon, Marousian court jester xxix, 70, 74–76
Zosimus, historian xiii, xvi, xxiv, xxx

Also available in the Christian Roman Empire Series

Volume 1. *The Life of Belisarius*
    by Lord Mahon

Volume 2. *The Gothic History of Jordanes: In English Version with an Introduction and a Commentary*
    Translated by Charles Christopher Mierow

Volume 3. *The Book of the Popes (Liber Pontificalis): To the Pontificate of Gregory I*
    Translated by Louise Ropes Loomis

Volume 4. *The Chronicle of John, Bishop of Nikiu: Translated from Zotenberg's Ethiopic Text*
    Translated by R. H. Charles

Volume 5. *The Ecclesiastical Annals of Evagrius: A History of the Church from AD 431 to AD 594*
    by Edward Walford

Volume 6. *The Life of Saint Augustine: A Translation of the* Sancti Augustini Vita *by Possidius, Bishop of Calama*
    by Herbert T. Weiskotten

Volume 7. *The Life of Saint Simeon Stylites: A Translation of the Syriac in* Bedjan's Acta Martyrum et Sanctorum
    by Rev. Frederick Lent

Volume 8. *The Life of the Blessed Emperor Constantine: In Four Books from 306 to 337 AD*
    by Eusebius Pamphilus

Volume 9. *The Dialogues of Saint Gregory the Great*
    edited by Edmund G. Gardner

Volume 10. *The Complete Works of Saint Cyprian:*
    edited by Phillip Campbell

For more information on this series, see our website at:
http://www.evolpub.com/CRE/CREseries.html

CPSIA information can be obtained
at www.ICGtesting.com
Printed in the USA
BVHW07s0731190818
524798BV00001B/13/P